The Game's Up: Essays in the Cultural Analysis of Sport, Leisure and Popular Culture

D1328661

ALAN TOMLINSON

Ashgate

ARENA

Aldershot • Brookfield USA • Singapore • Sydney

© Alan Tomlinson 1999

Published by
Ashgate Publishing Ltd
Gower House
Croft Road
Aldershot
Hants GU11 3HR
England

Ashgate Publishing Company
Old Post Road
Brookfield
Vermont 05036
USA

British Library Cataloguing in Publication Data
Tomlinson, Alan, 1950-
    The game's up : essays in the cultural analysis of sport,
    leisure and popular culture. - (Popular cultural studies)
    1. Sports - Sociological aspects 2. Mass media and sports
    3. Leisure
    I. Title
    306.4'8

Library of Congress Catalog Card Number: 98-74631

ISBN 1 85742 248 1 (HBK)
ISBN 1 85742 249 X (PBK)

Printed and bound by Athenaeum Press, Ltd.,
Gateshead, Tyne & Wear.

Contents

Preface and Acknowledgements

Two books entitled *Taking Sport Seriously* were published in the late 1990s (Donnelly, 1997; Allison, 1998)[1]. In both of these volumes, the editors were at pains to demonstrate the necessity to undertake rigorous research, scholarship and thinking on the place and impact of sport in contemporary society. It is a case that still needs to be made because the place of the study of sport in academic life remains a marginal one, despite sport's profile in the media and everyday popular culture, and a burgeoning volume of research on its political, historical, sociological and cultural dimensions.

Sport and other leisure and popular cultural forms are significant not just as reflections of social trends and cultural values but also as generative of such trends and values. The sport and leisure industries lead the way in the globalization of consumption; mega sports events produce the largest national and global media audiences in history; people's fragmented sense of self and identity can be stored up by consumer choices in leisure, or by chosen affiliations to sports teams and clubs. For all these reasons, it behoves social scientists, cultural analysts, and social and cultural historians to take sport, leisure and popular culture seriously. The growth of strong work in this field from the mid-1970s onwards, often linked to the development of sport and leisure studies programmes at undergraduate level and in postgraduate research centres, has been a welcome antidote to a snobbishness, in some quarters of academic life, which has dismissed sport and leisure studies as trivial, peripheral, and even bogus.

One such commentator is the philosopher pundit Roger Scruton, who in 1980 posited as an example of "factitious", relevance-based degrees, the hypothetical case of "Football Studies" — the kinds of courses and degrees "connected with the rise of humanities departments in the polytechnics ... usually put together out of pieces that have no obvious connection, in order to continue the illusion of an educational process that may in fact have ceased by the age of ten"[2]. Scruton observed quite rightly that 'relevance' is often claimed via the creation of a 'second-order' subject or a 'meta-discipline', and instanced the University of Warwick's Industrial Relations course in the same category as "Football Studies". Scruton indulged in a little tongue-in-cheek course development on this:

> ... there is the sociology of football (involving the study of the structure of crowds and the 'charisma' of players); the philosophy of football (beginning from Aristotle on *catharsis* and centring on the role of alienated labour in spectator sports); the psychology of football (containing dry reflections on how the motion of the ball is perceived by the human eye, together with much wetter reflections on 'football and the unconscious'); the ethics of football (including studies of social responsibility and the true origins of hooliganism in capitalist society); the history of football and its relation to class structures and so on ... Soon the academic world is saturated with teachers of football studies and the dole queues are swelling with their graduates[3].

His hypothetical example is parallelled, Scruton noted, in American colleges in the histories of 'Black Studies', 'Women's Studies' and 'Gay Studies', where he claimed that artificial links are also made between a jumble of rival disciplines and areas of claimed 'relevance' and 'social concern'. Scruton's main objection to such developments was that they have neither the scientific method to provide any basis for an 'established body of results', nor the 'more elusive discipline of the humanities'[4], and the 'critical intelligence' which flows from this[5]. Scruton's polemic raises important issues concerning the nature of new areas of intellectual work. But I have two main objections to his argument. First, he ignored the extent to which particular courses have specialized within, say, sport studies, so that they have a strong experimental science base, or a distinctive social science framework. In this sense students can emerge with adequate and even strong disciplinary bases. Second, such areas need to be researched in some depth so that the ideas of the likes of Scruton can be tested more fully. He used football himself, for instance, to make very big points about the nature of bonding and belonging in institutions (p. 48) and he cited competitive sport as the simplest example of forms of social participation which embody the values of a public life (pp. 142-143). In the second of these examples he described leisure as 'the essence of these forms'. If Scruton's recognition of the importance of sport and leisure is to be borne out, this can only be on the basis of research conducted in scientific terms on the basis of solid experimental methods, and in social and cultural terms through the sceptical eye of the critical intelligence. I would like to think that some 'second-order' areas where the disciplinary and foundation base has been clear have provided a scholarly research base for a fuller discussion of themes and topics which in Scruton's accomplished philosophical (or political?) hands remain sutured to the merely speculative.

Sport and the public forms of leisure are prominent in the cultural commentaries of our society, from the popular media to movies, from the novel and painting to poetry. J.B. Priestley, famously, cited football as the working man's art, in the opening pages of *The Good Companions* (Priestley, 1976)[6]; and reminisced about the echoing resonances through his own life of the "*thud-thud* of the ball, a sound unlike any other ... that unmistakeable call to the field"[7]. Ted Hughes could people one of his bleak natural landscapes and bring it alive with the rough ballet of the players:

> Between plunging valleys, on a bareback of hill
> Men in bunting colours
> Bounced, and their blown ball bounced. ....
>
> But the wingers leapt, they bicycled in air
> And the goalie flew horizontal
> And once again a golden holocaust
> Lifted the cloud's edge, to watch them.[8]

The wingers are depicted like salmon in one of Hughes' beloved fishing spots, and as supernatural fliers like ET's friends in the Spielberg film. The players are colourfully integrated in to the landscape, the flying goalkeeper at one with the order of nature. Hughes endows the simple game of football with a mythic resonance. But for all the literary and cultural representation of sport, its historical and social meanings cannot be assumed or merely taken-for-granted. If sport is as important as Scruton and literary figures such as Priestley and Hughes suggested it to be — even before Nick Hornby and *Fever Pitch*[9] — then it has to be investigated with the kind of rigour and thoroughness (and critical intelligence) that are brought to bear upon any other social institution or cultural practice.

But even within the social science community the study of sport and leisure has yet to be acknowledged as an area of central concern to beginning students. So the most prominent textbook in the field, by Giddens, has no chapter on either sport or leisure[10]. Given the discussion above, there is really very little justification for such an omission, other than conventional and narrow thinking. As work on sport and leisure continues to show its social science pedigree, more general sociological introductions will, justifiably, include coverage of these areas. It is interesting that in the more innovatively framed area of cultural studies, sport and leisure are seen as central to an adequate and comprehensive coverage of the field[11].

This volume of essays is based upon pieces produced between 1982 and 1992 with in addition a reworked version of a 1994 public lecture. The original essays and papers have been edited and amended to remove the sort of dated topical references that fade from both the popular and the expert memory, and the more arcane manifestations of specialist professional debate. Tenses have also been changed where appropriate, though — where dealing with trends and issues of the day — the essays were originally written in a conditional future tense, or a reflective present tense intended to be read in future years as forms of contemporary historical analysis.

The essays are organized as chapters in sections, but the emphasis on the notion of essay is deliberate. Samuel Johnson's dictionary (completed in 1755) offered, as its second definition of the word essay, the following: "A loose sally of the mind; an irregular indigested piece; not a regular and orderly composition"[12]. In old French, *essai* meant a trial, and in modern French the verb *essayer* refers to the process of trying and testing, and in its reflexive form to try one's hand. Such an emphasis on the attempt or trial was the main emphasis in the *essay* entry in Skeat's 1882 dictionary of etymology[13]. This collection of my own pieces retains this modern sense of the term, for they are concerned with interventions, tracing of trends, and agenda-setting in some core areas of the study of sport, leisure and popular culture. Whether they escape the parameters of Johnson's definition is for the reader and respondents to decide.

The essays are revised and collected together in this form because several colleagues in the field have recurrently commented that the pieces have proved useful and enduring in teaching courses, at undergraduate level, and in some cases as beginning points for more specialist graduate study. These colleagues include Garry Whannel, Peter Bramham, John Horne and Richard Holt. Lattterly, Ben Carrington has provided encouragement, support, and stimulation, including especially useful suggestions on the shape of this preface. The pieces have evidently sometimes been difficult to access, particularly when recommended to large numbers of students. This volume therefore retrieves their accessibility.

Those responsible for the Arena series of Popular Cultural Studies — especially Steve Redhead — provided support for the process of production of the collection. Although not involved in the eventual production process, Dave Morley (of Comedia/Routledge) was also most supportive in recommending structural and thematic principles for the collection. None of those named above bears any responsibility — it goes without saying, but has to be said — for the final shape of the volume.

The essays vary in tone and pitch, because they were originally written for different constituencies and in response to specific commissions (see Acknowledgement of Sources). But I do not believe that academic study and research should plough its own indecipherable jargonistic furrow, and not least of the essayist dimensions to the collection is the attempt to write about important issues, and to analyse and theorize, in clear terms and non-specialist language. The ways in which the essays have been received and used suggest that this has not been a wholly unrealistic aspiration. Indeed, the impact of the serious study of sport, leisure and popular culture, and its dissemination in appropriate professional spheres, can no longer be denied. The game is well and truly up for those to whom sport and leisure are mere epiphenomena; equally so for those who believe, idealistically and unrealistically, that sport and leisure cultures contribute some kind of 'world apart'.

My academic and intellectual debts are extensive, and include editors and others who commissioned and encouraged the pieces in the first place. The Chelsea School (Sport and Leisure Cultures), University of Brighton, has provided an infrastructure and an ambience supportive and conducive to the production of the volume. I am grateful for the responses of colleagues with whom I have worked over the years, particularly Graham McFee, John Sugden and Garry Whannel.

Personally, I am indebted to my daughters Alys and Rowan. Sceptical and indifferent observers of the world of sport cultures, they are nevertheless astute observers of broader leisure tastes and trends, and from such a base have offered invaluable support and perspective during the decade throughout which much of this material was first worked and written up.

Professionally, whatever merits the book has as an artefact are due to the exemplary copy-editing, typesetting and motivating skills of Myrene McFee.

Whatever deficiencies characterize the volume are, as I am sure the above-named and many others will not hesitate to point out, mine and mine alone.

Alan Tomlinson
Brighton, United Kingdom, December 1998

Notes

1   See L. Allison, ed., *Taking Sport Seriously*, Aachen, Meyer and Meyer, 1998; and P. Donnelly, ed., *Taking Sport Seriously, Social Issues in Canadian Sport*, Toronto, Thompson Publishing, 1997.

2   R. Scruton, *The Meaning of Conservatism*, Harmondsworth, Penguin, 1980, p. 149.

3   Ibid., p. 150.

4   Ibid., p. 152.

5   Scruton concedes that 'critical intelligence' is "difficult to define" (p. 152), but exemplifies it in, for instance, the "brilliant procedure of 'dramatization'" used by Thucydides. Somehow or another, those lucky enough to have a critical intelligence are able to understand facts of "a complex kind" (p. 154). But Scruton was insistent that such an aptitude could not be cultivated in 'second-order subjects'.

6   J.B. Priestley, *The Good Companions* (1929), Harmondsworth, Penguin, 1976.

7   J.B. Priestley, 'Sound of a football', in *Delight*, London, William Heinemann Ltd., 1949, p. 49.

8   T. Hughes, 'Football at Slack', in *Three Books — Remains of Elmet, Cave Birds, River*, London, Faber and Faber, 1993, p. 6.

9   N. Hornby, *Fever Pitch — A Fan's Life*, London, Victor Gollancz Ltd., 1992.

10 A. Giddens, *Sociology*, Cambridge, Polity Press, 1997.

11 A. Tomlinson, 'Sport, Leisure and Style', in D. Morley and K. Robbins, eds., *British Cultural Studies — An Introduction*, Oxford, Oxford University Press, 1999.

12 See *Johnson's Dictionary — A Modern Selection*, by E. L. McAdam, Jr. & G. Milne, London, Macmillan, 1982, p. 167.

13 W. W. Skeat, *The Concise Dictionary of English Etymology*, Ware (Herts), Wordsworth Editions Ltd., 1993, p. 137.

Acknowledgement of Sources

The chapters in this book are reworked and amended versions of, or draw upon material in, the following pieces:

Chapter 1 'Whose Feet in Which Time? Sport and Leisure in Contemporary Culture', professorial inaugural lecture, University of Brighton, 15 February 1994.

Chapter 2 'Physical Education, Sport and Sociology: The Current State and the Way Forward', in I. Glaister (ed), *Physical Education, Sport and Leisure: Sociological Perspectives*, London, NATFHE, 1984, pp. 44–53.

Chapter 3 'The Sociological Imagination, the New Journalism and Sport', in N. Theberge and P. Donnelly (eds), *Sport and the Sociological Imagination*, Fort Worth, Texas Christian University Press, 1983, pp. 21–39.

Chapter 4 'Whose Side are They On? Leisure Studies and Cultural Studies in Britain', *Leisure Studies*, Volume 8 Number 2, 1989, pp. 97–106; and see under Chapter 9 below.

Chapter 5 'Playing Away from Home: Leisure, access and exclusion', in P. Golding (ed), *Excluding the Poor*, London, Child Poverty Action Group, 1986, pp. 43–54.

Chapter 6 'Going Global: The FIFA Story', in A. Tomlinson and G. Whannel (eds), *Off the Ball — The Football World Cup*, London, Pluto Press, 1986, pp. 83–98.

1 Whose Feet in Which Time? Sport and Leisure in Contemporary Culture[1]

Methodology

In a classic British Telecom television advertisement of the late 1980s the punningly named Beattie (memorably played by the actress Maureen Lipmann) eulogized the academic achievements of her grandson — he'd actually failed most of his examinations, but at least he'd come in with a pass in Sociology — "he's got an 'Ology!" she screamed to an offstage family. The implication here was that sociology is some kind of easy option; or that 'ologizing is a form of obscure, pretentious or mysterious activity. Academics' concern with the familiar has also come in for some 'Ology bashing. In a review of a book on the history, politics and culture of the World (Soccer) Cup (Sugden and Tomlinson, 1994) the following tirade by Martin Smith exhibited the unreflective protectionism of a professional sphere, in this case the sports journalist:

> Talking heads, earnest young men with ology degrees, have been infiltrating football. The cloistered enclaves of our universities and colleges are also getting in the act ... trying to intellectualise the people's game, the beautiful game, the *simple* game ... But please, can we have our game back, Mister?

But I make no apology for the use and perpetuation of Ologies, and in this chapter and other chapters in this text survey a number of methodological concerns and emphases which have informed the approach to the study of sport, leisure and popular culture represented

in this book. All of them are expressions of a social historical and sociological concern with the place of sport and leisure in contemporary
culture, with how we understand the place of sport in contemporary
culture, and how the understanding of sport cannot be divorced from
the wider characteristics of leisure cultures or indeed society itself.
Sometimes the starting point for such interpretation can be a single
image, rather than a whole society. Take the image in Figure 1, by the
graphic artist Jac Depcyz. This was first published on the cover of the
Guardian Weekend (Saturday, 26 June 1993), an invitation to Pete Davies'
account of the USA build-up to World Cup USA 94, described as a "new
American dream". The image was also used to adorn the cover of a
book on soccer cultures, the World Cup and national identity (Sugden
and Tomlinson, 1994). It is an ideal image for raising central themes
concerning our understanding of sport. The Statue of Liberty — with
her gaze of haughty indifference, rather than Mona Lisa-like enigmatic
mysteriousness — looks comfortable enough as she holds the World
Cup aloft, a globe of the world itself spilling over the brim of the cup;
whilst she simultaneously balances a soccer ball on the fingertips of
the left hand. Not in the image, but associated with it in the minds of
many is the Emma Lazarus message: "Give me your tired, your poor,
your huddled masses yearning to breathe free..." — a slogan and a
comforting welcome for generations of arrivals to the New World.
Thus, in this image, one of the modern age's abiding icons of liberty,
hope, renewal and welcome is connected with the most popular team
sport of the age.

But it is not a comforting image. It is a disturbing one, for it literally
disturbs our assumptions about the place of soccer in world culture.
The USA's sports establishment does not like soccer. The country and
the sports public have recurrently rejected it as a mainstream sport. In
fact, in the build up to the 1994 World Cup indifference towards or even
hatred of soccer became a statement of patriotic commitment. The USA
women's soccer team was at the time the World Champion team, but
this was not widely known, and in the USA itself compounded the
problem of soccer's image. It has been convincingly argued that not
only is soccer in the USA the sport of minority ethnic communities, of
the middle-class educational institutions — but it is the sport, at its most

Figure 1 "New American Dream"

spectacularly successful level, of women (Sugden, 1994). This has created great problems for the game in gaining acceptance in the still-so-macho and nativist sports culture of the USA. And to compound the problem — soccer is played with the feet, appendages conspicuously absent both from this image and from the fundamental characteristics of the USA's dominant team-sports. In American football, baseball and basketball the feet are little more than aids to running, jumping and balancing. The major skills in these North American sports are based upon strength and manual dexterity; the showpiece of the American sporting physique is the torso. In capturing this truth, Depcyz's image— the statue holds the ball, goalkeeper perhaps as well as gatekeeper — also captures the essence of the relationship between the USA and soccer: the USA aspiration to become a world force in soccer could well be doomed to failure, despite a splendidly staged and memorably spectacular World Cup Finals event in the Summer of 1994. For you cannot very easily become a world power in soccer if your prevailing view of team sports includes the premise that feet are little more than aids to movement.

Accounting for the rise and significance of different forms of sport, leisure and popular culture, and of the social, political and economic significance of leisure practices, demands a recognition of the complexities and meanings of phenomena which at first sight might appear to be simple, straightforward and trivial. The questions which can then be posed are answerable only on the basis of a sensitivity to forces of history and to their impact upon inter-cultural relations and the forms a culture takes in different and distinctive societies. These points will be amplified and reinforced in the examples upon which I draw throughout this chapter, examples taken from a range of pieces collected in this volume, and from collaborative work with colleagues. Sport and leisure are everyday words with associations of unseriousness. These are associations which can be disputed. This can be done on the basis of another Ology, the science of the making and meaning of words.

Etymology

As recently as the 1880s, the words sport and leisure did not warrant their own etymological identities. For "sport", Walter Skeat, the innovative nineteenth-century etymologist, referred the reader to "port". For "leisure", the reference was to "licence" (Skeat, 1993).

"Sport" is defined by Skeat as mirth, derived from the Mediaeval English *disporten*, to amuse. It is cited as an abbreviated form of disport, with a double origin from Old French and Latin. The Old French *se desporter* meant to amuse oneself, initially to cease from labour. The Latin *portare* meant to carry oneself away (from work or labour in this context). So SPORT was seen as diversion, or removal from more serious aspects of life.

"Leisure" is defined by Skeat as freedom from employment, derived from the Mediaeval English *leyser*, and linked to older roots. In Old French, *leisir* (predecessor of today's *loisir*) meant to be permitted, as did the Latin *licere*. So LEISURE was seen as licence, as freedom: freedom to, as well as freedom from.

These are revealing roots, and in the early modern industrial period (at precisely the time at which Skeat was chronicling the origins of words) many leisure sports were indeed examples of diversionary cultural practice. For some, though, they were too diversionary. Often associated with secular forms of hedonism — the pub, drink, physical prowess, gambling, courtship and sex — they were seen by fun-hating factory owners and respectable religious bodies and individuals as distracting from the serious business of industrial labour or spiritual sobriety. It is this undesirable (for some) side of leisure sports that prompted reformist educators to rationalize and expand new forms of team games and athletic activity. They were driven, in this, by the sense that a form of leisure discipline could be cultivated in athletic activity, and by a belief that a healthy body could only improve still more a healthy mind. Sport was for them a form of character formation and social control, a view shared by many throughout the nineteenth and twentieth centuries (Bailey, 1978; Holt, 1989; Mangan, 1981). "We are developing a fat, flabby unhealthy, generation of children and I think it is time we did something about it", as a British conservative

5

politician put it during the Back to Basics drive of the John Major administration (Ian Sproat, appointed as Minister of Sport by John Major in August of 1993, cited in *The Guardian*, 28 January, 1994: p. 15).

For others, sport in its formative period was much more than character-building, social discipline or health reform. As working-class communities evolved in the appalling urban centres of nineteenth-century Britain, working-class males gave a new meaning to the term "professional" and disputed the amateur values on the basis of which many of the new sports forms had been premised. Disputes over the meaning of words were here rooted in oppositional practices — in these cases evidence of intense cultural conflict over what sports were really for, and how they related to wider aspects of the social relations of leisure. At the very point at which the meanings of the words were confirmed in their etymological pedigree, any narrowly definitive or authoritative interpretation of them was disputed by the vibrant cultural practices of everyday life. The upper-class values of amateurism and athleticism were undermined by working class appropriations of the notion of the "professional" — one upper-class objection to professional footballers was, as Tony Mason (Mason, 1980: p. 72) has shown so clearly, that they were not true professors, or teachers: they had nothing to profess (only, we might add, a better living to seek, a rather vulgar aspiration, perhaps, for true professors).

So sport and leisure in their relatively modern terms convey a sense of permitted diversion. Views of what constitute the limits of permittedness have always complicated any simple interpretation of this meaning. And the variety of activities and meanings, and modes of production and consumption of sport and leisure, do nothing to simplify this picture. But a central point is simple enough: despite the playful, mirthful associations of the terms, sport and leisure are not trivial. They embody deep and lasting meanings, as can be seen in, for instance, the respect and emotion expressed towards sports idols. The deaths in the mid-1990s of Bobby Moore, captain of the triumphant English soccer side of 1966 (Tomlinson and Young, 1999), and Matt Busby, legendary architect of three great Manchester United soccer sides, are testimony to this; and the extraordinary fixation of the USA public with the OJ Simpson murder case also demonstrated the way in which sports and leisure heroes can encapsulate the values and tensions at the heart of a society and its culture. In participation terms, the fact that so many people die in pursuit of sport and leisure, in dangerous contact sports or sensation-seeking activities, also reminds us of the seriousness of certain forms of involvement.

The seriousness of sport and leisure will of course vary according to the particular context in which the sport or leisure form exists, and what kind of sport or leisure form or practice is at issue. Categories and classifications are necessary to put in focus the relative significance of different levels and forms of sport, leisure and popular culture.

Typology

Concepts and models of sport and leisure have been produced, tested and refined, and many definitions have competed for credibility. The inconclusiveness of such debates does not worry me. If forced into a corner in such a context, I would emphasize that in sport the element of contest goes beyond the merely psychological, and must involve some element of physical exertion. Sport brings the body into play — the preparation of the body, bodily performance, the display of the body. Sport grants permission for a flaunting of the physical. This definitional emphasis is important for what is specific about sport in contemporary leisure cultures.

Participatory sport, though, is not one of the major leisure activities of our day. Campaigning bodies — such as Sports Councils — like to claim that it is, but a close look at the sources cited reveals that this rhetoric of recruitment (some might, more sceptically, call it an evaluative gloss on achieving set targets) is deceptive indeed.

Take the following claim, by the Sports Council (England) on participation rates in sport:

> By 1990, some two-thirds of adults regularly participated in some form of sport: 29 million adults in total. (Hart and McInnes, 1992: p. 123)

7

Inserted into a populist document such as the Council's strategy this amounts to a very significant claim — that the majority of the British population is regularly involved in physical activity. But what's the source for this? It's the General Household Survey (GHS), a reputable rigorous source indeed, but one searching for broad brushstrokes on the canvas of sport and leisure trends — the question on which the cited figure is based asks about participation in the last four weeks prior to interview. The figures are hardly an indication of commitment to the activity, or of mode or intensity of involvement. Darts and pool feature prominently, for instance, but can do so on the most fleeting or casual involvement. But even more importantly, the Sports Council disseminates an overall figure which includes "walking"; and in the GHS walking is any walk of two miles, for any purpose. You might have missed a taxi, or ambled along Brighton seafront, or run out of petrol — that won't stop you getting into the national participation figures on sports participation. It has been a commonplace to critique the use and abuse of statistics in, for instance, the former Soviet Union; we would do well to scrutinize the claims of the survey industries in our own society. And such claims become everyday wisdoms, reproduced as shared knowledge, more and more removed from their actual sources. Take this press cutting, for instance, which brings a cross-cultural dimension to the question:

A MORI poll last November revealed that only 46% of Britons play sport, compared with 64% in Italy, 63% in France, 61% in Germany and 59% in Spain. (Jon Craig article, *Daily Express*, 22 January 1994)

My own response to this is not shame at the lack of sportiness of the British, but rather incredulity at the methodologies employed across Europe for tracking these trends, and even more incredulity at the gullibility of the press.

For the key fact remains that sport and physical activity (or at least what is considered to be respectable physical activity — note how silent these survey sources are on the place of sexual anticipation and encounter within our leisure cultures) are minority activities — though

8

young middle-class males who do participate in sport develop into older, higher-class power brokers, so guaranteeing that the sports minority is an influential and powerful one.

Some of the growth or boom activities of the 1980s show still further the minority base of broad patterns of activity. Participation rates in athletics have risen dramatically, but from such a low base that it is still a marginal activity. Aerobics has been the growth industry in the field, but involvement can vary in intensity from the domestic setting to the church hall to the ritzy health club — and for the women who are the vast majority of participants it is an activity to squeeze in alongside persisting obligations and responsibilities for the running of households and the servicing of male needs. Swimming, with the growth of new facilities, is also reported as a growth activity. It is an interesting case for considering what is actually going on in leisure.

In indoor swimming centres, for instance, whole complexes have been designed to offer a multitude of experiences, a wide range of activities, rather than just the rectangular functionalism of the Victorian swimming bath. Whether people learn or reaffirm their swimming skills is not a concern in these developments — fun predominates in the leisure pool, profit depends on pleasure and pleasure is linked in one way or another with exotic lifestyle. So you can swim up to cocktail bars in Centrepark's Tropicana Centre in Rotterdam, by the port's main river, and await the evening laser show over the main water area; or swim naked under the external wall of the Centre's health suite to glance at the outside world of dilapidated barges and dirty wharfside eyesores before gliding back in to the paratropical indoors of this water world. When the bars are in the water itself swimming comes to take on new meanings. This is an example of what Raymond Williams (1983: p. 188) meant by the idea of "mobile privatization" and the mobility of "restricted privacies" — even where the family unit goes, the ideal is for the individual in the family to consume alone, or separately. Don't splash me on this side of the pool — you'll dilute my cocktail. In the Tropicana back in June 1989 I was sipping a lager by the poolside, while at the next table a mother was knitting. How do you make sense of this in surveys of leisure participation and involvement in sport?

It is indisputable that the strongest presence of sport in contemporary culture is ensured not in our public facilities or neighbourhoods, nor on the streets of our inner cities, nor out in the pastures of our rural communities. The Allied Dunbar Fitness Survey (1991) has shown us too that people who have not engaged keenly in sport in their youth rarely take it up in later life. Sport's presence is rooted most firmly in the popular media, and in the way in which it is transmitted via the media and consumed through the media. This is not to deny that in Britain there are a million or so (mainly males) who play soccer fairly regularly; or that suburban golf and tennis clubs are often oversubscribed. But it is to say that many more millions enjoy soccer as centrally heated domesticated theatre. As I have argued elsewhere (Philips and Tomlinson, 1992), the majority awareness of sport is of "spectacle, brought to us packaged, pruned and highly commodified, in the domestic sphere. 'Interest in sport' means [for the vast majority of those who would profess it] some degree of awareness of its presence on television. The main place of sport in contemporary popular culture — primarily through the rituals of domestic consumption — is as marketed product and media discourse" (p. 25). And the impact of the media on sport has not been benign or peripheral; as shown by Garry Whannel (1986a), it has been transformative. The production of sport by the media-entertainment industries is now the main source of most people's understanding of the meanings and messages of sport itself: much more pervasive and persistent than, say, the school or the family.

Consequently, it is examples from popular media forms within the consumer and media industries which have been the focus of much of my attention. However, I am aware that we must recognize different types and modes of sports involvement, and classify them. These would include self-generated participation, participation organized by others, spectatorship and fandom at various levels of intensity. In some of these the sports enthusiast consumes what he or she also produces (many sports clubs are premised on the commitment of what the populist neologiser Alvin Toffler [1981] has christened the "prosumer", in contexts rigorously explored by the American sociologist of "serious leisure", Bob Stebbins [1979]). And such models are valuable when we think of how media sport is consumed: for they help avoid misleading models of the passive consumer. Sports bars in North America are sites of camaraderie and community (predominantly male), of thriving sub-cultures of everyday life (Eastman and Land, 1997), and one unintended consequence of the Sky Television revolution in the broadcasting of football has been to stimulate such public cultures in the neighbour-hood centre of the British pub. But it is the constructed images of sport in the media that warrant close attention if its cultural impact is to be adequately assessed. It remains unresearched, but it is highly probable that the successful expansion of the ownership of colour television sets in this country was a direct consequence of male breadwinners' keen response to the entry of colourful sporting spectacle into the living room; and to the attractiveness of the sporting image on screen. Much the same could be said to account for whatever success satellite television has had in recent years. Cultural theory's framework for the analysis of visual spectacle is my next 'Ology — the Science of Signs.

Semiology

Let us take some images from the cultural event and sporting spectacle which, along with the football World Cup and the funeral of Princess Diana, has generated the largest simultaneous media audience in the history of humankind — the Olympic Games. The Games were on the rack at the turn of the 1970s and 1980s, after boycotts, tragedies and controversies: Black power salutes in Mexico in 1968; the tragic massacre of Israeli athletes in 1972 (another of those "where-were-you?" moments, alongside the death of JFK, England's winning of the World Cup and the death of Princess Diana); the boycott of Montreal '76 by black African nations; and the Carter-led Western boycott of the 1980 Moscow Games after the Soviet invasion of Afghanistan. There was no long queue for the privilege of hosting the 1984 Games. The International Olympic Committee had a straight choice which was not really any choice at all: Los Angeles, host to the 1932 Summer Olympics; or Tehran, in the Middle East cauldron of Iran. Unsurprisingly, the International Olympic Committee voted with the city of the angels. The 1984 Summer Games salvaged a very shaky looking movement, and it opened the show to the world with its own distinctive blend of showbiz, sport and spectacle; with cultural stereotypes, dancing, popular music and technological wizardry (see Chapter 11).

In the ever renewable traditions of media sport, the host nation's celebration of itself has become the focal point, the magnetic draw for the global audience. The full potential of this (though for a retrospective and minority audience in the cinema rather than in a mass networked form) was first exploited by Goebbels and Leni Riefenstahl in the filming of the Berlin Olympics (McFee and Tomlinson, 1999). Here the same processes are at work, though the neo-romantic and neo-classical emphasis in Riefenstahl's depiction of German history is very different to LA's jolly historicism in its showbiz version of American history. Group after group to which I've talked has confirmed that the pianos and the dancers lingered in the consciousness for much longer than did any particular sports event. And the whole thing got off the ground with a stunt vividly recalled by those audiences to which I've talked over the last ten years, when a Rocket Man descended from the heavens, into the heart of the Olympic stadium.

These are some of the dominant images of LA 1984. Hauntingly retained by the global audience, they are a monument to the spirit not so much of Pierre de Coubertin, aristocratic fin-de-siècle Rénovateur of the modern Olympics, but of Liberace and Steven Spielberg.

I am not USA-bashing here, but like the French negotiators in the GATT (General Agreement on Trade and Tariffs) talks I believe that USA culture and its assumptions about speaking for and to the world should certainly be interrogated. And it is not just the USA that is capable of such semantic appropriations — Seoul and Barcelona, and Albertville and Lillehammer, are open to comparable forms of analysis, showing how the Olympic myth is routinely arrogated within a given national culture (Tomlinson, 1996).

Whatever innate and relatively autonomous values sport and sports events and competitions might have, though, these are often over-ridden, in global sporting spectacles, by the wider social, cultural and political forces which make the event at all possible. It is the classical stuff of semiotic analysis: sport denotes competition, physicality, whatever. But at the deeper level, it connotes cultural values and political rivalries.

It is the interplay of such values and forces which underlies the process of meaning-production in sport. And the kinds of dominant meanings which are produced in and through sport are examples of my fifth 'Ology.

Ideology

By ideology I mean sets of values serving particular interests. Two ideologies have been particularly prominent in sport: sexism and nationalism.

Sexism and the Gendered Body

Sexist ideologies have dominated modern sports forms, and there is a distinguished body of feminist scholarship on this theme (Hall, 1996; Hargreaves, 1994). Suffice to say that as yet most social histories are of the publicly dominating male sports which documented their own dominant histories from the beginnings. And despite progress in sport towards gender equality, it is sobering to remind ourselves of the dates when women were first permitted to run in the longer track events — the 10,000 metres and the Marathon — at the Olympic Games: Barcelona 1992 and Los Angeles 1984 respectively. What kept women out were male-led presuppositions about the nature of the female body, about its alleged physical frailty and vulnerability. As women have made inroads into sporting territory traditionally dominated by men they have suffered from ideological backlashes: either they are seen as having surrendered their femininity (through body maintenance and accompanying muscle-development, and sometimes the use of performance-enhancing and sex-distorting drugs); or they are revered as Super-feminine women — they're sporty *and* sexy, drawn into the consumer industry of fitness s and fashion franchises.

A less explored dimension of the sexist bodily practices which characterize sport is the sphere of the masculine sporting body. The male body in sport has been much less prone to ideological pressure than has the female body. Whilst the tension around the female body is portrayed widely in girls' comics and women's magazines, the male body in all its shapes, sizes and distortions is much more tolerated. Think of some male sporting idols: the burliness of the rugby league player or of the cricketer (the portly Cowdrey, the beefy Botham, upholders of the bodily principles of WG Grace); the tiny flyweight boxer; the physical anonymity of the champion golfer or the motor-racing driver; the excesses of the Sumo wrestler. Despite male doubts in adolescence about weediness — remember the Charles Atlas ads which guaranteed that there was a way for the wimp not to have sand kicked into his face? — sport has offered lots of ways out of anonymity. Despite their far-from ideal bodies the partially lame Brazilian Garrincha and the stocky Argentinean Maradona dazzled soccer fans around the globe with their artistry. And in boys' comics this acknowledgement of what is acceptably physical is inclusive and accommodating. Here is a cast of characters from the comic *Roy of the Rovers* and its predecessors:

Limp Along Leslie — the physically impaired shepherd and part-time football star;

Billy (of Billy's Boots) — archetypal pubescent wimp, but a matchwinner with his magic boots on;

Nipper — anarchic streetwise adolescent;

Hot Shot Hamish — giant Scottish hard-man;

The Mighty Mouse — short, fat, caring swot; and

Alf Tupper — Tough of the Track, ragamuffin running hero with a training diet of fish and chips.

These are bodily images to give confidence to the young dart-throwing Jocky Wilson quite as much as to the young athletic Linford Christie. They gave reassurances of the accessibility of sport to the male readership, and brought all on equal terms into the fantasy world of Roy Race, linchpin of the boys' sports comic for 40 years.

Roy Race — Roy of Melchester Rovers — has now lost his Race against time. Glossy magazine formats, the computer-game phenomenon, the extension of broadcasting hours and the growth of specialist channels — these have all competed for the time and the favour of the adolescent male consumer. But from the mid 1950s Roy Race has symbolized an important aspect of sport — its cyclical nature, its

14

constant remaking, its dramatic narratives, its hero/superman motif. For millions of males who have followed sport, it has offered what is really a popular romantic genre, or a form of soap opera.

Roy has thrived not just in the pages of the comic text. The rhetoric of Roy of the Rovers has been prominent in male sporting gossip. There are many examples of this, and of the tacit understanding shared within the male sporting community. For instance, the Newcastle soccer player Peter Beardsley chose Roy of the Rovers as a metaphor for glorious romantic feats in the game (Tomlinson and Young, 1999). But my favourite remains the tribute to Roy Race and Melchester by the former West Bromwich Albion football manager Bobby Gould, later coach to the Welsh national side, who in 1991 defied club tradition and changed its away strip to red and yellow stripes: "I always wanted a team of mine to play in the Roy of the Rovers kit — I evaluated red and yellow as easy colours for the players to pick up" (*Daily Mirror*, August 1 1993, p. 35) — a splendid blend here of logic and confessional wish-fulfilment.

The male romance of sport can be blended with the adventure story. And the sporting triumph can so easily be simultaneously a national triumph. The remarkable success and impact of a particular blend of sport, masculinity, and nationalism can be found in the movie *Chariots of Fire*.

Nationalist Ideology

Colin Welland, scriptwriter of the movie, claimed that the film gestured "two fingers" to the establishment. Chapter 12 demonstrates the falsity of this claim, for without doubt *Chariots of Fire* is in the end a celebration of the theme of English/British nationalism.

Whatever the differences in class or race, the white pseudo-classical Puritanism of the runners stresses commonality and coherence. Lord Lindsay shares the final words in the film, with the faithful Monty as they leave the funeral of Harold Abrahams, Jew and Cambridge contemporary: "He did it Andy? He did what old boy? He ran them off their feet". But the 'them' in the end was the Americans. Despite anti-Semitic snobberies the runner Abrahams ran swiftly and determinedly into the Establishment. The movie is framed at the beginning by the ironic Blakeian hymn *Jerusalem* — 'And did those feet in ancient time...' — confirming the inherent Englishness/Britishness of the Abrahams achievement.

Chariots of Fire is a vivid evocation of how the sporting phenomenon can express a harmonious nationalism in which the divisions of ethnicity or separate cultures are transcended. Harold Abrahams, conscious of his descent from Lithuanian Jewish stock, is centre stage in the theatre as well as on the track, and his light operatic theme tune in the film is "To be An Englishman". Railing against the classically amateurist college masters — "yours are the values of the prep school playground ... and I shall carry the future with me", Abrahams eventually wins a victory claimed by the Masters as theirs, and becomes himself a part of an English establishment to which he was initially so opposed. *Chariots of Fire* shows how distinctive individual drive and motivation can be used by others to represent established national interests. Of course this is not inevitable, and glorious individualism prospers in top-level sport. But sport and leisure cultures will be misunderstood if the wider ideological context is put aside or ignored.

For sports cultures do so often operate in ideological fashion, and are fuelled by ideologies (Sugden, Tomlinson and McCartan, 1990). How else does Cuba's success in international sport make sense? In its last three Summer Olympic Games — Moscow in 1980, Barcelona in 1992 and Atlanta in 1996 — that small country of 10 million or so people, targetting particular Olympic sports, has finished high in the medal table. We need therefore, to unpick the ideological basis of sport which accounts for its profile in particular places and times. But this must be done with an open mind — taking care not to prejudge, and so turn intellectual work into my next 'Ology.

Theology

Theories can too easily become frameworks to defend, belief systems about how the world is shaped and how societies and cultures work.

In this, concepts are reified and interpretive work distorted. Examples are:

— European humanism — the work of Johann Huizinga, stressing play as a central element in culture;
— narrowly-based empiricism, producing, in what C. Wright Mills scathingly called abstract empiricism, the connoisseur of the cul-de-sac;
— over determinist Marxism — recognizing the importance of the economic but often — in say the work of Bero Rigauer — at the expense of a sensitivity to human agency and the generative capacity of the cultural.

But these too often seem like theologies, spiritual quests by the prophets of theory.

Similarly dogmatic theories — at times frenziedly supported by theologians of the idea — can be seen in emerging bodies of work on the place of sport and leisure in the post-modern condition; and on sport's place in an intensifyingly globalized world. Such theologies must be challenged by a more sustained and focused analysis upon the historical roots of sport and leisure, and its changing profile in a complex and changing world (as in, for instance, the seminal work of Elias and Dunning, 1986).

My own framework recognizes, along with colleagues such as John Hargreaves (1986), a need for critical method without predetermined theory. History as alive; culture as constantly being remade; corporeal culture as imbued with values; cultural texts as having ideological impacts; sports or leisure forms as socially produced. I have sought a blend of cultural studies and political economy in my work, with a central analytical concern being the analysis of how cultures relate to ideologies, and to the relations of domination and power characteristic of leisure and sports forms (see, too, Kellner, 1995). The concept of hegemony has been important for me here, in its recognition that power can be gained and sustained through negotiation, and is often based on the granting of consent by the subordinated to the powerful and dominant, and on the relatively unthreatening consequences of the granting of concessions within popular culture.

Sociology — No Apology

I could apologize for the limited breadth or depth of this opening essay — how wide, you may ask, was the range of examples? I could apologize for mentioning very few sports; for concentrating on instances of sport available in the popular media. But I will not, for the types of connections that I have demonstrated are essential to any understanding of the enormous significance of sporting spectacle in contemporary life, and the power of sport to generate as well as merely reflect key features of the day.

In 1994 the Republic of Ireland defeated Italy at the Giants Stadium in the USA World Cup in New Jersey. I was not at the game, for my ticket — in my co-author's baggage after our book launch in London's West End, en route to New York — was stolen. I had to watch the game in an Irish bar on the Upper East Side — even better for my memories, though surely worse for my ears, than being at the stadium itself. This was hardly deprivation, as Booker Prize-winning novelist Roddy Doyle (1993) reminds us, relating an earlier Ireland–Italy encounter at Italia '90:

> Come on, Ireland!
> They tried. They rattled the Italians. They hounded them and bit their arses. They ran and slid after them and got in their way. They never let us think that it was all over. They charged and ran back, and charged again. The second half. Schillachi hit the bar. Schillachi scored but he was offside. But the Irish kept at it, kept running and bullying. They were great and I loved them.
>
> Then it was over.
> We said nothing.
> The fans in Rome were still waving the flags, still singing. People in the pub were doing the same. I told Belinda I loved her.
> It was over.
> It was one of the great times of my life, when I loved being

from Dublin and I loved being Irish. Three years later, it still fills me. The joy and the fun and the pride. Adults behaving like children. Packie gritting his teeth. Being able to cry in public. Getting drunk in daylight. The T-shirts. The colour. Mick McCarthy's long throw. The songs. The players. Paul McGrath. The excitement and madness and love. It's all still in me and I'm starting to cry again.

They came home the next day. Nelson Mandela was in town as well, picking up his freedom of the city.

Roddy Doyle was, as that complex amalgam of the spontaneous fan and the reflective scribe, watching television, the medium which makes the consumption of such a wide range of sports involvement possible.

The popular media forms through which sport is widely consumed undoubtedly have the capacity to reiterate key cultural themes embodied in sport. Media sport and its evocative images can capture the range of human emotions as they are expressed through sport: the pain, the glory, the naked passion, the naturalistic escape: the images of sport remain poetically and seductively encapsulating of the range of human emotions and possibilities. This is the basis of the appeal of television sport's compilations of big sports events, particularly the Olympics. And popular anthems cement together the unique individual stories: in 1984 the BBC's compilation of this sort used Ultravox's *Gold* as the score for its visual depiction of medal winners; and Vangelis' elegaic score from *Chariots of Fire* for the more reflective moments. Parents of pubescent gymnasts and seekers of ennobling transhistorical themes would both recognize the appeal of such an anthem. The BBC Outside Broadcasting department was no exception to this.

Eighteen sets of British feet in the time of the 1984 Olympics were immortalized in gold. Can you name them now, beyond Daley Thompson? Few could answer in the affirmative, yet the sense of the familiarity and impact of the sporting spectacle remains undiminished.

There are no simple explanations to sport's cultural profile — at whatever level of participation or performative competence. Nor is the popular response to sport, and to sport spectacles as portrayed in the media, glibly dismissable or easily accounted for[2]. Sporting feats in ancient, and modern, times have had serious consequences for the nature of cultural life and leisure cultures within societies. Sport and leisure are too serious to be ignored by the social sciences. Sociological analysis of sport and leisure cultures is a task whose time has come.

Notes

1   Revision of Inaugural Professorial Lecture given at the University
    of Brighton, February 1994. This was an Open Lecture, written as
    much for the man or woman on the Brighton omnibus, and for
    colleagues from other disciplines, as for specialist theorists of sport
    and leisure. In fact, there is a bus-stop outside the Sallis Benney
    Theatre in Brighton where the lecture was delivered on a cold and
    snowy February night, and so the former constituency was probably
    quite well represented in the warm, darkened hall, with a lobby
    copiously provided with wine and snacks.

2   Justifying the new Sports Cabinet (comprising the Sports Ministers
    of England, Scotland, Wales and Northern Ireland under the
    Chairmanship of the Secretary of State for Culture, Media and Sport,
    Chris Smith), Sports Minister Tony Banks acknowledged the
    importance "for the psychology of the nation" of success in sport
    (speaking in July, 1998, BBC Radio 5).

I

Studying Sport and Leisure: Approaches and Trends

2 Physical Education, Sport and Sociology: Notes on Approaches and Alternatives

> How is it possible to consider the present, and quite specific present, with a mode of thought elaborated for a past which is often remote and superseded? When someone does this, it means that he is a walking anachronism, a fossil, and not living in the modern world, or at the least that he is strangely composite. (Antonio Gramsci, 1971: p. 324)

Introduction

In this essay I sketch out and offer a critique of some types of work which have focused upon physical education, sport and sociology, and indicate some alternative proposals. At the same time, the complex problem of the relation between a parent discipline and its offspring cannot be simply put to one side. On the contrary, this problem is one which must be confronted if anything like an adequate understanding of 'Physical Education, Sport and Sociology' is to be achieved. So we cannot talk solely about our own little sub-sociologies, for this runs the risk of becoming one of Gramsci's 'walking anachronisms'. In some respects, then, this essay might well have been sub-titled 'Against Ossification'.

In the following section I raise some very general points about why the label 'physical education' has such a malleable character. This is followed by a short discussion of ways of approaching sociological studies, and comments on various social scientific foci. Following this, I look more specifically at some of the problems involved in early sociological work on sport and physical education. Finally, and with reference to some examples of outstanding work from both within and beyond the area itself, I sketch out an agenda for a more adequately sociological study of selected aspects of sport and physical education.

Pinning Down P. E. — Some Problems

An historian of the physical education curriculum in public sector higher education during the last generation would have to don many masks — he or she would need to be a student of organizational growth and decline, and of the increasing professionalization of prospective teachers of the subject. As physical education was developed into an area of study in which degrees could be awarded for what was primarily academic work, so the demands of being a teacher of physical education in higher education may have altered in very significant ways. I offer no substantive empirical base for these remarks, but it does seem pretty clear that the subject of physical education found its way into high-level programmes of study before its own subject-matter had clearly emerged, or even been identified. The problem was straight-forward: what to teach?

Although this was a pretty straightforward problem it was further complicated by the fact that the question was most often being posed within institutions which specialized in the education of teachers. This meant that the study of education, as such, was in some cases divorced from the study of physical education. The latter was seen, in some ways, as being essentially practical, whilst academic work was seen as a separate and distinct activity. This dilemma was not exclusive to the world of physical education. In the colleges of (teacher) education a split between the education/practical staff and the subject-specialist staff was a long standing one. But in physical education the status order was perhaps reversed. Whereas many tutors of English, History or the Sciences may have felt themselves somehow elevated above the level of the practical education tutor, in the world of physical education the subject-specialist was seen as the a-theoretical practitioner, and 'real' academic work was reserved for the scholar of the general educational process. Physical education became trapped in the dichotomy of theory-practice.

I cannot consider the drift, in the world of British physical education of the 1970s, towards human movement studies, in a bid for entry into the academic world. All I will say is that this was one indication of the attempts within physical education to gain for itself an academic respectability of sorts. It was an attempt to say 'Look, we're more than mere P.E. specialists, we actually analyse an important dimension of human behaviour'. The drift towards this kind of claim was one kind of response to the question I posed earlier: what to teach? In a similar process of diversification, physical educationists interested in the social dimensions of physical education became very involved in 'leisure studies'. Now, leisure is not always human movement, yet such areas were taken up, often together, in this general search for 'what to teach' when physical education was seeking an academic base.

Another kind of response was to spot the discipline and run with it. Many physical educationists diversified their interests and became philosophers, psychologists, physiologists, sociologists and so on. But many of them did not look at physical education so much as sport. For 'human movement' (and, to a lesser extent, 'leisure studies') are wide-ranging categories. Also, when we take the education out of the physical — if the education is siphoned off by 'education' experts in the colleges — what have we left but the 'physical'? The forms of study for the emergent area of physical education could only become, in those circumstances, the 'physical', or general examples of 'movement' — in other words, anything to do with human beings moving, in virtually any setting or context. The idea of movement could be approached from any point of view, in any context. I suppose there were some limits to its application. There were no references to Wilhelm Reich, for instance, in the emerging human movement literature: sexual relations, one of the most interesting dimensions of human movement, and most universal of leisure practices, were not incorporated into the field as a significant topic; explicitly *sexual* bodily communication did not feature in human movement studies.

There were, then, some sorts of limits imposed upon the new field of study; but not many. And so the field had no apparent boundaries. Coterminous with the attempt to evolve such interdisciplinary areas of study, the option of spotting the discipline and running with it also became a popular one. Get yourself a subject (say sport), get yourself a discipline (sociology, or psychology) and you're away. What this had to do with *physical education* itself did not seem to be asked. Physical education was very much taken-for-granted, not as a distinctive sphere of study (and long before P.E. became an examinable school subject) and served as a stage upon which any vaguely appropriate script could be acted out. Fourth-year B. Ed. Physical Education students, for instance, began to study leisure policy, sports psychology and so on without necessarily knowing why. Sport and leisure were increasingly seen as physical education itself; studying things from the newly erected platforms of sub-disciplines seemed to be enough legitimation in itself for this kind of work.

The late Alan Guy once suggested to me that the very newness of physical education as a profession for men meant that by the 1950s male teachers of the subject were already extremely insecure, as the switch between different professional bases of and approaches to the subject was taking place. This would certainly be worth further study. The pressure to 'go academic' and produce the B. Ed. degree in the subject produced a crisis of confidence and identity among many physical educationists, but it would be extremely interesting to further explore the forms that this crisis took. Were women physical educationists, with a more secure base as a long-established profession, confident enough to attempt a broader definition of their subject — from physical education to human movement? Were men, less secure, more likely to find security in the specialist discipline, particularly those within the experimental natural sciences? Either way, when these responses emerged in the late 1970s and early 1980s, producing an interesting range of B. Ed., B. A., and B. Sc. courses, physical education may well have been not so much reconstituted as a subject, but reduced to an *a priori* backdrop to all sorts of mixtures of the old and the new. And throughout it all, whatever the swish sophistication of submissions to the validating body of the field, the CNAA, it is not impossible that within the broader academic subject area, work was being done that was not altogether different from a whole generation previously — for that is where 'physical education' seemed to be a safe, secure and uncomplicated world.

'What to teach?' That remained the core of the problem. The study of physical education is concerned with the specific and the general relevance of what goes on in the physical education curriculum. With an adequately wide notion of 'education', such study certainly includes matters beyond the specialized school curriculum, taking in the study of ways in which physical activity has had a socializing and educative role to play in different societies and cultures. Also, physical education should be understood *in relation to* other kinds of cultural experience. Physical education must not be viewed purely normatively, it cannot be simply assumed to be 'a good thing'. In Wolfenden the school/non-school participation gap was seen, by physical educationists, as a problem to be overcome by educational and action-research initiatives. But Paul Corrigan's (1979) work, and the work of researchers like Phil Cohen and David Robbins (1978), shows that the Wolfenden Gap is a deeply rooted aspect of cultural relations. 'Physical education' itself is a value-laden notion. It is the study of that phenomenon — its prevalent values, its dominant practices, its evolving forms — with which the physical educationist must be concerned if the development of physical education studies is to include a more coherent and fully developed rationale (see Kirk, 1992, for a comprehensive critique which provides an evaluative basis for such a rationale). I switch now to the problem of sociology.

Sociological Approaches on Sport

Introductions to sociology have often become lists of 'perspectives': a tour through the supersession of one fading 'ism' by another 'ism'. In the Leisure Studies and the Physical Education literature, for instance, there emerged as the field(s) developed an increasing number of papers on such matters, representing interesting contests for dominance among competing perspectives. But across and beyond such 'isms' one can identify four main ways of approaching sociological work, ones that anyone interested in sociological work — whether their interest is in behavioural patterns in public urinals, the social life of Olympic gold medallists, or the consumption of television programmes — should consider when clarifying or choosing an approach, or combination of approaches.

First, there is the middle range theory approach, in which central concepts and themes are focused upon. This can also be an interesting form of the history of ideas. Concepts such as 'power', 'conflict', 'bureaucracy', 'alienation' might be used in this approach, and developed as themes with reference to particular social settings.

Second, a more general-theoretical approach would stress the competing 'paradigms' or frameworks that have been seeking control in the development of the discipline. This would be another, more orthodox kind of history of ideas, in which the sociologist constantly relativizes and puts in context the offerings of previous sociological perspectives. Functionalism, for instance, is seen as the social product of a liberal-democratic consensus; phenomenology is, in this sense, a thoroughly appropriate development in sociology (as opposed to philosophy) out of the radicalism of the 1960s; neo-Marxist studies are the product of a conflict-ridden society in crisis.

Third, a stress on social structure includes emphases such as 'the social structure of modern Britain', 'society today' and so on. This has usually taken the form of considering respectively a number of interdependent social institutions. More critically, such an approach might consider the balance between consensus and conflict within and between such institutions.

Fourth, a social problems approach sustains one of the strongest roots of the discipline — in 1933 most members of the American Sociological Association said that their primary interest was social work (Easthope, 1974: p. 14). It is still an interesting way of setting up a consideration of social relationships, by posing important questions concerning the genesis and reproduction of, for instance, inequality.

The first approach might be the most revealing way forward for sociological work on physical education and sport, along with the third approach. The second approach is perhaps necessary, but difficult to put over to students whose main interests may be in forms of physical activity. The fourth approach is really the Sports-Council type of approach, what Wright Mills saw as a form of liberal practicality, or "a moralising sociology of milieux" (Mills, 1970: p. 100) — which could well become a more illiberal practicality within the "administration of social services in a welfare state" (Mills, 1970: p. 104). We need only think of how money becomes available for sports and community development in the inner-city to see how the social problem approach can turn into a form of administrative control. Such approaches might be equally applied to the institutional past and to the present.

Sociology, in staking its claims to the territory of the present, has often turned away from study of the very processes that have created the present. So the past has been sadly missing in much sociological work. It is the second type of the third approach that could also overcome this defect; and if concepts are employed on the past as well as the present, then the first approach would also offer much to a sociological understanding of the development of physical education and sport. In the final section of this essay I offer a programme for such work. Before doing that, though, it is necessary and revealing to consider some of the weaknesses and strengths of particular contributions to the area.

Not the Way Forward at All: Some Flaws in Work in the Field

The following critique concentrates upon two writers; this may not fairly represent the range of work in the field of physical education and sport. As areas of study grow there is always room for the emergence of specialists on specialisms. Some years ago I heard a Professor of American Studies lecture to a professional association on the nature of work done in American Studies over the last thirty years — this boiled down to a content-analysis of professional journals and a classification of significant texts in the field. I have had no time — and am not sure whether I in fact have the inclination — to tackle such a task, and so my criticisms should not be taken as criticisms of a whole field. But the flaws which concern me are so basic, so important, that they must be pointed out so that the whole of the field does not become affected by them. I concentrate upon two problems: the world-history problem; and the problem of the sub-discipline.

By the world-history problem I mean the tendency in physical education to try and study every example of physical education/ activity, usually in its sport-related forms, that there has ever been. In most areas of study world-history has faded, yet physical educationists continue to offer massive world-historical syntheses. The students of literature might specialize on, say, the nineteenth century. Not so the unfortunate students of physical education. They are bombarded with every society known to us, with every mention of physical activity that can be pieced together. The only thing missing in this global history of physical education is some account of the nature of physical education/activity between the decline of the Roman Empire, and the emergence of feudal society — perhaps the Barbarians' activity is not classifiable as physical education! Now, what is lacking in such approaches is any real sense of what physical activity/education is as a cultural experience in the specific social setting. It is much more worthwhile to do selected case-studies in depth than to do all of history in the most superficial manner.

The most representative example of this tendency is Earle F. Zeigler's (1979) *History of Physical Education and Sport*, in which a variety of renowned specialists cover world history. Robert Glassford and Gerry Redmond's contribution is on 'physical education and sport in modern times'. This is a big title, and clearly demands some kind of organizing principle. Remarkably, Glassford and Redmond have none that is clearly used or adhered to. Their task is undertaken on the basis of either a developed sense of understanding of the field, or what can only be a touching naiveté. Most lacking is a concern with the way in which people lived their lives; a stress on culturally distinctive factors of social life and the analysis of particular influences of a period. Overall, a sense of how forces are imposed by some on others, and lived out by all in various distinctive ways, has come to the centre of historical consciousness. Glassford and Redmond do not share this consciousness.

Glassford and Redmond employ no organizing principle. This is not just disappointing; it is also ironic. For at the beginning of their chapter they offer a not uninteresting taxonomy of 'value shifts', a 'series of ethics', which can be seen as "guiding principles for sport and physical education programmes" since 1800. These are the ethnocentric, biocentric, egocentric and athropometric ethics, stressing the nation-state, a kind of nature-bound romanticism, an 'individualistic' athleticism, and 'the world' respectively.

This is a chronologically interesting model for analysing development in physical education. The authors say that in contemporary global ethics — their athropometric ethic — there is as yet no 'parallel physical education' programme. What they reveal here is that physical education is a direct reflection of social influences — or that they expect it to be. Their kind of social analysis is a crude form of the "sport reflects the society in which it occurs" (Glassford and Redmond, 1979: p. 133) model. Of course it does. But how? These writers do not even work with the model that they present at the beginning of their account.

Glassford and Redmond are not short on background historical detail. The nineteenth century is an 'age of progress', we are told, due to changes in technology and the effects of a whole range of inventions. We are given the dates of the appearance of steamboats, rubber, bicycles, tyres, cars, aeroplanes, aqualungs, the steam press, cameras, telephones, lamps, dynamos, cinema and radio — these "were representative of profound changes which contributed to the evolution of modern sports" (1979: p. 141). Some link is suggested, too, by the focus upon sporting events of the first commercial motion picture and wireless test. The relation of all this, though, to the particular value-shifts identified earlier on, is simply not considered. Instead, Glassford and Redmond make two interesting points about developments in sport, before pulling the carpet from under their own feet with the most sweeping of a-historical conclusions.

First, they assert that "the most dominant factor in the evolution of sport since 1800" is that "*Sport has become utterly serious*" (1979: p. 158). Second, they recognize the "inexorable emergence of a huge international mass-production recreation and sport industry, replete with specialized paraphernalia, catering to the ever expanding leisure market (Vickerman, 1975)". Interestingly, they quote an economist here, and not a social historian. There is a massive absence in their account; people, social relations and experience are simply left out. Yet they are there, prominently, in the unused model at the beginning of the chapter. People are mentioned in their account, but these are the innovators. De Coubertin, for instance, is said to have carried out "the most important single act in the history of sport" (1979: p. 144), yet in terms of their model surely it is the ideologically contested Olympic Movement which defies categorization as what they call the anthropometric ethic. There was scope for consideration of what a dominant ethic might do to the social life of a people, but this simply did not happen. And then near the end of the chapter, as if all the effort of making the social and historical points has finally proved too much for them, they escape into an idealist corner. Their history of the modern world finally gets slotted into a global history, an utterly idealist one which denies their own fundamental premise that sport reflects society. In 1947, they say, Robert Henderson made "perhaps the most significant" assertion in sports history:

> *That all modern games played with bat and ball descend from one common source: an ancient fertility rite observed by Priest Kings in the Egypt of the Pyramids.* Therefore, for Henderson, such popular activities as baseball, cricket and tennis are 'merely vestigial remains of religious rites of ancient times' (1947, pp. 3-7). It would be difficult to find a more thought-provoking analysis of the transformation from (religious) 'holy-days' to (sport) 'holidays' in all of sport literature. (Glassford and Redmond 1979: p. 161)

It depends, of course, where you look. Glassford and Redmond start with the point that sport reflects society. They reassert the point at the end. But just before this, they offer us a 'Book of Genesis' version of social development in which sport X begat sport Y, sport Y begat sport Z and so on — until, in the end, all things are attributable to what came first. The present is the product of the past, but these writers show no real sense that different periods have specific sets of social relations and cultural conflicts. Glassford and Redmond's world history of sport is an idealist history of cultural forms. It is, in Gramsci's sense, fossilized.

The second problem is related to the issue of the sub-discipline. If the physical educationist chooses to 'spot the discipline' and run, as I put it earlier in this paper, he or she often runs to some newly carved out space within the sub-discipline. To a certain extent this is inevitable and indeed the only practical alternative. No-one could claim to read *all* the literature of sociology. Sociologists have usually specialized in one or two fields, and called themselves sociologists *of* this, that or the other. But Eric Saunders has picked up the distinction between the 'Sociologist *of* something', and the 'Something-sociologist'. The former is said to be a student of social behaviour, the other a sports theorist. But is not sport a form of 'social behaviour'? How can *any* sort of sociologist be interested in anything but central questions about social behaviour?

Saunders goes on to say that the 'sports sociologist' will direct attention to "gaps in sports theory, whilst the sociologist of sport is concerned with gaps in sociological theory ... " (Saunders, 1976: p. 51). Here, I think, is the crunch point. How can this distinction be accepted? Surely *any* sociologist is interested in questions of social structure and social relationships. And if work on sport shows us something about social relationships, surely that is bound to be connected to our understanding of, to use Saunders' term, 'social behaviour'. Let me take the example of someone who has done a great deal more than most in Britain to develop serious sociological work on sport. Eric Dunning is not only interested in sport. He is interested in social theory and, particularly, Norbert Elias' configurational sociology. Now, whilst Dunning is at pains to make theoretical and methodological points in the context of sociology as a discipline — such as that sociology must be developmental, and that theorizing must be object-adequate — it would be absurd to say that he has 'theorised' the social but not sport. His work increases our understanding of sport, raises general sociological issues, and fuels wider sociological debate (Elias and Dunning, 1986).

In the end, I do not think that Saunders' distinction holds. What is this 'sports theory' that has some kind of 'sociological' base but that is not necessarily designed to advance our understanding of 'social behaviour'? It sounds to me like a neatly constructed little area within a sub-discipline — a specialism within a sub-discipline. It is likely that the flight towards this kind of over-specialization would produce examples of intellectual lag, where debates from the parent-discipline will take time to filter down. Points initially made in the sociological literature might constantly be remade. Some years after a key, influential article has been debated in sociological circles another writer can pick the points up and make them to a new and somewhat over-specialized audience (as in, for instance, Haywood, 1977). If this flaw does not produce fossils, it certainly does produce composites. Sport cannot be seen as something set *apart* from other spheres of social life. A sports theory set apart from central sociological questions can only be a dis-located theory, a theory of human practice out of context. Such a 'theory' fails to make the link between particularized milieu and wider public context, between biography and history, that is at the centre of the sociological imagination (Mills, 1970).

Alternatives

Dunning's work has been instanced as an alternative to some of the flawed approaches characteristic of the early field. More work shows the availability of further alternatives. A further model of scholarship, from someone within the professional world of physical education, is Tony Mangan's work on athleticism (Mangan, 1981). This does not contribute merely to our understanding of physical education. It helps us understand how particular kinds of dominant ideologies are produced. Through certain kinds of sport, cultural relations of a specific kind get *re*produced. No one could read Mangan and not concede that physical education and sport can have a powerful ideological function. Five other areas of work have provided critical alternatives.

First, the study of the development of the physical education curriculum, and the emergence of physical education as a profession, has been developed in critically framed theoretical histories. Which social groups or individuals developed the 'profession'? How were they encouraged by, and representative of, the institutions of the state? Such a study needs to be thoroughly conceptualized, rather than merely descriptive, and should explore the role which physical education has played for both elements in the dominant culture and for other social groups. Perhaps the key question here is the extent to which physical education has or has not contributed an ideology — rather than a mere set of values. It seems to me that writers in the field have often used 'ideology' when they have in fact been talking about 'values'. So this area of research would enlighten us in new ways on the ideological function which physical education might have had in different phases of the development of modern industrial capitalism (Evans, 1986; Hargreaves, 1986; Kirk, 1992).

Second, a fully developed ethnographic study of the place of physical education in the school curriculum would be invaluable. Is physical education transformative, or merely reproductive, with regard to dominant values? Paul Willis has flirted with this subject but it is undeveloped in his work. In the odd footnote, in *Learning to Labour* (Willis, 1977: pp. 86-88), he suggested how sport may combine a sense of individual or group freedom with a set of orthodox values to produce a form of incorporation *into* the dominant culture. This is precisely the process that Angela McRobbie's (1982)work on the activities of adolescent working-class girls has revealed to us. Girls reading *Jackie* escape from the world of a dominant school or parental culture, only to prepare themselves for life in a world bounded by the culture of femininity. Now, is this what happens in some sports in the physical education curriculum? Or to what extent — and we should all read and re-read Paul Willis' study to think seriously about this — can physical education/sport constitute a form of 'cultural penetration', to use Willis' own term? Corrigan (1979) has also shown the conflictual relationship between formal school sport and youth cultures. Work on Asian youth (Fleming, 1995) has picked up some of these challenges.

Third, we need to identify, and not take-for-granted, the 'dominant values' of physical education and sport. Who decides what in the area? Are the governing bodies of sport a series of interlocking elites? How does the relation between generations affect the structure and practices of sports bureaucracies? What *is* the role of the Sports Council in post-war Britain with relation to different levels of physical activity and sport? If the answers to these questions suggest that the dominant values are too diverse for any definitive analysis, then we would still need to account for the development of sports elites and the emerging significance of the state in providing for sport; and the relative effectiveness of different policy communities in sport (Houlihan, 1997).

Fourth, there is a need for more genuinely penetrating work on the 'lived experience' of physical education and sport — a version of the second point, but in settings way beyond the school. What is the significance of forms of physical activity such as sport for, say, girls, blacks, housewives, and city bankers? And which sports? Whenever any of my students discuss the idea of gender-specific forms of cultural reproduction through sport, I urge them to read Shirley Prendergast's article on the meaning of stoolball in the life of young housewives/ mothers in Sussex villages (Prendergast, 1977). We need more studies like this, which situate the sports activity as a cultural form in a particular context of wider influences or determinants. Carrington (1998) has produced powerful work of this kind on black identity, cricket and community.

Finally — and this ending is really a beginning as must be the case in all arguments of this kind — we need a more sophisticated understanding of the materialist basis of sports development. What are the *real* relations which underlie sports? John Hargreaves pieced together, from critical work on leisure by social historians, a pioneering skeletal account (Hargreaves, 1982: pp. 37-38). Such an account has been fleshed out in his own (1986) and others' (Gruneau, 1983) theoretical work on sports development.

The sociological study of physical education and sport must retain, or acquire and develop, a sense of the material basis of physical education and sports, and of the wider social relations in which they are situated. This would inevitably challenge the professional rationale for and rhetoric of physical education. Educationists often see themselves as having some degree of agency in their lives, some capacity to affect the world around them. If we are potential agents, and can work with notions of what the world could be like as well as what it is, then we should recognize an element of potential agency in our own professional practice. Physical education, if it is to be more than a set of taken-for-granted activities and values or a crude form of social control, must be studied and, if necessary, made and re-made as a significant element in our wider culture. Alternatives to old flaws can re-shape the study of the area so that physical education becomes the focus of sociological enquiry, rather than claiming an isolated area of expertise, marginally located with nothing to say to or about the social.

3 The Sociological Imagination, the New Journalism and Sports Writing and Research

The Sociological Imagination

No serious examination of the sociological imagination is possible without recognition of C. Wright Mills' seminal statement. At risk of repetition bordering on superfluity, then, I will consider some of his main points. For Mills, the sociological imagination comprises the capacity to make connections between the 'larger historical scene' and the individual's 'inner life' and 'external career' (1970: p. 11). He makes the same point in several different ways. It is the sociological imagination through which we can grasp the relations between 'history and biography'; and with which we are able to see the relations between the remotely impersonal and the 'most intimate features of the human self' (Mills, 1970: pp. 12 and 14). A primary distinction with which the sociological imagination works is that between 'personal troubles' and 'public issues', and sociological insight is particularly focused upon cases where personal troubles outgrow particular individual settings (or 'milieux' as Mills calls them) and become public issues of social structure. For Mills, the main problem with which the sociological imagination should deal is the problem of reason and freedom in modern society. I argue in this chapter that unorthodox sources can operate in sociologically imaginative ways which can help us explore some dimensions of this problem.

The sociological imagination is, in Mills' view, "coming to be felt as a need" in the contemporary world, and it has also flowered in many areas beyond academic sociology, emerging as "the common denominator of our cultural period" (Mills, 1970: pp. 29 and 20)[1]. Some of the most perceptive of social commentators have exhibited what is undeniably their own particular version of the sociological imagination, sometimes in marked preference to early forms of scientific sociology. Randolph Bourne, for instance, moved from traditional English studies at Columbia just prior to the First World War, into the area of sociology. In Max Lerner's view, Bourne saw the term 'sociology' as a catalyst which "included loosely within itself all the groping toward collective living that (his) generation was making" (Schissel, 1965: p. xx). But rather than slot into the scientific sociology of the time, Bourne's thinking operated on the level of the social commentator and social critic, producing innovative and penetrative writings on education, the pacifist question and the state. His central preoccupations became, in Max Lerner's words again, "the relation between political power and cultural creation, and the new world forms and modes of thinking that can be fashioned to replace nationalism" (Filler, 1943: p. vii). Bourne epitomized the attempt of his own generation to give adequate consideration to the individual in the machine age, and to recognize that 'culture' was a necessity rather than a luxury of civilisation (Filler, 1943: p. 133). In his own way Bourne pointed to the paramount importance of an understanding of the creative dimensions of human actions. In his concern with the agency of the intellect or the role of the intellectual, and with the oppressive nature of the state, Bourne could be seen as a North American, albeit less theoretical or revolutionary, version of the Marxist critic Antonio Gramsci.

In this context Bourne also offered some thoughts on the social significance of collegiate sports. He was not the first to do this. Thorstein Veblen had already argued that athletic games combined "futility" with a "colorable make believe of purpose", whilst at the same time functioning in an economic sense as a significant form of training and organization (Veblen, 1953: pp. 172 and 245). Bourne's comments of 1915 on college sports, though, highlighted still further the formative influence of "the good old Anglo-Saxon conviction that life is essentially a game where significance lies in terms of winning or losing" (Schissel, 1965: p. 69). He was more concerned than Veblen to get at the core values of sports (Veblen tended to see them all as 'predatory'), and these in Bourne's view were inextricably linked to the values of an essentially practical, winner-take-all society. Bourne argued that critical thinking was dismissed in undergraduate life in favour of a Peter Pan world of sporting techniques and races for different goals: "The game is won or lost. Analysis and speculation seem superfluous" (Bourne, 1977: p. 214). He saw sports as the embodiment of American cultural values. The task, he then implied, is to contest the terrain that they occupied in college life, and to foster instead the critical spirit of the intellect.

This was provocative stuff, critical in a classically sociological fashion, and pointing to the central issues of the age. The social critic has been an important bearer of the sociological imagination, and offers insights into our social experience which must be taken seriously and might have the status of the hypothesis. George Orwell, for instance, observed that international sport was simply a surrogate form of war (Orwell, 1968: pp. 40-44). It is thinkers like Bourne and Orwell who show us that imaginative sociological thinking about sport is not confined to the halls of academia and to the funded research project.

Other less formal or academic spheres in which the sociological imagination has operated include the writing of fiction and sports writing. Novelists have often argued that particular types of novel — whatever their literary flaws — have lasting significance as social documents evocative of their time and place. The sprawling, prolix novels of Thomas Wolfe, for instance, prompted J. B. Priestley to comment that "Fifty sociological treatises on the recent American scene would not tell us as much about the place and the people as Wolfe does" (Priestley, 1972: p. 12). C. L. R. James has looked at Melville's *Moby Dick* and has asked how a book from the world of 1850 could contain so much of the world of the 1950s. Melville's work, he suggested, was a journey towards the creation of Captain Ahab, a character which sums up 'the whole epoch of human history'. In creating 'types' in the context of historical settings and social processes fictional constructions can formulate problems in the classical sociological sense. Thus, in James' view, Melville is a key representative writer of industrial civilisation, in whose work "the divisions and antagonisms and madnesses of an outworn civilisation are mercilessly dissected and cast aside" (James, 1977: p. 159). This is why fictional forms can be of genuine interest to the analyst of social formations, and are indicative of both the constraints and possibilities which are so often in tension within specific forms of cultural expression and practice.

Our insight into social phenomena can also be enhanced by social actors who develop into social observers of their own (often former) spheres of activity. In this category we can place the previously unreflecting, or coercively constrained, social actor who breaks through and 'tells it like it really is'. The 'pro football' establishment in America has been exposed as a big problem in itself by savage contributions to radical critique and the genre of the 'sports' novel (Parrish, 1972; Gent, 1973).

More generally, Charles Page has observed that painters and sculptors have made 'insightful imaginative reconstructions' of sport, and that it would be short-sighted to ignore these when we are considering the relationship between sport and society. He argued against a sociological provincialism which ignores the contributions of non-sociologists, and suggested that sports writers have often contributed 'meritoriously' to the sociology of sport. Page called George Plimpton a 'participant observer', and noted that other writers work in distinctively sociological ways. Such writing might be of general interest, but it is also a literature 'of sociological utility' (Page, 1973: p. 14). But he said nothing about the sorts of uses to which such writing could be put. In the following section I explore the characteristics and the thrust of selected examples of 'new journalistic' writing on sport in an attempt to illustrate more specifically the utility of one category among such sources.

Selected 'New Journalistic' Treatments of Sport

Big claims have been made for the new journalism, most of all by Tom Wolfe, the most 'successful' New Journalist of all. Wolfe sees this type of writing as a successor to the novel, a successor so effective that it "would wipe out the novel as literature's main event" within ten years (Wolfe, 1975: p. 22). We need not take too seriously a contention so trenchantly put, but it is worth dwelling on the excitement that early writers in this genre felt over what was in many respects a revelatory innovation. Wolfe attributes the breakthrough to Jimmy Breslin, who discovered that "it was feasible for a columnist to actually leave the building, go outside and do reporting on his own, genuine legwork" (Wolfe, 1975: p. 25). Breslin's background as a freelance for *Sports Illustrated* and other magazines, and his columns from 1963 onwards for the *Herald Tribune*, made him an influential as well as pioneering figure.

Wolfe points out that Breslin made it his business to be at a scene before any main event, so that he could gather off-camera material, the novelistic detail that gave life to his writing. Wolfe himself started work on the *Herald Tribune*, and experimented with the techniques of fiction for the documentation of real events. His particular interest was in 'point-of-view'.

It is not appropriate to develop here a critique of Wolfe's account of the characteristics and significance of the writings of new journalism. I want simply to raise some points about why this writing has focused, among other things, upon sport, and how the writings are of use to the sociologist. In Wolfe's terms, the breed of journalists "somehow had the moxie to talk their way inside of any milieu, even closed societies, and hang on for dear life" (1975: p. 41). John Sack, for instance, joined an infantry company as a reporter and went to war. Hunter Thompson ran with the Hells' Angels in California for eighteen months. This capacity for empathy was a central part of the new journalist's method. And, as I have already noted, Charles Page referred to George Plimpton as a participant-observer, and in so doing gave sociological recognition to Plimpton's enterprise.

Wolfe refers to Plimpton's work as 'extraordinary feats with the sports world', and to his strategy as one of "hanging back in the shadows with a diffidence and humility that provoked his 'subjects' into asking him to join in as one of them" (1975: p. 67). I would not want to suggest that such adventures have always been greeted with rapturous praise. Morris Dickstein has referred to "the harmless participatory manner of a George Plimpton" in his dismissal of Tom Wolfe's writing (Dickstein, 1977: p. 140). But if Plimpton's achievements are harmless in terms of the wider issues of the age, his technique did enable certain revelations to be made. In his 'inside story' of the breaking of Babe Ruth's record he employed the novelistic technique of varied point-of-view in the context of a single event, managing to evoke some of the resonances in the life of a society which can be set off by a seemingly superfluous sports event (Plimpton, 1974). This is one of the kind of things Charles Page was suggesting could be done by the sociologist of sport when he wrote of the study of particularly dramatic, at times traumatic, events in the world of sport (1973: p. 9). Spending time with the Detroit Lions in 1963, Plimpton also opened the window upon some specific characteristics of group culture in professional football. Consider this passage, following on from Plimpton's account of his rendition of his old College song at pre-season training:

> Nobody put down their forks to listen. It was apparent that the singing was secondary to the indignity to which the rookie was put; he was being embarrassed, so that he would keep the rigorous caste firmly in mind. (Plimpton, 1964: p. 23)

This is an astute and first-hand interpretation of an initiation rite — hazing — in a particular occupational subculture. In making his own 'rookie' mistakes, Plimpton revealed to us the unwritten rules of football life, its normative code, including the preferential treatment of the quarterback (1964: p. 41). Plimpton was a genuine participant, not just an observer. This gave him access to initiation ceremonies such as the rookie's ordeal on an unprecedentedly accessible scale — as one of the rookies, he actually 'oversaw' it himself. Plimpton evoked the paradoxes of the sporting life, the exhilaration of fitness and camaraderie alongside the constraints of control and discipline. He used contrasts in his observations — two girls playing 'purposeless', spontaneous tennis are contrasted with the team, drilled with machine-like precision in its training routines (1964: pp. 308 and 322). This implied, but neither stated nor developed, an interpretation of the significance of different types of sports. In the end the interpretation faded out on a note of ambiguity. In some ways, then, Plimpton is harmless, and his biography of the team is not placed in any hard context of history. But after reading Plimpton, we feel we know more about the experience of the professional footballer and the sport's cultural patterns.

Plimpton's work offers the sociologist an ethnographic source full of usable detail.

The other writers considered in this section are Norman Mailer, Gay Talese and Hunter Thompson. Wolfe himself has not really written a great deal on sport, and his writing is in some ways less penetrative than the other writers considered. For Wolfe, the demonstration of moral points is subservient to the attempt to prove "one's technical mastery as a writer" (Wolfe, 1975: p. 66). In other words, form dominates content in his work. Dickstein condemns him for failing to let himself go, and for abandoning any critical perspective so that Wolfe's work has, in the end, no sense of context at all[2]. Wolfe himself claims that the new journalists work with a "strange sort of objectivity, an egotistical objectivity ... an objectivity of sorts" (1975: p. 66). An English critic, Richard Hoggart, has suggested that Wolfe's work is little more than a search for poise, style or form. Wolfe, as indicated above, is aware of this. Hoggart suggests, though, that this tendency prevents Wolfe's work from becoming representative of anything. It remains a mere symptom of the age of modern mass communication, an age in which the medium and the stylistic poise are more important than the message; in such circumstances manner triumphs over matter (Hoggart, 1970). Style and content combine more effectively in the sports writing of Norman Mailer, Gay Talese and Hunter Thompson.

In Norman Mailer's book on the George Foreman/Mohammed Ali fight, for instance, we see a writer, to use Dickstein's words again, reporting "most deeply on what was happening both inside and outside his own head" (Dickstein, 1977: p. 143). In this way Mailer manages to situate the social actor — and himself — in wider social and historical contexts. And at certain points Mailer moves explicitly into the realms of the sociological imagination. He is trying to find an appropriate context in which to place the boxing match, and given that this fight is to take place in Zaire, he has been reading his way into African culture by consulting authorities on Bantu philosophy. His source excites him, pointing out that the Bantu philosophy 'saw humans as forces, not beings'. That is, men and women are more than just the parts of themselves, more than the result of heredity and experience. They have, Mailer's reading implies, a future, a projective, a creative potential which is framed in terms of past influences:

> A man was not only what he contained, not only his desires, his memory and his personality, but also the forces that came to inhabit him at any moment from all things living and dead ... so the meaning of one's life was never hard to find.
> One did one's best to live in the pull of these forces in such a way as to increase one's own force. (Mailer, 1977: p. 42)

This is the framework in which Mailer begins to make sense of the Foreman-Ali fight. It is clear to any of us that boxing is more than a mere contest between two opponents. It is also more than just a form of entertainment available to the highest bidder. Mailer begins to probe into the context of the contest, and this shows how the commercial dimensions of the sport and the undeniable personal rivalries have deeper resonances. The social meanings of sport are not simply there to be read off from the activity. Mailer has often believed that Ali's mind has been built upon whims and contradictions. His response to Ali's incredible victory over Foreman changes this. Ali fights as a Black Muslim, as the representative of the black race in a sport whose champions are almost exclusively black. Mailer's great insight is this: that Ali gains his inner resources of strength from his sense of himself as a significant human agent, as a force for change. Mailer concludes that Ali must live with a highly developed sense of anxiety given "the size of his world role and his intimate knowledge of his own ignorance" (Mailer, 1977: p. 42)[3]. In this book Mailer begins to link a cultural event to vital social processes, and in doing so can offer an interpretation of the cultural event which is framed in terms of that event's external determinants. Without the participatory techniques of the new journalism, and the use of fictional devices for documentary writing, these insights could not have been arrived at or presented in such an effective way. Mailer talked to and ran with an apparently unfit and lethargic Ali just a few days before the fight. Such intimacy with the subject matter is what enables Mailer to move towards an interpretation of the fight in terms of supra-individual forces.

It was a piece written in 1962 which first alerted Tom Wolfe to the existence of a style of writing which was to influence him so dramatically. The piece was written by Gay Talese, on Joe Louis (Talese, 1962). Wolfe's recollections of the piece show his own specific concern with style rather than substance. To Wolfe, the qualities of the piece derive from its use of literary devices such as point of view, scene switching and use of time sequences. Wolfe nowhere talks about what the piece is actually saying about a famous sports figure.

Talese, though, is not merely a technician. He does have something to say. As a middle-aged man, he was implying, Joe Louis is learning to live with a dignity appropriate to his former fame. In other pieces, too, Talese offers memorable interpretations as well as observations. Although Talese himself sees the 'new journalism' as a "more imaginative approach to reporting" (1981: p. 9), and then goes on to briefly discuss a few ways in which this can be achieved, his real significance is bound up with the interpretative shape which he imposes upon his material. This is worth looking at in more detail, with reference not just to the piece on Louis but to a piece on Floyd Patterson.

If ever we are tempted to understand sport on the basis of a kind of reductionism which sees only the commercial base to and economic dimensions of the sporting spectacle, we should turn to Talese's picture of the twenty-nine year old, financially secure and physically unmarked Floyd Patterson, in his mountainside retreat after being knocked out for the second time by Sonny Liston:

But Patterson … cannot believe that he is finished. He cannot help but think that it was something more than Liston that destroyed him — a strange, psychological force was also involved, and unless he can fully understand what it was, and learn to deal with it in the boxing ring, he may never be able to live peacefully anywhere but under this mountain. Nor will he ever be able to discard the false whiskers and moustache that, ever since Johansson beat him in 1959, he has carried with him in a small attaché case into each fight so he can slip out of the stadium unrecognized should he lose. (Talese, 1981: p. 69)

Patterson conquered his fear of heights in order to learn how to fly. This was a way of ensuring that after a defeat he could get 'out of town, fast'. Talese shows us how a champion boxer can be a mass of contradictions, a cowardly winner. In defeat Patterson would never face people. Here we see the dilemma of the dramatically successful individual, whose background leaves him few resources to draw upon when success in the sphere of his expertise is no longer guaranteed. Talese show us the raw human emotions behind the outer surface layer of stardom. This same general point is true of Talese's portrayal of the legendary baseball player, Joe Di Maggio, who set a record of fifty-six consecutive hits in 1941. Talese wrote his piece twenty-five years later, and captured the meaning of Di Maggio to millions of fans. The scene is the stadium in New York one day in 1965, when a veteran player has been talked out of retirement. Di Maggio is present on the occasion:

> The banners had been held by hundreds of young boys whose dreams had been fulfilled so often by Mantle, but also seated in the grandstands were older men, paunchy and balding, in whose middle-aged minds Di Maggio was still vivid and invincible, and some of them remembered how one month before, during a pre-game exhibition at old timers Day in Yankee Stadium, Di Maggio had hit a pitch into the left field seats, and suddenly thousands of people had jumped wildly to their feet, joyously screaming — the great Di Maggio had returned, they were young again, it was yesterday. (Talese, 1981: p. 124)

Sport has the capacity to do this sort of thing to people, to offer them unforgettably intense and meaningful moments, and is all the more effective because it could be you or us out there performing. As Di Maggio remarks to a 'man from New York' who calls him a great man — "I'm not great .... I'm not great .... I'm just a man trying to get along" (1981: p. 117). Talese shows us how sport, and sports celebrities, can live on in the popular memory, even though the former sports star is an individual just like any other individual, 'trying to get along'.

But it is in some of the writing of Hunter Thompson that the sociological imagination meets with the new journalism with most devastating effect. Thompson's writing is made up of what he calls gonzo journalism — a "style of 'reporting' based on William Faulkner's idea that the best fiction is far more true than any kind of journalism" (Thompson, 1980: p. 114). To do this sort of reporting effectively, Thompson believes, requires the skills of the journalist, the photographer and the actor, "because the writer must be a participant in the scene, while he's writing it — or at least taping it, or even sketching it" (1980: p. 115). In Thompson's view Tom Wolfe fails to break genuinely 'new' ground mainly because of his reluctance to participate.

The participant observer of California's Hells' Angels attributes this failure to Wolfe's crustiness: "Wolfe's problem is that he's too crusty to participate in his stories. The people he feels comfortable with are dull as stale dogshit, and the people who seem to fascinate him as a writer are so weird that they make him nervous" (Thompson, 1980: p. 116).

Thompson has no problems in this department, bursting his way into any setting that the job demands — football teams (1980: pp. 51-84); Mohammed Ali's inner circle (1980: pp. 578-622); international deep-sea fishing contests (1980: pp. 445-447); Jean-Claude Killy's aeroplane (1980: pp. 84-103). Thompson's writing on sports is also bound up with writing about his own drug-crazed 1960s existence. Setting out as a sports reporter to watch both horse and motor racing (Thompson, 1980: pp. 29-43; Thompson, 1972), he produces a "vile epitaph for the drug culture of the Sixties" (Thompson, 1980: p. 118). But this is part of his achievement. By entering sporting settings in his own terms he is able to polarize things to emphasize the nature of sports values by looking at them through the eyes of the marginal individual. John Leonard of the New York Times has called him "our official crazy, patrolling the edge". Nelson Algren suggested that his hallucinated vision of the 60s "strikes one as having been the sanest" (Thompson, 1980: dust-jacket). By pitching himself into particular milieux, Thompson is able to depict the main characteristics of those settings. He shows us the owner of the Oakland Raiders manically coaching three of his key players on a training field at twilight (1980: p. 65). The 'international' deep-sea fishing champion in Cozumel is shown up for the charlatan — in 'sporting' terms — that he really is, and we are given behind-the-scenes detail on the elitist 'sports' culture (1980: pp. 445 ff.). In going behind the scenes here, Thompson is producing material which undermines 'official' versions of social reality (Peter Berger's first motif of 'debunking' in his model of sociology as a form of consciousness), and in his investigative voyeurism he is able to show what can actually go on under the surface of social life (Berger's 'unrespectability' motif applied to the respectable [Berger, 1966: Ch 2]).

Thompson shows us an aging Mohammed Ali still finding sources of motivation in his role as underdog after his defeat by Leon Spinks. Ali, for Thompson, is a perfect contemporary myth:

> Myths and legends die hard in America. We love them for the extra dimension they provide, the illusion of near-infinite possibility to erase the narrow confines of most men's reality. Weird heroes and mould breaking champions exist as living proof to those who need it that the tyranny of the 'rat race' is not yet final. Look at Joe Namath, they say; he broke all the rules and still beat the system like a gong. Or Hugh Hefner, the Horatio Alger of our time. And Cassius Clay — Mohammed Ali — who flew so high, like the U2, that he couldn't quite believe it when the drone bees shot him down. (Thompson, 1980: pp. 429-430)

At his most effective Thompson points to connections between individual experience and social forces. One such piece was written in 1970, on twenty six year old French ski-champion Jean-Claude Killy. Killy won three gold medals at the 1968 Winter Olympics and then put himself in the hands of Mark McCormack: "The only sure thing in the deal was a hell of a lot of money, both sooner and later. Beyond that, Killy had no idea what he was getting into" (1980: p. 90). Thompson's piece covers Killy's appearances at the Chicago Auto Show and in Boston, where the skier is selling Chevrolets. Here is Thompson's description of Killy at work:

There was a hint of decency — perhaps even humour — about him, but the high-powered realities of the world he lives in now make it hard to deal with him on any terms except those of pure commerce. His handlers rush him from one scheduled appearance to the next; his time and priorities are parcelled out according to their dollar/publicity value; everything he says is screened and programmed. He often sounds like a prisoner of war, dutifully repeating his name, rank and serial number ... and smiling, just as dutifully, fixing his interrogator with that wistful, distracted sort of half-grin that he 'knows' is deadly effective because mishandlers have showed him the evidence in a hundred press-clippings. The smile has become a trademark. It combines James Dean, Porfiro Rubirosa and a teenage bank clerk with a foolproof embezzlement scheme.

Killy projects an innocence and a shy vulnerability that he is working very hard to overcome. He likes the carefree, hell-for-leather image that he earned as the world's best ski racer, but nostalgia is not his bag, and his real interest now is his new commercial scene, the high-rolling world of the money game, where nothing is free and amateurs are called losers. The wistful smile is there, and Killy is shrewd enough to value it, but it will be a hard thing to retain through three years of auto shows, even for $100,000 a year. (1980: p. 86)

The smile is not always retained. When Killy is asked to comment on IOC President Avery Brundage's request that for breaking the Olympic's amateur code he return his Olympic medals, the response is not the programmed one:

But when a Montreal Star reporter asked Jean-Claude how he felt about turning in his Olympic medals, he replied 'Let Brundage come over here himself and take them from me'.

It was a rare public display of the 'old Jean-Claude'. His American personality has been carefully manicured to avoid such outbursts. Chevrolet doesn't want him to say what he thinks, but to sell Chevrolets — and you don't do that by telling self-righteous old men to fuck off. You don't even admit that the French Government paid you to be a skier because things are done that way in France and most other countries, and nobody born after 1900 calls it anything but natural ... when you sell Chevrolets in America you honour the myths and mentality of the marketplace: You smile like Horatio Alger and give all the credit to Mom and Dad, who never lost their faith in you and even mortgaged their ingots when things got tough. (1980: p. 92)

Thompson here demonstrates the way in which the sport performer becomes transformed into a commodity form, caught up in the inexorable economic forces of a particular mode of production. Killy's partner in promotion for Chevrolet is former American football superstar O. J. Simpson:

O. J. 's mind is not complicated; he had had God on his side for so long that it never occurs to him that selling Chevrolets is any less holy than making touch-downs. Like Frank Gifford, whose shoes he finally filled in the USC backfield, he understands that football is only the beginning of his TV career. (1980: p. 94)

Simpson is presented as a black capitalist, using his blackness as a market force, rather like the Joe Louis of Gay Talese's pioneering piece of reporting (Talese, 1962). Killy understands his new life but does not warm to it:

...locked into a gilded life-style where winning means keeping his mouth shut and reciting, on cue, from other men's scripts. He is a handsome middle-class French boy who trained hard and learned to ski so well that now his name is immensely saleable on the marketplace of a crazily inflated culture-economy that eats its heroes like hot dogs and honors them on about the same level ...

His TV-hero image probably surprises him more that it does the rest of us. We take whatever heroes come our way, and we're not inclined to haggle. (1980: p. 103)

Thompson does not simply dismiss Killy as a 'witless greedhead'. He sees him as a victim of social forces, but as a willing one too — a 'good soldier' of capitalism (1980: p. 104), who corrupts his 'completely original act' by working as hard at selling Chevrolets as he did at his sport. Thompson's interpretation of Killy as an instance of advanced commodity exchange is given further emphasis by his own romanticism. He sees Mohammed Ali as a black 'Gatsby' (1980: p. 622) and compares Killy's smile to Gatsby's (1980: p. 88). They are both presented as doomed romantics, as individuals who have been almost wholly taken over by specific socio-economic forces. So Thompson offers us a sense of how social forces are lived, of the interrelationship between different elements of our social life. Sport cannot be seen as a merely non-productive phenomenon. It is play, but it is also a focus for consumption. Sports performers can never be detached, innocent actors in a cocooned world of sport and play. They might come into our consciousness as exciting performers. In order to stay there, other that in the 'popular memory', they must become subservient to the forces of their time and place.

Another sport-related Thompson piece, after a decade of retirement, centred on the Honolulu marathon of 1980. He starts his piece off in typical challenging fashion, asking why "8,000 supposedly smart people ... get up at four in the morning and stagger at high speed through the streets of Waikiki for 26 ball-bursting miles in a race that less than a dozen of them have the slightest chance of winning?" (Thompson, 1981: p. 24). He believes that the Marathon might represent the "last refuge of the liberal mind, ... the last thing that works. Physical Fitness" (1981: p. 26). Doctors, lawyers, relatively affluent professionals, and many others from 'two generations of political activists and social anarchists' are now, after 'politics failed and personal relationships proved unmanageable', into running. In doing this, they have also created a major rapid-growth industry. But why running? "Nothing else has worked, and the ability to run 26 miles at top speed might be a very handy skill for the coming ordeal of the 80s" (1981: p. 83). To contextualize individuals, it is necessary to make connections between individuals and contexts. In locating marathon running within a context of failed dreams, unachieved interpersonal Utopias and frightening futures, Thompson addresses issues central to any but the most arid of sociological imaginations.

The Sociological Pertinence of the New Journalism

At its most effective, new journalistic writing can inform sociological thinking, and its techniques inform sociological work. When the writer balances content with form then it can be a rich source indeed. This balance, though, must be carefully maintained. Wolfe is so impressed with form that he recollects Gay Talese's piece on Joe Louis almost purely in terms of its literary techniques. It is a beautiful piece, playing with time and mood in extremely evocative ways, and starting and ending with the same scene. But, as Hoggart pointed out, to concentrate on manner rather than matter is to run the risk of offering a partial and incomplete reading. Generally, though, when the balance is there, new journalistic writing can show what lived realities really are like, and can situate these realities in the context of their external determinants.

It can do this by shifting from one perspective to another, as Mills recommends; by suddenly talking not just about sport but about economic and political processes with which sports are connected. It can also, at its best, illustrate contradictions and tensions. Joe Louis' work as a black salesman is hardly the best way of acting out his sense that blacks are unequal and exploited. When Killy's 'Gatsby'-like smile slips, we see a complex human being and not merely a commodity. The new journalistic sources can help us formulate the biggest sociological 'problem' of all: sports may be repositories of 'inner meanings', but they do not exist in autonomy. They represent the value systems of the time, and in so doing can embody the tensions, contradictions and antagonisms of the age. Hunter Thompson, in particular, recognizes this. His strategy in seeing the mainstream as problematic, as a problem to be explored, is a genuinely sociological premise.

The sociological imagination can work in many ways. Anthony Giddens suggests a threefold exercize of it, involving three types of sensitivity — the historical, the anthropological and the critical (Giddens, 1982). This first form of sensitivity does not always or necessarily characterize new journalistic writing on sports. Such writings contribute, obviously, to the investigation of particular contemporary moments. But the anthropological and the critical dimensions combine in the most effective pieces. In entering scenes from the outside, the new journalist can undermine the ethnocentric basis of commonsense views of the world; and in showing what things are really like can be critical, albeit in an iconoclastic rather than future-oriented or projective way.

New journalistic writing highlights sport as a problem in the classical sense. The sociological imagination is not the exclusive property of the trained, professional social scientist. Problems should not be reduced to 'social problems' in the sense of the 'liberal practicality' in which a middle-class public makes an issue out of the troubles of lower-class people (Mills, 1970: p. 96). Sociological knowledge should not be ordered into organized facts for ready transmission as the settled view of things. And the exploration of values, value conflicts and the varied nature of cultural experience cannot be collapsed into tidy and quantifiable generalizations. New journalistic pieces on sport formulate sport as a problem of values, and when 'the interplay of ideas and facts' (Mills, 1970: p. 99) works, they are of genuine use to the sociological researcher into sport.

To conclude on a bold note I will suggest just what 'sociological utility' these sources have. They can be critically framed presentations of lived sports experience, and they can also highlight how general social processes are lived and experienced in specific settings. They are, at their best, a form of mediated ethnography. All reported experience is, of course, to some degree mediated by the reporter or the ethnographer. But in our formulation of the problem of the nature and place of sport in society, mediated ethnographies may be better than no ethnography at all. Until genuinely ethnographic data produced by covert and / or overt professional observers become available, the penetrative push of the new journalist will remain one source — albeit an uneven and at times bizarre one — on which the sociologist should draw in the exercize of any genuinely sociological imagination.

Notes

1   Mills' vision of how sociological work should be done is not news, of course, to sociologists of sport. His vision is at the heart of one of the most sophisticated early discussions of 'sociological perspectives' on sport in Richard S. Gruneau's 'Sport as an Area of Sociological Study: an introduction to major themes and perspectives' (Gruneau, 1976).

2   It is worth quoting Dickstein at length on this. He claims that:

> Wolfe has no notion of the kinds of social forces that impede both manners and morals *and* politics, no feel for what Trilling calls 'a culture's hum and buzz of implication'; 'a dim mental region of intention' that underlies a culture and shapes its character at a given historical moment. This is the implicit unity of mood or moral temper that the cultural observer must seek out, by which, for instance, the style of confrontation in the politics of the sixties is closely related to the style of self-assertion in the poetry and sexuality of the period, which in turn is related to the unexpected impulse of the journalist, in covering these and other developments, to do *his* own thing in an authenticating subjective way. And to determine *why* the culture should be moving in this direction, and to make some distinctions and judgments about it, required someone with greater analytical acuity, with more political sensitivity and novelistic vision, than Tom Wolfe. (Dickstein, 1977: p. 143)

3   This insight is all the more revealing when looking at the predictably brain-damaged figure of the Ali of today.

Whether he in fact changed things is not so much the issue as the fact that he himself, and many followers, believed that he had the capacity of change things. Revolutionaries do not always initiate revolutions but this does not mean that they are not dynamic human agents themselves. For a few years at least Mohammed Ali fought for his own beliefs, whilst also acting out the dreams of millions. If nothing has changed, and if Ali has now exchanged his assertive revolutionary role for the role of the victim, this in no way eradicates his former significance as a symbol of his time. No other conclusion is possible for anyone who has seen the montage-documentary *When We Were Kings*.

4 Leisure Studies and Cultural Studies in Britain

Introduction

The Leisure Studies Association (LSA) staged its second international conference in June/July 1988. The Conference lasted for 5 days and attracted 143 presentations of various kinds, from speculative working papers to state-of-the-art overviews of areas of study. Most of the 264 delegates who attended the Conference were from academic backgrounds, from colleges, polytechnics and universities. One count from the Conference Handbook has shown that only five delegates were working in the sphere of leisure management; and only two were from the world of local policy-making, that is they were councillors. This worried Eileen McKeever of the Institute of Leisure and Amenity Management (ILAM), the United Kingdom's aspiring and perhaps emergent umbrella body for leisure professionals, as she reported in the LSA Newsletter of November 1988. From her side of the theory/practice fence she clearly mourns the under-representation of the leisure provider/policy-maker at the LSA Conference. She does not seem to be alone in this. From the other side of the fence Bill Bacon, in the same newsletter, expressed great concern about the same problem: "I was extremely worried during my stay at Brighton at the growing gulf that seems to be developing between the world of recreation, the academic and the teacher and that of the practitioner, the manager and the supplier of leisure services".

If I interpret him correctly, Bill Bacon is chiding the professional practitioners for their neglect of research, debate and informed exchange. There were many excellent papers, he observed, from which great relevance could have been gleaned, 'for practice as well as theory'. Both Bacon and McKeever go on to discuss the possibility of closer links between the practical leisure professional and the academic practitioner, implying that LSA should consider forging links with ILAM.

Bacon and McKeever make some valid points. There were more practitioners, certainly, at the LSA's first international conference in 1984, and it did seem in the Summer of 1988 that the profession itself took little heed of the deliberations and thoughts of academics. But this was not a deliberate attempt to freeze out the practitioner. The practitioner changed since the early 1980s. S/he must, particularly in the public sector, market rather than manage; profit-maximize rather than develop; measure performance-indicators rather than pump-prime. Leisure professionals might look a bit reflectively 'soft' if they were caught with their hands full of worrying research and their heads full of challenging ideas. It is no wonder that in its second international conference the LSA did not reach as mixed a constituency as it had done four years earlier. People from both sides of the fence had less time to sit on that fence together, to attempt to build common pathways from one side to the other. At its second international conference the LSA continued to reflect important trends, but by then most leisure professionals were probably too busy pruning their marketing skills and polishing their new corporate images to take time out to think about the state of knowledge in the field of leisure; or to learn from the comparative insights which were widely available at a conference where presenters came from more than twenty countries across four continents.

Whatever the outcome of the practice/theory issue in the professional world of leisure and leisure studies, it would be a sad day indeed if intellectual and academic skills were marginalized in favour of market analysis and the fatuous futurology of trendspotters. Academic analysis and rigorous research tell us things we don't always want to know. They describe failed dreams as much as realized ambition. They seek to explain not just the fads of the here and now, but the larger-scale trends that have shaped us. As leisure is talked about by influential people, more and more in terms of what Bob Tyrrell of the Henley Centre sees as a post-industrial mass middle-class society (Tyrell, 1990), it becomes even more urgent to *think through* just what a variety of leisure cultures there are, have been and might still be. Cross-cultural and historical insights are indispensable here. The 1988 Conference offered plenty of those. But something else is also essential. Without theory there is nothing; without concepts lists of facts are simply signposts to nowhere.

Sagacity, Critique and Academic Careerism

Throughout the later 1970s and in the 1980s there were various attempts to cross disciplinary boundaries, and to bring together different perspectives from the sociology of leisure, Leisure Studies and the British Cultural Studies tradition. One such initiative was taken by the Leisure and Recreation Study Group of the British Sociological Association/Leisure Studies Association in 1980, when a Workshop on "Leisure and Social Control" was organized, hosted by the Centre for Contemporary Cultural Studies at the University of Birmingham (Tomlinson, 1981). This was an attempt to wrench Leisure Studies and the sociology of leisure out of a rather cosy parochialism in which major writers in the field addressed themselves neither to each other nor to sociological work on different but clearly related aspects of social life. The sociology of leisure, in particular, remained in its own theoretical backwaters, becalmed by its combination of simplistic taxonomies and empirical reportage.

The 1980 Workshop proceedings were published in 1981, and are still available as Number 19 on the Leisure Studies Association's Publications list. A major contribution to these proceedings was the identification of startling gaps in much of what John Clarke and Chas Critcher called the "conventional wisdom" in Leisure Studies. One of these gaps was the common lack of any adequately historicized conception of the social; this could only be remedied by seeing history not as mere prelude or background, but as process, as forcefully formative. Another was the need to snap Leisure Studies out of its essentially patriarchal framework, and so to expose many of its universalizing assumptions about leisure, which in great part derived from an exclusive focus upon the experience and values of adult males in full-time employment. Many contributors to the Workshop also argued that leisure should not be over-individualized, that leisure should be understood as integrally connected to wider relations of culture, status and power, rather than being seen as some kind of separate or autonomous sphere of social life.

Despite such initiatives, the conventional wisdom has a grip on things, for some very common and, hierarchies being what they are, deep-rooted and understandable reasons. New books might challenge established wisdoms. But older books can keep oracles busy on professional circuits, even when their wisdoms have been shown time and time again to be pretty jaded, their critical edge blunted in the haze of Conference banquets and committee politics.

It was John Kenneth Galbraith (1962: ch.2) who invented the term "conventional wisdom". For a long time, whilst working on his classic exploration of the contradictions of the affluent society, he struggled to find a concise yet telling term to describe the way in which "acceptable ideas have great stability" and people "approve most of what they best understand". He used the term to refer to the set of stable, acceptable and predictable ideas which can come to be affirmed and celebrated as religious rite: "Scholars gather in scholarly assemblages to hear in elegant statement what all have heard before … the structure of ideas that is based on acceptability".

Cultural studies challenges the premises of the early Leisure Studies in ways which widen rather than resolve the practitioner/researcher relation.

Leisure Studies and the Early Sociology of Leisure in Britain

Research and writing on leisure have developed higher profiles as a response to a perceived problem: the problem of the "leisure society". Large-scale theories about the nature of the advanced industrial society, about the beneficial effects of automation, about the spread of affluence, suggested to many in the 1950s that industrial societies stood on the threshold of a new social order. Some claimed that leisure itself would become the major formative influence upon the direction the modern society would take. There was a peculiar yet persistent combination of ideas at work here. An idealist stress on leisure and its humanizing potential (derived from post-holocaust European thinking), blended with North American theories concerning the end of ideology, to suggest or at least imply that in some way or another leisure was something available to all, a sphere in which choice, creativity and freedom could be given almost unlimited expression. A further influence, grafted on to these, was the developing industrial sociology which was soon to add leisure (the adjunct to work) to the expanding repertoire of the sociologist of industry. In Britain, certainly, among the geographers and sociologists who contributed to the development of Leisure Studies, these themes were central and enduring. Classical social theory — a concern with relations of power and inequality, with the workings of ideology, and the nature of contemporary conscious-ness — was not drawn upon. Its concerns were not so much sidelined as ignored, in a formative phase for Leisure Studies in which con-tributors were happy to chug away producing head-counting surveys of what people did and, on a much more limited scale, of why they thought they did what they did. Work in this tradition was primarily concerned with charting distributional patterns of leisure participation, rather than developing interpretations of the place of leisure in social relations.

At least three sets of interests coalesced to form the alliance which consolidated the growth of Leisure Studies in this formative phase. A reformist strand in liberal sociology implied that to identify problems in the social order, to glimpse cracks in the social structure, could diagnostically point to beneficial changes. At the same time, in the burgeoning public-sector professions, leisure provision was reframed, elevated into a profession in which social democratic administrators saw sport, recreation and leisure as one further sphere of expertise for the caring provider (unaware, at this stage, that this might involve attempts at reintegrating millions of unemployed people into "respectable" forms of activity). The third set of interests was that of the environmentalist, two types of which were prominent, though of common motivational origins in socially committed geographical studies: one with a concern directed very much towards issues of access to and conservation of the countryside; the other with a concern for the planned development of the built environment, a fancy brief of sorts for the enlightened town-planner. Established figures in the formative phase of Leisure Studies in Britain came from the ranks, then, of the liberal sociologist, the public-sector provider and the environmentally-aware geographer. The Leisure Studies Association, set up in the mid-1970s, represented an initiative out of if not a full-blown synthesis of these interests. Some even thought that this was enough, that a new applied science was under way. Away from the UK, in the University of Ottawa, such interests fuelled, for a few years at least, the fires of a Faculty of Recreology. In North America throughout the 1980s some specialists continued to offer the services of the Leisurologist.

In the UK the self-labelling has been of a less flamboyant kind. But the sets of interest have remained influential in the work produced on the basis of public funding. In the early 1980s, for instance, when the London-based Sports Council and the then Social Science Research Council funded a large-scale project on work and leisure, the work was commissioned from a Department of Geography where the research was then carried out on the basis of analytical categories imported from America and adapted by Stanley Parker some fifteen or so years earlier (Parker, 1971).

This alliance, then, this overlapping of interests and concerns, has produced a substantial body of material, but little of this has been influenced by any more critical or even comprehensive form of social theory. This is the case even in the sociological contributions, where some concern with social theory might have been expected.

The early sociology of leisure in Britain offered more than the well-intentioned but naive administrative humanism which was the driving motivation for many providers and policy-makers. It certainly conceptualized leisure, and explored its relationship to some of society's main institutions. But much sociological work on leisure also exhibited several fundamental flaws. I will consider just four; I am sure that other commentators could find more.

First, too much dependence was placed upon an over-simplistic notion of the connectedness of work and leisure, guaranteeing neat classifications of the work-leisure relation. The survey method was vital for a lot of this work, and the more penetrating interpretative offerings of ethnography remained untapped. What these more penetrating studies have reminded us (in critically informed debates about the ideological nature of the labour process, for instance [Willis, 1978]; and in social histories of leisure practices [Bailey, 1978]) is that work and leisure are always part of a society's general relations, often bound up with that society's cultural features and ideological processes. It is not enough to simply freeze a couple of apparently autonomous spheres of life and then study lines of possible connection between them. Work and leisure are ideologically constructed dimensions of the production/consumption dynamic. Leisure has often been defined expressly to fit a particular idea of this dynamic. Some of the more antediluvian examples of the early sociology of leisure show little sense of this, and look barely capable of coping with, say, the growth of the informal economy during periods of acute unemployment. Most taxonomies imported from earlier social contexts or intellectual climates will simply not do any more, if we are to understand the range of meanings in the leisure activities of everyday and working life.

The second flaw is that this early work shows little capacity to deal adequately with questions concerning power. Too many writers overstressed the voluntaristic nature of leisure and left it at that. Yet clearly as members of communities and primary groups, as citizens as well as individuals, we make personal choices which are determined by and contribute back to structures of power and domination. A concern with status in some approaches simply meant that people could, if they so chose or strove, accrue status through forms of leisure, consumption and display (see, for instance, Hoggett and Bishop, 1986; and Stebbins, 1979). That is undoubtedly in a real but limited sense true. But striving and choosing are not merely voluntaristic acts; statuses available to different individuals are never unconnected to wider relations of privilege and wider patterns of cultural practice.

A third criticism is that the early sociology of leisure tended to rob practices of their meanings. Leisure activities are not always as they might at first appear to be. They might be provided by some for particular purposes, but used by most for something else, or developed by others for specific and different purposes. Any perceptive analysis of the relation between the rational recreation movement and many working-class practices in the second half of the nineteenth century makes this unambiguously clear. The same could be said of the relation between youth movements or providers and the young people who make up their clientele. When we look closely at what some people say others should do, and at what those others actually do, we will not be short of examples which show that the meaning of leisure is often disputed. In some contexts the meaning of the practice is appropriated. In others it is simply imposed on a relatively powerless group. In still others it is a matter of negotiation with other people, or with apparently impersonal forces such as the state or the consumer market. In no cases at all should some simple single dimension such as freedom be attributed to leisure. Key historical work, especially, if read and genuinely absorbed by the sociologist, warns against such incomplete readings of the contexts in which the meanings of leisure are produced.

My fourth criticism is not specific to the sociology of leisure. It is a point concerned with the contemporary history of ideas, with the growth of new fields. Quite simply, specializations often prosper, once established, by keeping the boundaries of the specialism relatively narrowly defined. In the sociology of leisure and sport in the UK, for instance, it is notable that specialists most prominent in this field show nowhere that they have actually read each other's work. It is almost as if particular branches of branches had grown up — the sociology of leisure in the civilizing process (Elias and Dunning, 1986); the sociology of leisure in the family (Rapoport and Rapoport, 1975); the sociology of leisure in gender relations (Deem, 1986; and Hargreaves, 1994); the sociology of leisure and work (Parker, 1971). Such forms of specialization have at least two effects: first, they fragment our general understanding; and second, they confirm specialists as band-leaders of small bands, seen as somewhat marginal by the bigger orchestras occupying the more prestigious parts of the disciplinary territory.

The early sociology of leisure in Britain has, then, often remained a-theoretical in terms of contemporary sociological debates, and too often — despite honourable exceptions — a-historical in terms of temporal analysis. It has been kept well-fed by the professional and cultural apparatus that grows up around any conventional wisdom. Its practitioners may deny that they are members of any such club, but with self-perpetuating international jamborees and conferences, with the set books lined up on the shelves, such denials do not sound convincing. But such cosiness of the conventional wisdom is one of the aspects under challenge from the more critical perspectives available in Cultural Studies.

Cultural Studies in Britain

Cultural Studies stems from roots very different to those of Leisure Studies. If the typical figure in the emergence of Leisure Studies has been the liberal applied social scientist, often an exponent of pluralism, the typical figure in Cultural Studies has been the New Left social theorist, literary critic or social historian, frequently expounding the relevance of an intellectual or cultural Marxism or neo-Marxism. In its most formative phase Cultural Studies in Britain emerged from the crisis in English Studies, and pushed towards a focus upon the serious analysis of popular culture and everyday life. Two major and not always smoothly compatible methodological emphases have continued to be at the centre of initiatives in Cultural Studies: the ethnographic study of everyday life, as a means of studying cultural practices; and the semiotic analysis of popular cultural texts, as a way of understanding the ideological work which is accomplished in much of our not-so-innocent cultural activity, or leisure. In the best work on youth culture and subcultural style (Hebdige, 1979; McRobbie, 1982), both these emphases have been drawn upon in framing and then working on the particular problematic. The most convincing work in Cultural Studies has produced concrete case-studies but, under the influence of theory from feminism to French structuralism, has never left these case-studies cocooned in an inconsequential descriptive and localized context.

Particularly under the influence of Stuart Hall and his colleagues at the Centre for Contemporary Cultural Studies at the University of Birmingham, work in Cultural Studies also stressed the importance of social and political context and praxis. Detailed work should be contextualized in terms of socially and politically acute moments. For central to Cultural Studies has been the concern with the relation between culture and ideology, with the ways in which the practices of the popular or subordinate classes have related to the reproduction of, and shifts in, the dominant culture. Also drawing where appropriate upon some variants of critical and interpretative sociology (Hollands, 1985), work in Cultural Studies has been consistently concerned with investigating the relation between popular consciousness and the political process.

The three major analytical concerns of Cultural Studies have been outlined in successive statements and pieces by Stuart Hall and Richard Johnson(Hall, 1980b; Johnson, 1986/87). They are: the formal analysis of popular texts (films, television, magazines, comics, for instance); the situating of these texts to explore how they are variously read, received and consumed; and observation and analysis of lived cultures, of cultural experience, through the development of ethnographies of everyday practices. Contemporary Cultural Studies in Britain needs, in Johnson's view, to pursue two vital questions. First, how do subjective forms become popular on the level of "principles of living"? And second, how do popular pleasures operate in specifically political fashion? There has not been any simple consensus over the definition of scope of Cultural Studies, but these sorts of questions convey its major concerns.

Several of the central tenets of Cultural Studies (shared, too, with a Critical Sociology) can be seen as ways round some of the problems identified in the earlier discussion of Leisure Studies and the sociology of leisure. First, research in Cultural Studies does not separate the present from the historical. It must be recognized that contemporary beliefs and practices are produced and reproduced in history. Second, always be ready to see the familiar as strange, the at-first-sight innocent as redolent with significant meaning; do not see the everyday world as a natural world, but as one which is culturally and ideologically constituted in still-shifting relations. Third, recognize that there is no simple culture, but that we need to talk about cultures and relations between cultures. We should be interested not just in the consumer market but in its relation to traditional working-class culture, and the questions concerning transformation and power that must be asked when looking at such a relation. For it is often within cultural relations — the switch from comfortable neighbourly pub to brightly-lit theme bar — that leisure practices can be seen to have their specific meanings. For Leisure Studies the implications of this should be clear: never abstract leisure activity from its context in cultural relations. Fourth, Cultural Studies reminds us of the range, diversity and varied richness of the cultural; often our understanding of the cultural has come from what Raymond Williams liked to call a "selective tradition", from which we gain only a partial understanding, as quite as much is left out of such a tradition as ever finds its way in. There is a retrieval project, to identify and illuminate what was left out. Fifth, Cultural Studies has been concerned with struggle and intervention, in which the analytical itself is a form of practice, or more accurately, praxis.

I do not want to suggest that Cultural Studies offers an all-embracing panacea. Some tendencies are in need of careful and searching critique. Some contributions too often, for instance, accept the premise that the more dazzling the language, the more penetrating the insight. This is a recurrent characteristic in much twentieth-century European critical theory. Without wishing to perpetuate any stodgy Anglo-Saxon a-theoreticism, I would question any such premise. Interpretive and critical work need not adopt an obscurantism bordering on the incommunicable. Work in the Cultural Studies tradition has tended, too, to take for granted whatever is meant by the dominant culture, rather than subjecting it in turn to rigorous scrutiny and analysis. But despite such problems, the promise of Cultural Studies remains, on the basis of its capacity to throw light on key questions which orthodox Leisure Studies and the early sociology of leisure neglected. These include the ideological nature of leisure itself; the relation of everyday life to power, privilege and domination; and the conditions of cultural transformation, on both grand (the rise of a creatively subversive industrial proletariat, or of the women's movement) and more localized (the punkdresser as meaning-innovator, or bricoleur) scales.

Leisure Studies and Cultural Studies: Contrasts and Tensions

I mentioned at the beginning of this critique that there is a tension between the two approaches. This tension revolves around big questions concerning what kind of society we now live in, what kind of forces shape us, what scope there is for forms of human creativity and agency.

Leisure Studies has represented a particular kind of praxis, an operationalization of one vision of the good life by a faction of the caring/providing public sector professions. Cultural Studies has produced cultural analysis and cultural commentators whose form of praxis has been cast in more aspirantly transformational form, often linked to projects designed to mobilize collectivist strategies and ideals.

Leisure Studies has relied, in its sense of action and development, upon a distributional awareness of the availability of and need for facilities. Its vision has been one of increased participation, imposed downwards upon potential markets. Cultural Studies has been much more concerned with the study of the category of "experience", with how popular subjectivities are constituted from below. There is often a sense in provider-sponsored studies of leisure facilities that some swisher marketing technique along with a well-intentioned plan of animation or provision will be enough; people will then flood in, releasing a leisure potential lying dormant within everyone not yet converted. Work in Cultural Studies shatters any model of such a smoothly functioning leisure market.

Cultural Studies has also questioned the way in which Leisure Studies has tended to fragment the social world, in the latter's commitment to a vision of the world of leisure as the good society. In its emphasis upon the interconnectedness of the different sites of social life, Cultural Studies has sought to embrace the true complexity of the cultural, so rejecting any simplistic or idealistic conception of leisure.

Leisure Studies has offered an emergent profession an analytic academic underpinning, not least the wealth of data on distributional dimensions of leisure that became available as the field developed. The usefulness of this should certainly not be underestimated. If the study of leisure further develops under the influence of Cultural Studies, such achievements should not be cast aside, like the fading record collections of an ageing fan. But to listen closely to the voices of those materially located within different leisure cultures in a society, and to theorize them, is to shift Leisure Studies some way from a bureaucratic technicism which has tended too often to misrepresent or betray the subjects for whom it has claimed to speak. Cultural Studies, conceived in ways compatible with the critical sociological imagination can contribute to such a shift.

The Sociological Analysis of Sport and Leisure, and British Cultural Studies

Paradigm-hunting and perspective-baiting is a necessary evil in critical social science. We need to locate our own intellectual roots, and to situate them *vis-à-vis* alternative perspectives. Inevitably, this will at times involve a degree of parody in the presentation of respective positions; and so sometimes, in the eyes of those in the position under scrutiny, a degree of misrepresentation. Eric Dunning argues that critics of figurational sociology often fail to understand the subtleties of the figurational framework. The same can be said of portrayals of British cultural studies. I have argued elsewhere against such misrepresentations, in an exchange with John MacAloon (Hargreaves and Tomlinson, 1992). Here, before delving in a little more detail into the history of ideas of British cultural studies, I will respond to a couple of points made by Eric Dunning about the cultural approach.

Eric Dunning, at a conference in Vienna in June 1992, commented that the term culture, in its inherent relativism, distorts the necessary balance in sociological work between description and analysis; and that it also perpetuates the false dualism between social structure (presumably seen as a kind of contextually determining force), and culture (seen, I think, as a form of agency involving a set of values and beliefs). Let me take these two points one by one.

First, there is no *necessary* distortion or loss of balance between description and analysis when using the concept of culture. Indeed, it can be seen as a powerful relational concept, rather than as a relativist term, facilitating the analysis of *cultures* and cultural relations. With such an emphasis, ethnography, for instance, can be simultaneously descriptive and analytical; indeed, if it were not so, ethnography would be little more than the random collection of data on any and every aspect of social life. As Robert Hollands has argued, what we need to work towards, for the best ethnography, is a sense of structural ethnography (Hollands, 1985). If we do this, there is no inexorable relativism in our use of the concept; nor is there any necessary distortion between the descriptive and the analytical.

The second point made by Eric Dunning addresses one of the classic dualisms of contemporary social thought — the made (often inherited structure) and making (often idealized agency) elements of human being. Theorists more erudite and eloquent than I have addressed this problem, in the classic theoretical tomes of the social sciences, and on occasion in terms of sports cultures and their social development (Gruneau, 1983). My intent here is simply to record the awareness of this problem that has characterized work within British cultural studies. This is not to say that there have not been excesses of the very kind to which Eric Dunning is referring.

Indeed, in cultural studies in the 1970s and the early 1980s the rival sub-paradigms of 'structuralism' and 'culturalism' evoked passionate exchanges, critiques and disavowals among cultural studies researchers and academics. There seemed to be irreconcilable differences between theorists for whom the social world was a network of all-embracing and deeply entrenched structures, and theorists for whom the essence of the cultural was the capacity for meaning-production in human beings, and particularly for the subordinate classes in society. But very early on in these debates — no sooner had the schisms been identified (Johnson, 1979a) — Stuart Hall was urging a form of bridge-building, declaring that "neither structuralism nor culturalism will do" (Hall, 1980a). Richard Johnson (1979b), too, expressed regret at having outlined so clearly such labels. And much intellectual energy has been expended upon reconciling such extremes, and seeking a theoretical synthesis which recognizes both the determined and the to-be-determined in social being.

This latter is of course the Holy Grail of social theory, and bold attempts are recurrently made to resolve or overcome the dualism. I think here of the exciting fusion of phenomenology and structuralism represented in Berger and Luckmann's (1971) work; figurational sociologists' claim to having reached the site of the Holy Grail (Elias, 1978; Goudsblom, 1977); and of course Anthony Giddens' structuration theory, which comprises a major statement on the resolution of this dualism (Giddens, 1984). I make no claim that cultural studies has resolved this issue; but it is unfair to accuse cultural studies, or approaches emphasizing or prioritizing culture, of perpetuating the dualism.

John Clarke, documenting his own journey through the British cultural studies territories of the 1950s, 1970s and 1980s (along with Stuart Hall, through from the Centre for Contemporary Cultural Studies at the University of Birmingham, to the Social Science Faculty at the Open University) highlights the most productive tension in the development of cultural studies — the aspiration to overcome the very dualism to which Eric Dunning refers: "Cultural studies has been founded in precisely this tension between the reductionist pressures of orthodox Marxism and the idealist tendency to separate culture from social relations" (Clarke, 1991: p. xv). One commentary on Birmingham cultural studies (Turner, 1990) also recognizes the centrality of this tension in the Centre's work, and points out that Gramsci's "theory of hegemony does not allow for power to flow 'bottom-up', and severely qualifies the economistic assumptions of the effectiveness of power imposed from the 'top-down'" (Turner, 1990: pp. 215-216).

The more 'culturalist' strand in this project developed out of a radical English studies and a preoccupation with the study of popular culture (particularly the changing culture of traditional working-class communities); popular culture was seen as warranting serious analytical attention, and new forms of popular culture were given critical attention as texts in themselves (Hoggart, 1958). Critical Marxist work in social history stressed the project of retrieval, of subordinate groups' histories and narratives of struggle (Thompson, 1963): and previously unconnected spheres of the social and the cultural were explored in innovative ways involving new methodologies for cultural analysis and the recognition of a more broadly conceived sociology of popular consciousness (Williams, 1963). These three books by Hoggart, Thompson and Williams constituted what Stuart Hall has called "the originating texts, the original 'curriculum' of the field ... responses of different kinds to a decisive historical conjuncture ... cultural interventions in their own right" (Hall, 1980b: p. 16). Under Hall's stewardship at the Centre for Contemporary Cultural Studies more European influences (Althusserian Marxism, semiotic theory, Gramsci's work) were brought to bear, and cultural studies' integrating strand became a critical analysis of the media and their framing ideologies, and the study of the modes in which the media are consumed and experienced, framed in terms of feminist as well as class-cultural analysis.

But the most rigorous work in this tradition always recognized the full complexity of the phenomenon under scrutiny. Chas Critcher, for instance, was always interested in football culture in its fully lived forms, in everyday lived cultures as they articulated with media forms and other forms of representation and consumption (Critcher, 1979). Leisure and the media, in Critcher's view, can only be understood in terms of the patterns of lived culture as well as the structural patterns identifiable in media texts (Critcher, 1992). Also, Whannel's work (1992) on textual analysis, political economy and consumption provided an important example of how to integrate several central concerns of the cultural analyst.

In this sense, then, cultural studies and the critical sociology of cultural consumption have developed as a multi-faceted sociology of consumption, in which the analysis of the role of ideology in modern cultural relations and formations has been the central thrust. And this central problematic has been arrived at via other routes in critical theory and critical theoretical accounts of modern culture. John Thompson, for instance, has proposed a general framework for cultural analysis which he calls a 'depth hermeneutics' involving 'different types of analysis' which are linked on the 'path of interpretation' (Thompson, 1990). These different types of analysis constitute, for Thompson, a comprehensive methodological approach to the analysis of ideology and modern culture — in which there are three principal phases. I will outline these with reference to the modern Olympic Games.

76

The first phase is that of social historical analysis, concerned with "the social and historical conditions of the production, circulation and reception of symbolic forms" (Thompson, 1990: p. 282). To understand the modern Olympic Games, then, it would be necessary to contextualize the moment of their emergence and creation in fin-de-siècle Europe, and, even more specifically, the material and ideological basis of the values of the 'founder' of the Games, the Baron Pierre de Coubertin (MacAloon, 1981; Tomlinson, 1984). And such analysis would not be one-off and fixed. The social and historical conditions obviously change, and each Olympiad and Games constitutes a form of remaking, what elsewhere I have called a 'necessary arrogation' (Tomlinson, 1989) of the claimed ideals and values of Olympism. Second, Thompson emphasizes the formal/discursive analysis which is necessary to any systematic study of the structural features, patterns and relationships of the forms. In this phase, the rituals and major characteristics of the Olympic Games would need to be subjected to rigorous analysis; this would include rituals of a local, lived character, in, say, host cities and nations, and their relationship to the spectacle of the Games (MacAloon, 1984); ceremonial rituals within the protocol of the Games themselves; and media presentations of the Games phenomenon, most significantly in the contemporary era, in televisual form. And third, at the level of interpretation or re-interpretation, we need to be concerned with "creative construction of meaning ... an interpretive explication of what is represented or what is said" (Thompson, 1990: p. 289). At this stage of Thompson's depth hermeneutic the meaning of the cultural phenomenon is what is at issue. In terms of the Olympic example, the relative importance of different dimensions of the Games — as drama, local culture, corporate enterprise, physical display, nationalist swaggering or whatever — would need to be considered.

It is precisely such debates about re-interpretation in which theorists are engaged when to some observers they seem to be defending esoteric intellectual fiefdoms or adhering in reductionist fashion to one particular framework.

Thompson's framework has been criticized in some quarters as an over-inflated version of what some in cultural studies have been trying to do for some time (Barker, 1991). More sympathetically, I feel grateful for the availability of a general and widely applicable methodological and analytical framework for work in the critical sociology of culture and cultural analysis (although I would take issue with the implied relativism of the hermeneutic if in the end all interpretations were to be deemed equally authentic on an explanatory level). And there does appear to be an emerging consensus in British work around these themes. John Thompson's study includes as its chief empirical focus an analysis of mass communications, and he reminds us that there are three aspects of the mass communications process: the production/ transmission/diffusion of forms; the construction of media messages; and the reception/appropriation of media messages. This is what Thompson calls a 'tripartite' approach. It is shared with commentators on the sociology of consumption (Warde, 1990); with many cultural/ media theorists aware of the complexity of the production-consumption dynamic; and, in whatever skeletal early versions, with some leisure theorists (Tomlinson, 1983).

The best cultural analysis has avoided the Scylla of any structuralist reductionism and the Charybdis of cultural relativism, and has consistently sought to capture the dynamic of the made and the making. The cultural imagination is no more inherently distorted than is the sociological imagination: as C. Wright Mills so inimitably expressed it, the best sociological analysis will countenance neither abstracted empiricism nor grand theory (Mills, 1970). Similarly, the best cultural analysis needs more than just descriptive ethnographies or all-embracing theories. Exemplary work is this vein, Critcher's on football for instance, has — as argued above — explored the culture of football in its fully lived forms, concentrating on the everyday lived culture of the professional player and the fan (and, vitally, the relation between them), and the media forms through which football has been consumed.

I would argue, therefore, for cultural analysis/studies and the cultural analysis of sport and leisure as a project concerned with classic sociological questions. The most fully developed and effective cultural studies offers an awareness of contexts as well as texts, determining forces as well as particularized and distinctive lived cultures. This central concern — how do cultures operate ideologically, or reach towards new horizons of human possibility? — is best developed on the basis of a methodological/interpretive open-mindedness. Work on key theoretical concerns such as hegemony has — despite criticisms, particularly from social historians (Golby and Purdue, 1984) — demonstrated this (Gruneau, 1988; Clarke and Critcher, 1984), as long as the researcher does not impose a predetermined theoretical framework upon the object of enquiry; hegemony', for instance, is an analytical tool, a concept in the intellectual tool kit, not a theory in itself.

Although it has been argued that "the British version of cultural studies … is a global diaspora without a 'homeland'" (Turner, 1992: p. 204), the impact of innovative work in this field has not been trivial or marginal. Work on cultural practices and ideology (Willis, 1977) has been among the most influential critical sociological work of the last two decades. Indeed, two polls taken in 1973 and 1980 show the impact of cultural studies upon the British sociological profession in the 1970s. In 1973 a chart listing those sociological works perceived by sociologists as the most highly regarded explanatory texts was topped by Durkheim, with *Suicide*. Number 2 in the chart was Weber's *The Protestant Ethic and the Spirit of Capitalism*. In 1980 a follow-up poll saw Durkheim at Number 2, but there was a new Number 1 — Paul Willis' *Learning to Labour* (Heath and Edmundson, 1981). Some might not warm to the balance in Willis' work between description and theory, but that particular version of the cultural studies approach could hardly be accused of perpetuating false dualisms or marginalizing the explanatory. Indeed, during his late 1970s / early 1980s North American tours Anthony Giddens, when asked to specify an empirical study which exemplified the processes to which structuration theory pointed, cited Willis' classic ethnography. And in his textbook Giddens has described *Learning to Labour* as a "brilliant study of cultural reproduction" (Giddens, 1989: p. 430).

Concluding Comment

The cultural studies project has not, then, been some quirky eccentricity on the margins of British social scientific life. It has been more than that. It has been a way of recognizing the legacy of the past in the present, of addressing the question of how culture(s) can come to operate ideologically (in the interests of some rather than others), of accounting for why and how subordinate groups respond in the way that they do to those who hold power over them, of exploring the relation between lived cultures and forms of (media-based) representation, and of examining the ways in which dominant views of the world achieve and retain their positions of dominance. It has also, in a radical way, revitalized the theory/practice debate, by abandoning premises of pseudo-neutrality and stressing that cultural analysis is always a potential form of engagement or intervention. Any emphasis on understanding the institutions of society needs to be balanced with a sensitivity to the complexity of lived cultures, and to the cultural meanings and relations of symbolic forms in that society. Thus might false dualisms be avoided. The study of sport and leisure need be neither over-romantically celebratory of the cultural, nor over-deterministically structuralist in emphasis. An open-minded and balanced cultural studies / critical sociology thus has much to offer to the social scientific study of sport and leisure. Whether the product of such approaches will be of value to the practitioner is an issue of less immediate importance than the need to accomplish — and disseminate in accessible forms — empirically adequate and conceptually informed and theorized studies of sport and leisure forms and practices. Once accomplished, such work has the capacity to reinvigorate both academic and professional debates concerning the nature and place of leisure studies in contemporary culture and society.

5   Playing Away from Home: Leisure, Disadvantage and Issues of Income and Access at the Heart of the Thatcher Years

It is in the world of leisure, away from the home, that the divide between the privileged and the poor finds one of its most observable public forms. Consumers have emerged as a new kind of 'leisure class'. Raymond Williams has captured a central characteristic of this consumer culture in his idea of 'mobile privatisation' (Williams, 1983). By this he means that more and more, in the world of leisure, people have chosen to do things in immediate social groups, or on their own. They will go 'out' when it pleases them. Improvements in transport and communication, increased private car ownership and improved road networks have made much of this possible. It all backfires, sometimes, in the motorway jams, in fraught social relations inside the over-full car on the Bank Holiday weekend. But people pack up and set off again next Bank Holiday, making individual decisions about where to go and what to do — what's the latest spectacle, where haven't we been yet? 'Mum, Dad, the telly says we should go …'.

There's plenty to do, we're reminded, as a consumer. And the images in Sunday supplements and other forms of media advertising constantly urge us to do it. In consuming and spending, we do our little bit to boost the flagging economy; our leisure becomes in turn productive. But many people have little opportunity to express such consumer choice. Such people are doubly disadvantaged. Denied the basic requirements of the consumer — regular work and disposable income — they are also excluded from the 'leisure life-style'. Not

81

admitted in the first place, they are then branded by their exclusion. Yet talk of the new 'leisure society' conjures up images of a world of limitless possibilities for those with time on their hands, but little money in their pockets. Clearly, their possibilities will be very different from those open to the more economically privileged.

Idle Time and Useful Leisure

Leisure has always been determined by power and privilege. The world of leisure has been a world of inequality as much as of opportunity. It has also been a sphere in which disputes over what is 'acceptable behaviour' have been prominent. Not infrequently, leisure has been seen very openly as a means of transforming the consciousness of the populace. In the nineteenth century the 'rational recreation' movement attempted to 'civilize' the more boisterous elements in the working-class popular culture, to formalize and standardize leisure activities in ways that would make them 'self-improving'. Ideologues from the churches and from the newly emergent commercial bourgeoisie formed alliances to attack certain notions of leisure as dangerous and to attempt, through leisure, to achieve forms of class conciliation. Arguments and conflicts concerning 'time' have often been linked to the question of leisure. E. P. Thompson showed clearly how the industrial worker's unproductive use of time (when not occupying measured time at work) was of great concern to the urban bourgeoisie. He quotes the views of one 1821 moralist, on manual workers left with:

> ... several hours in the day to be spent nearly as they please. And in what manner ... is this precious time expended by those of no mental cultivation? We shall often see them just simply annihilating these portions of time. They will for an hour, or for hours together ... sit on a bench or lie down on a bank or hillock ... yielded up to utter vacancy and torpor .... (Thompson, 1993: p. 395)

It is this sort of concern which is at the heart of debates about the 'problem' of leisure, a century and a half on. The unconstructive use of public space is still seen as threatening. The question of how time and public space are used — idly or constructively, rationally — has been a recurrent one in the modern period.

But as recently as the 1920s and the 1930s, the work-leisure relationship was pretty blurred, very different in a traditional working-class experience from that in the burgeoning middle-class suburban culture. People lived and worked in working-class neighbourhoods and communities which offered a rich texture to their everyday lives — maybe not much in terms of material comforts, and often virtually nothing in terms of conspicuous consumption. But accounts of life in the inter-war period show us that, despite the rosy glow of the popular memory that might idealize such conditions of living, neighbourhood and community were still important contexts for leisure. Local, collective and often self-generated activities still thrived. At the same time, the embryonic consumer culture was under construction in the rise of suburban culture: radios, cars, fashion, holidays, paperbacks. Consumer horizons were certainly expanding, but not for everyone. Spectator sport was popular, but not always for the spectacle. Alun Howkins has pointed out that admission to Lords cricket ground in the 1930s was one of the cheapest ways of getting a seat for the day if you were unemployed, with nowhere to go and limited options about what to do (Lowerson and Howkins, 1981: p. 95).

'Idle' time, it has often been thought, could be made respectable — and therefore less threatening — if turned into 'leisure' time (Clarke and Critcher, 1984). In the 1980s in Britain, the same issues were being raised. 'New' notions of discipline, around concerns of time and work, are being debated. This is one new form of a very old problem for a dominant culture seeking to hold on to its dominance: how to speak to diverse elements in the society and to convince them of their integral place in that society. Unemployed youth with little spending power and no options in the leisure market will understandably be sceptical about such attempts. People labouring away at cleaning offices in the early mornings of grey, cold autumn days; underpaid hirelings of multinational fast-food chains; non-unionized employees of rurally splendid theme parks; disgracefully paid waitresses with only temporary and casual work; invisible labourers cleaning up the refuse of the consumer society at play — all these figures, bent and exploited presences in the consumer landscape, whose role is so necessary as service labour to the consumer 'leisure class' — all these will also be sceptical about the claims that we are a 'united society' in which the individual is free to choose, able to determine his or her own destiny.

Two Nations of Leisure

For we are not just free agents in the social world. Options as to what we do away from home will be open, or limited, to us on the basis of a number of things: money, time, desire, confidence. And we will respond to possibilities differently in terms of our class, age, gender or race. Just because resources or facilities are there is no guarantee that they are accessible to all. Take the example of the squash court, one of the booming leisure activities of the 1960s/70s. Figures in the 1980s showed this to be one of the most evenly distributed of male sports activities across the age range. Though 'regular' squash is played most among males between the ages of 20 and 34 (1 in 10), 7 per cent or so of the 16-19 year-old males and 4 per cent or so 35-59 year-olds polled played regularly. Given what the Henley Centre for Forecasting describes as the "large body of people who remain unconvinced of the attractions of sport" (*Leisure Futures*, Autumn 1985: p. 87), this looks like a pretty steady and evenly distributed participation rate in squash. But let's look more closely at who might be playing, and how they go about fitting squash into their lifestyle. Other figures have shown the class bases of participation. Clearly, 'male', in the Henley Centre's use of the Central Statistical Office's figures, is a very undeveloped category. 'White, suburban, middle-class professional male' might be a more adequate expanded category. Buying kit, shoes, racket, balls, and paying fees and so on are premised on adequate disposable income. United Kingdom spending on sports clothing and footwear has risen from an estimated £275m in 1979 to a quite staggering £780m in 1984 — a massive increase.

84

All sorts of developments may have fed into such an increase —
for instance, the school gates of many well-to-do neighbourhoods have
become informal fashion parade grounds, mostly for women's 'leisure'
or 'jogging' fashions during the years of the 'body boom'. But we know
that the increase in squash playing has drawn in people who are able
to spend on sports clothing and footwear. Looking good, not just feeling
good, has been a central concern of people contributing to the physical
renaissance that is evident in a few boom sports. And quite simply, this
has cost money — levels of disposable income which for increasing
numbers would be the difference between desperate survival and
ordinary comfort.

Also, less obvious but of equal importance, getting on court is no
simple matter. Where squash has boomed, you might need a telephone,
a diary, some flexible working hours, as well as all the kit, before
starting. The squash game is set up just like the business meeting.
Punctuality; precision; short, sharp and decisive action; the game often
needs to be set up organizationally, played promptly and somewhat
privately. It is the leisure activity *par excellence* for the thrusting young
professional. But if you work on a factory floor for a set number of
clocked-in hours, or if you are unemployed and have no phone to hand,
even the basic requirements for booking are not part of your cultural
repertoire. Leisure is not and never has been a social space wide open
to any newcomer.

The world of leisure has never been open and accessible in this
way. The professional forecasters, high-tech crystal-ball gazers of the
Henley Centre don't mince their words on this: "The *'Two Nations'*
phenomenon is becoming more pronounced and will continue to do
so for the foreseeable future" (*Leisure Futures*, Autumn 1985: p. 3).
They then offer several dimensions along which the 'two nations'
phenomenon can be seen: north vs south; poor vs rich; unemployed
vs employed; tenant vs occupier; youth vs non-youth; urban vs rural.
Yet, around most of these dimensions, it is the accessibility of different
groups to commodity culture which is the major dividing line between
the privileged and the poor. The culture of consumption in leisure is
becoming increasingly remote and impossible a prospect for those
excluded by both social and economic disadvantage. 'Mobile

privatization' might have become a significant aspect of the contemporary culture of consumption for some, but it is clear that many groups and individuals are unable even to consider the option of following the trend. Leisure activities are not the product of free individual choices made in a social world of wide-open possibilities.

Away-from-home activities are not, apart from motoring, dominant among younger age groups. Eating out increased in the early 1980s, but very much in terms of overseas tourist markets and fast-food expenditure. And the latter, as any parent of young children knows, is hard to see as leisure rather than familial obligation. The top five away-from-home entertainments, in the Henley Centre's 1985 time-use survey, were the pub (surely one of the longest reigning chart-toppers of all time), motoring, dance-clubs/discos, sports clubs and the cinema. Age is a big factor here. Young adults make up a high proportion of pub-goers and, not surprisingly, of dancers. As we look at figures for dance-activity through the life cycle, there is a dramatic fall-off after middle age — so, too, with sports clubs, though not so dramatically. And, perhaps more surprisingly, there is the same trend in cinema attendance. The general pattern to emerge from close consideration of the top five examples of 'playing' away from home is clear enough: after early adulthood more and more people spend more and more of their spare time in and around the house. Televisions, gardens, home improvements, home screenings, home entertaining. These constitute the core elements in a consumer culture which develops the home as self-governed leisure centre.

But leisure activities outside the home have clear boundaries formed by class and gender, not just age. It is not simply 'women' who play bingo — which attracts 13 per cent of women — it is middle-aged to elderly working-class women. And much of the drinking in pubs throughout the land — as any early evening commuter pint-drinker will know — is by males. Motoring is perhaps the activity most evenly distributed across age bands, with a slight peak amongst people in the 46-55 age groups — driving around, maybe, with a new sense of freedom, now that the children are no longer with them.

Generally speaking, the most obviously growing parts of the leisure market seem to be sports clubs and the pub. For the sports club, the potential member needs, as noted earlier with reference to squash-playing, a range of cultural competencies, as well as money. For the pub, money is always needed. Other 'growth' areas include theme parks, the death-knell for the ties of community and neighbourhood which were at the heart of earlier experiences of free-time and leisure. The English theme park Alton Towers is clean, tidy, efficient, good fun undeniably. It is also functional, crowded, anonymity-inducing, slick. And for an average size family in the mid 1980s it could easily run to £40 or £50 for the day. What better image of unequal access in leisure than this: an ancient country house in remote Derbyshire countryside catering for the hedonistic needs of suburban crowds, whilst an increasing proportion of the country's urban population wonders how it might eke out the basis of subsistence?

It is worth taking a look at the stark facts of consumer ownership and of leisure participation. Although in some sense increasingly sophis-ticated forms of mass production have made a range of consumer goods available at relatively accessible prices, that accessibility is far from universal. There has certainly been an increase in the domestic avail-ability of the telephone. In 1973, only 45 per cent of all households had one. In 1984, 78 per cent of households could boast this vital form of communication with the outside world — a sizeable increase, but still leaving almost a quarter of all households without one. Proportionately, more owner-occupiers than tenants have had telephones. A car, vital for so many forms of leisure, was owned in 1983 by only around half of households (the figures on this vary, from 43 to 59 per cent). Of the tenants of local authorities and new towns in 1983, only 29 per cent had a car available (Central Statistical Office, 1985: Table 6.12, p. 99).

Much leisure away from home — as testified in the pervasiveness of the credit card and cheque card notices in restaurants, cinemas, shops, petrol stations and transport termini — is premised on formalized personal finances. But, as Jan Toporowski (1986) has shown, only a minority of poorer households have bank accounts or access to financial aids and institutions.

Table 1: Participation[1] in selected social and cultural activities in Great Britain: by socio-economic group[2] and by sex, 1983 (%) [Source: *Social Trends*, 15 1985, Table 10.3]

	Professional employers and managers	Intermediate and junior non-manual	Skilled manual and own account non-professional	Semi-skilled and un-skilled manual	Full-time students	All persons[3]	All males[3]	All females[3]
open air outings								
seaside	9	9	6	6	6	7	7	8
country	5	3	2	2	2	3	3	3
parks	4	5	3	3	2	4	3	4
entertainment, social, and cultural activities								
going to the cinema	9	10	5	4	27	7	7	8
visiting historic buildings	13	11	6	5	7	8	8	8
going to the theatre/opera/ballet	8	7	2	2	7	4	4	5
going to museums/art galleries	5	4	2	2	4	3	3	3
amateur music/drama	4	4	2	2	11	3	3	3
attending leisure classes	3	3	1	1	1	2	1	2
going to fairs/amusement arcades	1	2	1	1	2	1	1	2
going out for a meal[4]	61	51	34	27	46	40	41	40
going out for a drink[4]	56	55	61	50	61	54	64	46
dancing	10	13	9	9	31	11	10	12
home based activities								
listening to records/tapes[4]	69	70	60	54	93	63	65	62
gardening	58	47	46	39	20	44	50	39
needlework/knitting[4]	14	42	11	30	22	27	2	48
house repairs/DIY[4]	55	35	45	27	22	36	51	24
reading books[4]	68	70	44	45	74	56	50	61
Sample size (= 100%) (numbers)	2,391	5,632	4,115	5,658	550	19,070	8,751	10,319

1 Annual averages of participation of people aged 16 or over.   2 Full-time students are covered separately.

3 Includes armed forces, and persons who have never worked. These are excluded from the analysis by socio-economic group.

4 The high participation levels are partly attributable to the fact that these items were prompted.

The inequality of participation in leisure activities is starkly displayed in Table 1. In only dancing, drinking and attendance at fairs (deep-rooted traditional activities in working-class as well as youth culture) is there a significantly even participation rate by different socio-economic groups. In most cases, activity increases proportionately with income.

'But everyone at least gets a holiday', it might be objected, in the age of paid holidays. But you are only paid if you have work. And there are many examples of paid work which leave little room for expenditure on leisure. So even having a break away from home is far from a general trend — 42 per cent of adult residents of Great Britain took no holiday in 1983. More people took more than one holiday a year in the mid-1980s, but these were those for whom the holiday was already part of their social calendar: they simply chose to get away more. The leisured get more leisure, while the rest stay at home. As *Social Trends* (1985) put it: "In 1983 58% of adults in social classes D and E did not have a holiday compared with only 22% in classes A and B; over a third of those in classes A and B, but only 11% in classes D and E, had more than one holiday".

Those already immersed in a consumer-based leisure culture, those already 'doing the business', know exactly what's what. Leisure becomes a public statement of status and relative privilege. It stresses exclusivity quite as much as open opportunity. Roger Daltry, former Who rock star, is the spokesperson for those riding high on the wave of consumer leisure: "This does the business. The American Express card shows exactly who's who".

Exclusion from the Leisure Utopia

In a very important social document on the life of young people in Wolverhampton in the mid-1980s, we see a social world far removed from the consumer world, a very different cultural landscape indeed (Willis *et al.*, 1985). There are no neat work/leisure distinctions here, no tidy categories of leisure activities. Young people in Wolverhampton know what they want: they want work. For that is what provides the promise of consumerism, to play one's part in the cycle of production-consumption. Denied their role at the point of production, many young and unemployed people are also disqualified from participation at the point of consumption. Doubly disadvantaged, such young people as those studied by Paul Willis and his collaborators make up a population of the excluded.

They know what they want to do, but are unable to do it if they are unemployed or underpaid. They want to drink, buy clothes and music. The most common activities among those in the study's sample (a mixture of employed and unemployed youth) who had visited the town centre during the day were shopping and window-shopping, meeting friends, using the library, and 'signing on', and then going to the pub, to the job-centre, and 'hanging about'. There is not a lot about sports clubs, and even pubs do not feature prominently, in this picture of inner-city leisure culture among the young.

As Paul Willis points out, when we look closely at the experience of inner-city youth in Thatcher's England, it is clear that "for the first time in modern history, a whole social group face the prospect of the effective disappearance of work and the wage for a very prolonged period" (Willis *et al.*, 1985: p. 1) — perhaps, for some, for the whole of their lives. No amount of palliatives will make 'leisure' a substitute for work, when the full promise of leisure is premised upon the power of the consumer in the market place. And once we recognize the specificity of different groups' experience, the problem is compounded still further. Unemployed black youth in Wolverhampton are particularly disenfranchized from the leisure democracy:

The high level of unemployment within the black community makes leisure facilities an important factor ... There are no real social leisure or formal leisure pursuits which are relevant for young blacks in Wolverhampton. Social leisure pursuits such as discos, pubs and other evening adult meeting places, or formal leisure pursuits such as institutionalized activities, mainstream youth clubs and unemployed activities do not attract young blacks. They concentrate, therefore, on activities with an acceptable cultural content where they feel more comfortable. (Willis *et al.*, 1985: p. 86)

A full and adequate grasp of the diversity of the experience of different groups reveals different scales of exclusion from the leisure utopia. But, in the last instance, the divide is clearly between two unequally positioned cultures. And when well-meaning initiatives to open up access to the underprivileged are made, the consequences are far from the ones anticipated by the well-intentioned leisure provider. Two examples illustrate this, both also showing the importance of definitions of time.

In sport and leisure centres throughout the land, schemes for ease of access of the unemployed to the facilities have met with mixed response. Conceived very much as contemporary forms of 'improving' initiatives which will solve the problem of 'idle time' among non-productive people, they have been unevenly and sometimes naively developed. And they have in a very real sense been imposed. One survey of schemes provided for the unemployed by local authorities revealed that only 6 out of 285 respondents made any systematic attempts, "either before or after launching a scheme, to assess the likely wants of the intended customers" (Glyptis, 1983: p. 296). Most attempts at provision were much more rooted in 'faith' and 'hunch' than in any coherently developed view of what the relationship of the unemployed is to the 'leisure society'. "Traces of obligation and haste, rather than enthusiasm and positive planning" were said by Sue Glyptis to be characteristic of this 'hasty initiative' (Glyptis, 1983: p. 296).

To counter this, pre-launch surveys of interests have been recommended (Glyptis and Riddington, *nd*). But such a strategy, a form of market-research on the under-privileged, would have to break with the tradition of the provider mentality. Too often, 'sport and leisure for the unemployed' has been a slogan for keeping what providers see as potential trouble-makers off the streets. Although more progressive authorities — the Greater London Council and Sheffield, for instance, — sought, before their abolition by the Conservative administration, not to impose 'wants' from above, concessionary rates in prescribed times can only be the wooden spoon in the competitive consumer society. The general trends work against the success of such schemes anyway, when public provision — be this in terms of libraries or playing fields — is fast being eroded, to be replaced by expensive private provision. In the 'mixed economy' of leisure, authorities in the affluent south-east have been the most likely not to bother to run schemes at all. Again, the leisure society is clearly an unequally accessible and a divided one.

But we should hardly be surprised that the unemployed do not always jump with joy at the offer, even when it is made. Some studies have shown how the psychological effect of unemployment has been to drive individuals into privatized retreat, into hiding in the home. Playing badminton or swimming at a cheaper rate in off-peak time on the basis of your UB40 is a pretty public declaration of your partial, marginal membership of the consumer/leisure culture; it is to accept the wearing of a badge of exclusion, to be granted access as stigma. On the municipal golf courses of Sheffield City council, it is told, as we move towards the second millennium in a modern sophisticated civilization, that there are fist fights on the greens. Unemployed, given access, play the course in truly leisured style, taking their time. Employed players must hurry; time is money; work beckons. Rather than 'Playing through, please', the greeting from one foursome of employed drivers to another group of leisurely-paced out-of-work players is more likely to be: 'Get out of the way, you idle buggers'.

Freedom, Free-time, and the Leisure Myth

We live in a society in which we are said to be free to make our own choices. We choose our husbands, wives, lovers, television channels, newspapers, politicians. The freedom to choose, we are told, is a central principle of liberal democratic societies.

This conflation of 'freedom of choice' and 'individualism' is the core of the New Right's ideological grip in the time of the crisis in welfare democracy (Bull and Wilding, 1983). For the majority of the British working people are still in work; Thatchernomics claims to have conquered inflation: consumer goodies are cheaper, swisher and more and more accessible. 'Don't leave home without it', we are reminded by some of the most reactionary popular figures of the day — Sevy Ballesteros, for instance. And so many don't: with Amex or Visa or Mastercard snugly tucked into their credit card wallets, armed for active service on the consumer battlefields of western capitalism. Within all of this, leisure is presented as the sphere in which individual freedoms are expressed (you can do what you want), and in which badges of individual success can be displayed (the new suit, the pricey trainer, the Sony Walkman) in public declarations of individuality and privatized living.

And for the unemployed, the poorly paid, the disadvantaged, there is always hope. For if Alan Sugar did it, why not me? If the millionaire electrical chain-store dealer started with just one barrow and a couple of cardboard boxes of stock, then who can deny the New Right's claim that freedom to succeed is there, if only the individual tries hard enough?

There are, of course, many ways of opposing and contesting this view of things. Choices only exist in contexts. Those contexts are ones in which relations of power and privilege determine how much freedom we actually have in the choices we make. We will not be very likely to make our million if we come from an ethnic inner-city neighbourhood, where work itself is not part of our experience, where the idea of 'working' for wages is a merely abstract principle, where you and your mates may never have worked in your life. This is the converse side of the Amex vision of life, of Roger Daltry's call to us to make sure that we 'don't leave home without it'. Ideologue of youthful counter-cultural assertion in the 1960s/70s, Daltry is here speaking to and for the 'yuppie' generation whose world is so far apart from the dislocated world of the poor, the unemployed, the underprivileged. Structural shifts in the balance between work and leisure in the contemporary period have produced a divide of massive significance between a glossy, vibrant and conspicuous culture of consumption, and a shadowy culture of dislocation and exclusion. When these cultures meet, in the dark and violent nights of disturbance in the inner-city, in the broken windows and looted shelves of video-cassette recorder stores, the myth of the New Right's ideology of opportunity is shattered. In the desperate plight of the inner-city, in the exclusion of so many from the 'leisure society', this cultural collision finds its most dramatic form.

Unemployment figures show pretty clearly the extent of changes in the work structures of industrial capitalism. At the end of 1984, one estimate put the number of unemployed (seen as those seeking work) in western industrialized nations at 31.2 million. It is still possible to put to one side the 1 in 7 or 8 in, say, the United Kingdom, to say that they are the exception, the atypical. But when the figures are taken on a world scale, we find that the 1 in 10, or 1 in 6, or 1 in 7 add up, within the industrial system conceived world-wide, to a figure bigger than the population of a number of individual countries. Unemployment looks to be a structural feature of contemporary industrial society. Figures for the end of 1984 mark out Japan (2. 7%) and Sweden (3%) as prominent exceptions to the general rule; but the Netherlands (17%), United Kingdom (13. 9%), Canada (11. 2%), West Germany (10. 6%), France (10. 3%) and Italy (10%) demonstrate the scale of the problem. And grasping this as a structural feature of contemporary societies, it becomes clear that a consumer culture of leisure is a mark of a great social and economic divide. The unemployed and the poor will not be written to by Roger Daltry's sponsors. Plastic money is only a prospect for those with plenty. Here we see once more the falsity of the pluralist notion of free choice and open opportunity in leisure. In the public spaces of leisure we see the incompatibility of a buoyant consumer culture (in which time is money and pleasure is consumption) with a culture of deprivation and, ultimately, exclusion experienced by a substantial and growing proportion of the population.

II

Studies in Football Culture

6 Going Global: The FIFA Story

> The Prussians are a bunch of bastards ... dirty square heads, mindless sheep without the slightest initiative and ready for the slaughter. (Henri Desgrange, founder of Tour de France and sports paper editor, August 1914, [quoted in Holt, 1981, p. 195])

> We must have the World Cup *because* we have nothing. (Carlos Ditterhorn, President of the Chilean Football Federation, on his country's successful candidature to host the 1962 Finals, made whilst earthquakes were shaking his country)

Large-scale international sports were trapped, from their beginnings, in a major tension. They represented an attractive cosmopolitanism and meeting ground between cultures. But equally, they were always a forum for the assertion of particular national strengths. It was as if nations wanted to reach out to each other for a handshake whilst simultaneously puffing out their chests in pompous self-satisfaction. On the eve of the First World War the core values of French sporting patriotism are uninhibitedly expressed, in the opening quote above, as Europe is about to enter one of its most tragic international conflicts.

Nations struggling for a focused self-identity in their formative days were not slow to seize on sport as a potent weapon. Ironically England — the nation which acted as a model for the global expansion of football — was to play a pretty minor part in the early politics of international football and the World Cup itself.

The game of football was exported to the world by all-confident Britons. Football became one of Britain's most successful cultural exports, more resoundingly universal than, say, Shakespeare, and more smoothly adaptable than, say, a Gilbert and Sullivan opera. Football was exported as one of the means whereby allegedly uncivilized nations might be rendered civilized. The character-training bred in the public schools would fuel the ethos of the gentleman-amateur. Yet, Britain, though offering the game to the world, did not then lead the internationalization of the game. As the game took a grip on the world, and as international matches assumed a tone of emphatic modernity — travel, tactics and the competitive element all packaged into assertive national formats — Britain stayed at home. The world governing body, FIFA (Fédération Internationale de Football Association) initially got off the ground with no help from the British and, particularly, with indifference bordering on contempt from the English footballing authority, the Football Association.

In the last quarter of the 20th century, FIFA has not been slow to˙ celebrate its eightieth birthday with a self-confident ring of modernity. Hailing the achievements of its President, João Havelange, the organization chose to stress the direction FIFA has taken during his decade at the helm. With Havelange, FIFA has followed "another direction, that of universality ... the Brazilian President ... applied methods in football which were long known in social, economic and political life" *(FIFA, 1904-1984)* p. 26). FIFA presents its President as an uncompromising man of action, who offered a then-uncertain organiz-ation a "necessary dynamism". FIFA's self-image projects a cosmopoli-tan and confident universality. Its headquarters — nicely placed in safe little Switzerland, non-aligned location par excellence — offers simultaneous translation, regular glossy communications for different interest groups within their worldwide constituency, and a sharp here-and-now image: "The administration is managed in the form of a modern firm". The firm has made many deals in Havelange's time.

Fall on any FIFA publication and you'll fall on a number of lucrative contract deals. On the back of a copy of *FIFA News* a few years ago: "KLM, the 'official FIFA airline'", salutes FIFA for its worldwide achievements in "doing work for young people".

FIFA, then, has successfully developed and then kept
national dimension to football, whilst itself shifting with the t....., y..
sustaining a historical commitment to youth. From a small grouping
of seven founder-member European associations in 1904, FIFA had
developed by 1986 into a giant organization with 150 members and a
dozen or so aspirant members jostling for space on the waiting list.

How did this achievement take place? And why was England,
benevolent sponsor of the world game, sitting on the sidelines so often
in the earlier days of the FIFA story? The first years of the FIFA were
presided over by a French engineer/newspaper editor (for a brief 2-
year spell); then an English civil-servant from Blackburn (an integral
contributor to Blackburn Rovers' domination of the English Cup in the
1880s); before the French lawyer Rimet took over for several decades.
FIFA after 1974 was in the hands of a suave, sleek Latin American
lawyer/businessman of European extraction. The pendulum of word
footballing politics has swung dramatically towards the Third World.
England moved rather late towards asserting control in the world
game, but when the Third World made its bid for ascendancy in the
politics of the game, support was assured from other emergent
nations. English influence was to be transitional rather than transformative.

FIFA started life in 1904. After seeking the unresponsive English
Association as leader and figurehead of the initiative, a group of
Europeans founded the organization at a meeting in Paris of the
representatives of seven nations: Belgium, Denmark, France, the
Netherlands, Spain, Sweden and Switzerland. British associations,
right in the centre of the key phase of the game's worldwide growth,
initiated in many cases by Britons, were conspicuously absent. The
Frenchman Robert Gúerin had suggested the formation of a European
federation of nations to Frederick Wall, Secretary of the Football
Association in England. Wall's response was in the classical mould of
the phlegmatic English upper class:

The Council of the Football Association cannot see the advantages of such a Federation, but on all such matters upon which
joint action was desirable they would be prepared to confer.

Not much imaginative dialogue here! But note the rider to the lack of co-operation: 'to confer' was seen as very much acceptable. Clearly Wall was hedging his bets. The English would not be willing to risk assuming the leadership of an unproven initiative, but they were happy to be, in principle, available in a consultative advisory capacity.

Clearly Wall was suspicious to the point of an utter lack of confidence concerning the competence of this group of what he saw as upstarts. For several years the FA had deflected the advances of its European neighbours. Belgium had approached them at the end of the 1890s, wanting to arrive at some form of international collaboration. The Dutch had approached the FA in 1902 suggesting the formation of an international association which could focus upon the widespread European development of the game. Both these approaches were not so much rebuffed as set aside to languish in the bureaucratic proced-ures of an inefficient FA; it was as if to rush into action were considered ungentlemanly. So the response to the French approach prior to the 1904 formulation of FIFA was part of the general pattern of England's separatist superciliousness.

Two decades after FIFA was formed its first President, Guérin, and the Dutchman Carl Hirschmann said that they had never been able to understand why the British gave no lead to FIFA. Guérin recollected that after meeting Wall twice in 1903 he saw that for the moment at least he could get no further:

Tiring of the struggle and recognizing that the Englishmen, true to tradition, wanted to wait and watch, I undertook to invite delegates from various nations myself.

Britain was clearly playing the role of the patrician, but as soon as FIFA looked strong enough to survive, the English FA was ready to join the project. France had played its first international match less than three weeks before the meeting at which FIFA was formed. Denmark's first international was not to take place until the 1908 Olympics in London, the year of Switzerland's first international matches. Spain played its first international at the 1920 Olympic Games. So FIFA's founding fathers were really babes in arms. Three of them — Sweden, France and Spain — helped form FIFA before national Football Associations had been formed in their own countries. In 1902, in the first international match between non-British countries, Austria beat Hungary 5-0. Other more experienced nations, not just the British, were also notable by their absence from the 1904 initiative.

It is not surprising, then, that the FA became more involved through the proffering of advice and expertise. A special FA committee asked Continental nations to a conference on the eve of the 1905 England-Scotland match in London, after which the British Associations accepted FIFA's general objectives and expressed a willingness to co-operate. The English FA then soon decided that the only way to defend the game against misinterpretations, and against intrusions into the principles of amateurism, was to dominate it. This was achieved by getting D. B. Woolfall, the Blackburn man, elected as FIFA President. (Guérin had resigned after his efforts to organize a first international competition came to nothing: when his deadline for entries was reached, there were no entrants). This was how Woolfall summarized the attitude of the FA after meeting with other nations in Berne in 1905:

> ... it is important to the FA and other European Associations that a properly constituted Federation should be established and the Football Association should use its influence to regulate football on the Continent as a pure sport and give all Continental Associations the full benefit of the many years experience of the FA.

The stress was on the 'proper' procedures, on the 'purity' of the game, and on the importance of 'experience'. These were the terms on which England was willing to hold hands with the Continent. This was a trait which de Gaulle was to find to galling in that other tale of Britain 'going into Europe' a half century later.

Early attempts at a World Cup had foundered, and with them the optimism of the Frenchman Guérin. The Olympic Games provided a form of official World Championship, but in fact many of the outstanding players of the era were denied, by their professional status, participation. FIFA bumbled along quietly for a few years — a growing, rather a sleeping, giant — and then started to consolidate its position in truly global terms after the Great War.

Non-European members began to join before the War: South Africa in 1909/10, Argentina and Chile in 1912; the USA in 1913. Great Britain continued to take top honours in European-based Olympic tournaments, in 1900, 1908 and 1912.

After the Great War the face of world football began to change. In a controversial Final in Antwerp in the 1920 Olympics, Belgium took the honours when, as they were leading 2-0, the Czech team walked off the pitch and into Olympic infamy, claiming that dubious refereeing decisions were no accident. And in 1924 at the Paris Olympics, Uruguay defeated Switzerland in a Final that was to ring out the old age of amateur domination of the world game.

FIFA was to tussle with the ideological tensions which were at the heart of such a transformative period. The World Cup, beset by nationalist jealousies, rivalries and conflicts, was to emerge as one of the forums for international jousting. Figures on FIFA's growth (listed below), and figures in Table 1 (opposite) on the escalating scale of the World Cup itself, show clearly the truly global dimensions of this expansion.

Year	Number of Associations
1904	7
1914	24
1920	20
1923	31
1930	41
1938	51
1950	73
1954	85
1959	95
1984	150
1998	200

Table 1: The World Cup Finals

Year	Winner	Venue	Attendance	No. of Games	No. of Teams	Global Distribution of Teams
1930	Uruguay	Uruguay	434,500	18	13	8 Latin American, 4 European plus USA
1934	Italy	Italy	395,000	17	16	2 Latin American, 12 European plus USA and Egypt
1938	Italy	France	483,000	18	15	1 Latin American, 12 European plus Dutch East Indies, Cuba
1950	Uruguay	Brazil	1,337,000	22	13	6 Latin American, 6 European plus USA
1954	W. Germany	Switzerland	943,000	26	16	3 Latin American, 11 European plus Turkey and Korea
1958	Brazil	Sweden	868,000	35	16	4 Latin American, 12 European
1962	Brazil	Chile	776,000	32	16	6 Latin American, 10 European
1966	England	England	1,614,677	32	16	5 Latin American, 10 European plus North Korea
1970	Brazil	Mexico	1,673,975	32	16	5 Latin American, 9 European plus Israel and Morocco
1974	W. Germany	W. Germany	1,774,022	38	16	4 Latin American, 9 European plus Australia, Zaire, Haiti
1978	Argentina	Argentina	1,610,215	38	16	4 Latin American, 10 European plus Tunisia and Iran
1982	Italy	Spain	------	52	24	6 Latin American, 14 European plus Cameroon, Kuwait, Algeria, New Zealand
1986	Argentina	Mexico		52	24	5 Latin American, 14 European, 2 African, 2 Asian plus Canada
1990	Germany	Italy		52	24	5 Latin American, 14 European, 2 African, 2 Asian plus USA
1994	Brazil	USA		52	24	5 Latin American, 13 European, 3 African, 2 Asian plus USA
1998	France	France		64	32	5 Latin American, 15 European, 5 African, 4 Asian plus USA, Jamaica

This has been a steady and even rate of growth in membership, with only one significant interruption — after the First World War. The expansion of membership from the late 1980s onwards was consequent upon the collapse of the Soviet Union and the growth of ethnic nationalisms, and a strengthening of the continental federations representing new and smaller nations. The balance of participation between different blocs of nations can be seen in Table 1. Spoils are evenly divided between Latin America and Europe — eight winners each — a proportionately bigger achievement by the South Americans, perhaps, as they include one Brazilian triumph on European soil. No European side has yet won the World Cup on the American continent.

As the tournament has expanded in scale, goals have not increased in number. Quite the reverse. The average number of goals per game in the first tournaments was round about four. The highest ever number of goals per game was in the 1954 Finals — well over five. This fell to under four in Brazil in 1958. In the five tournaments up to 1978 the figure stayed below three. A technically-based caution has crept into the matches.

But this should not lead us to contrast any stained present with any pure past. The World Cup has never been covered in, and so bolstered by, any mythology of idealism comparable to, say, the Olympic myth. World Cup history is riddled with examples of open conflict and corruption which have never been smoothed over by the reassertion of any uniting ideology. At the very first World Cup the journey proved too much for most European sides and the hosts, Uruguay — Olympic champions in 1924 and 1928 — were so insulted by this that they stayed away from the next two World Cups. On their own sub-continent, their 1930 World Cup triumph was not unanimously acclaimed. After Argentina lost the Final, a mob stormed the Uruguayan Consulate in Buenos Aires, to be dispersed by gun-toting police. In 1934 the Finals were exploited unashamedly by Mussolini, who claimed the "azurri" (the blues) for his own. Argentina refused to travel to the 1938 Finals in France, after having their own candidature as host-nation rejected. Mexico also withdrew; Cuba sneaked in as last minute replacements. In 1950 in Brazil, only

Yugoslavia, of the Iron Curtain countries, made the trip. Germany was still, five years after the end of the war, not accepted as a FIFA member. Scotland felt unworthy of the honour of participation — coming second in the British championship, a qualifying performance designated by FIFA, was not a proud enough achievement for them. They had announced that they would compete only if they won the British championship. Losing to England at Hampden Park, they stuck obstinately to this haughtily rigid stance. Argentina did not even compete on its own doorstep, over a disagreement with the Brazilian Federation. And France, generously invited (as FIFA and World Cup pioneers) to replace Turkey (another withdrawal) even though they had failed to qualify, themselves withdrew in a dispute over venues and travel schedules.

In the 1958 qualifying rounds all Israel's opponents refused to play them. Wales, drawn out of a hat containing the names of other qualifying groups' runners-up, played off with the isolated Israelis, beat them twice and marched on to Scandinavian glory. Controversy reached hysterical heights in that tournament when the Swedes progressed further and further, and in their semi-final against the holders, West Germany, placed their own cheer-leaders on the pitch to whip up the crowd — German cheerleaders being restricted to the running-track. They were forbidden from engaging in these extreme jingoistic practices for the Final against Brazil.

Conflicts and tensions have been a recurrent characteristic of the World Cup story. Tales abound of the plotting of Mexican hosts during their lobbying of FIFA for the privilege of hosting the 1970 Finals. Sir Stanley Rous must have seen some of the writing on the wall for his 1974 re-selection defeat when a big majority backed Mexico. And Argentina's military junta was expressing an early Malvinas spirit in backing the 1978 Finals, and using the national victory to divert attention from internal problems. But these examples do not leave the Europeans with a comparatively clear bill of moral health. Albeit more quietly and less dramatically, the European nations had always given world football their own political inflections, as early disputes in the development of FIFA show.

Although the most obviously tense political relations between countries followed the end of the Great War, when a breakaway group of nations sought to isolate their previous enemies, the most recurrent conflict within FIFA during the 1920s concerned definitions of amateurism. FIFA — kept together during the war by the secretarial labours of the Dutchman Carl Hirschmann, and spurred into action again after the end of the war by Jules Rimet, the President of the French Football Association — called a conference in Brussels in 1919, where the English would not sit down alongside their former foes. FIFA wanted normal sporting relations restored, but delegates from the British Associations and from Belgium, Luxembourg, and France too, passed a resolution ostracizing the "former enemy nations of Austria, Germany and Hungary". A resolution was also passed ostracizing "neutral associations" if they kept up playing contact with the defeated countries. This went too far for the neutral countries, who were unwilling to be dictated to in quite so complete a fashion. Denmark, Finland, Norway and Sweden expressed their intention to continue to keep up playing contacts with all countries. Italy expressed the same view. The boycotting group formed a new Federation of National Football Associations, and the English FA withdrew from FIFA. In 1920 Jules Rimet was made provisional chairman of FIFA. In 1921 he became official President, a post he held for the next 33 years.

The new splinter group was a fragile body. Belgium and France soon had doubts about the proposal to boycott 'neutrals'. And within four years, helped by the need for British co-operation concerning Irish football in the newly partitioned Ireland, FIFA had persuaded the British Associations back into the fold, agreeing to the major pre-requisites laid down by the British. One key point of tension remained: the definition of the amateur. It might seem odd that in a period of increasingly full-time commitment to a professionalizing game, British Associations should produce rifts in the international relations of sport by defending old notions of amateurism. Such defences have to be seen as a form of rearguard action, an attempt to impose traditional and established values on a situation fast getting out of control; and on the domestic English front, a manifestation of the tensions between the old-guard administration in the Football Association, and the more fully developed professional ethos of the Football League.

Having been wooed back into FIFA in the early 1920s, by 1928 the British again resigned. The 'amateur' issue had been a lurking threat to FIFA harmony, and when in 1926 the International Olympic Committee approved of 'broken time' payments for competitors in the forthcoming Games, the old English dog could no longer be held on its leash. The amateur/professional issue was clear enough to the FA, who had negotiated definitions decades before.

In October 1927, at the Lime Street Station Hotel in Liverpool, five Englishmen, four Scots, three Welshmen and five Irishmen gathered to work out their stance concerning this issue. Liverpool, a major channel of communication and exploitation to the corners of the globe in earlier days — perhaps an ironically fitting context for the meeting of these 17 honest Britons who were to cock a snook to the world and draw inwards into a not-so-splendid isolation. And what a contrast! The International Olympic Conference and FIFA had met in cosmopolitan Paris in 1927, to approve 'broken time' payments — a recognition of the diversity of sporting reality in the modern world — Paris, home of the modern. The British response was to meet in one of the temples of an old industrializing nation, and to reaffirm without any deviation whatsoever the British definition of amateur:

> Players are either amateur or professional. Any player registered with this Association as a professional or receiving remuneration or consideration of any sort above his necessary hotel and travelling expenses actually paid, shall be a professional. Training expenses of amateurs other than the wages paid to a trainer or coach must be paid by the players themselves. A player competing for any money prize in a football context shall be a professional.

This was pretty unambiguous stuff. Even professionals playing for their country were to experience this honest rigidity in later years. Sir Stanley Matthews recollects his first game for England against Wales at Cardiff a few weeks after the appointment of Stanley Rous as FA Secretary:

> On the Saturday morning he got us all together to pay our fee and he had all these notes piled up on the desk and he paid us I think we had £6 or £8. We had expenses and we had little tickets and it said 'travelling', say from Stoke to Cardiff, 'afternoon tea' and you had to put your price in, you know in those days afternoon tea was 1/6d. and if you overcharged (the Treasurer) already knew the prices and he'd say 'you've overcharged sixpence'.

Sir Stanley Matthews also recollected the letters of selection internationals received, addressing them only by their surnames. It is clear that the FA, though seeking to catch up with the modern world, was still rooted in traditional relations of class privilege and deference. This was the tension at the centre of the English FA's conflict with FIFA.

The British were not alone in their concern for amateurism. In 1925 — before the Olympic 'broken-time' decision had been taken — A. Verdyck, the Secretary of the Union Royal Belge des Football Association, wrote to Frederick Wall. This letter was not publicized widely, and was marked for issue to "members of the Council only". In the letter it was suggested that the President of the Belgian Association, Count Joseph d'Oultremont, had been granted the power to meet with the English FA as part of the Belgian determination to "fight energetically against sham amateurism". Verdyck noted that at a recent FIFA meeting it was clear that some member Associations "do not desire to fight that evil and to take the necessary measures to outroot it" and to "cleanse football", The Belgian saw the British as obvious allies in their attempt "to bring cleanliness in Sport". It might have been expected that the English would make a generous response to such a flattering approach. But an FA conference decided that it would be undesirable to meet with the Belgians. Indeed, the Belgians would be informed that the FA was clear on its rules and principles, and need not make matches with other nations/Associations which flaunted them. No meeting — but plenty of advice at a not-so-friendly arm's length.

This clarity led to the decision, taken at Sheffield in February 1928, to withdraw from FIFA. The resolution to resign was passed unanimously by the delegates of the 'Associations of the United Kingdom'. The FA Conference Report stresses how the representatives of all four UK countries were convinced that "they should be free to conduct their affairs the way their long experience has shown to be desirable". The English FA was authorized to write to Carl Hirsch–mann; and Frederick Wall's letter played all the old tunes in this refrain of the old guard. Britain's professional/amateur distinction was summarized and the FIFA acceptance of 'broken-time' payments criticized: the UK Associations "are satisfied from their experience in years past that it will not work out satisfactorily". Note, again, the patrician refrain, reaffirming constantly the wisdom of the elder:

The great majority of the Associations affiliated with La Fédération Internationale de Football Association are of comparatively recent formation, and as a consequence cannot have the knowledge which only experience can bring.

Resignation, then, but not total withdrawal. Wall noted too, that the UK Associations would like to maintain "friendly relations". And British teams continued to play internationals during these years of separatism. But they were not present at the birth of the World Cup. It took the trauma of world war and post-war modernization to bring the FA more truly into the fraught community of world football. When Stanley Rous took over from Frederick Wall at FA headquarters there were only five staff. No wonder Wall responded slowly in his previous 39 years at the FA. Rous soon changed things, building up a staff of thirty and a base for England's true re-entry into world football, Nearly twenty years after their resignation, the British Associations rejoined. Rimet had built up good working relations with Rous, and the British celebrated their re-entry by hosting a Great Britain vs. FIFA match at Hampden Park, Scotland, at the end of the 1947 season. 135,000 saw the British rout this world-side 6-1. The receipts of £35,000 were gifted to FIFA.

Victorious from the war, triumphant on the pitch, magnanimous in their renewed membership — the British came out of self-imposed isolation very much in their own terms. But they were soon to find that although they had crushed the might of the Rest of the World, parts of the world were ready to expose the vulnerabilities of a British game which for so long had assumed a superiority which had really long gone. The 1-0 defeat suffered by England at the hands of the USA in Brazil in 1950 — England's first World Cup — was seen as a dramatic aberration. The Hungarian rout of England in 1953 at Wembley was a confirmation, though, of the changing balance of power in world football. This was also to be expressed in the shifting patterns of power between the nations, especially in the emergence of the Third World countries as equals not just on the playing field, but also in the boardroom. This is clearly seen in the symbolic impact of two of FIFA's most prominent figures — Sir Stanley Rous, English son of a grocer turned gentleman and conversationalist with Royalty (if only once a year at the Cup Final); and Dr. João Havelange, Brazilian lawyer and millionaire businessman of Belgian extraction.

Jules Rimet reigned as FIFA President from 1921 until 1954. The Association had 20 members when he took over, and 85 on his retirement. FIFA had, in his stewardship, spread its wings worldwide. Rimet, in his youth a keen spokesman for the socially harmonizing effects of sport and, professionally, a lawyer, laid the foundation for FIFA's launch into the 20th century.

The French had not marched confidently into the international sporting scene. Their initiative was itself born of the crisis of a declining imperialist power, looking for a new role in a world in the making. Nations, as the redrawn map of Europe after the Great War showed so clearly, were fragile unities. International prominence in sport was becoming one way of showing national strength. FIFA's development from its early foundations and from the consolidation of the Rimet years was challenged by a late 20th century emergence of the Third World. In the reactionary view of the English sports journalist Brian Glanville, "Havelange has ruined the World Cup, has sold it down the river to the Afro-Asians and their ilk" (*World Soccer*, October 1984, p. 14); and throughout this, Glanville also claims, "the European countries have truckled to ... the ineffable Havelange" (*World Soccer*, November 1985, p. 18). But if FIFA is fully understood in the context of world politics, the shift in power relations in the game must be seen as more than just some obsequious submission of abdicating rulers. The symbolic impact of the sporting occasion is such that it has always fuelled emerging nationalisms, as well as dominant and extant ones; and has also stimulated individual ambitions. This is most dramatically revealed in the reluctant secession of Stanley Rous to the rampantly determined Havelange in 1974.

The Belgium lawyer Rodelphe Seeldrayers and the Englishman Arthur Drewry had led FIFA for brief spells after Rimet's resignation in 1954. Sir Stanley Rous (plain Mr. Stanley Rous before being ennobled for his services to the staging in London of the 1948 Olympics) took over from Drewry, in 1961. Secretary of the English Football Association from 1934 to 1962, he had led the British Associations back into FIFA in 1946. Rous took over at FIFA in his mid-sixties, the retiring age for male workers. He grasped this new challenge with typical energy and commitment. Walter Winterbottom, England's first manager, comments that "in our own country he took us out of being an insular Association Football League and got us back into world football and this was tremendous". But Rous was entering a relatively unscripted drama when he stepped onto the international stage.

Rous was a highly influential figure in the English game. He had been a referee of international repute after playing as an amateur. A son of the lower middle classes (his two elder sisters were school teachers) he studied at St. Luke's College, Exeter, and then taught at Watford Grammar School. He was part of a socially mobile and developing service profession, no inheritor of established privileges. He played football at College, then in the Army during the Great War, but his major impact on the game, initially, was as a top-class referee. In many respects he went on to modernize the English game, establishing a more efficient bureaucratic base, introducing teaching schemes for all levels of the game — coaching, playing, refereeing. But this mission was not an innocent one. Britain itself was in crisis after the Second World War, losing an Empire and looking for a role. The educating of football players as coaches — of practitioners as educators — was one way of retaining "a valuable cultural link", as Stephen Wagg (1984: pp. 77–78) has put it, with former British colonies. Rous advised many newly incrementalized players/coaches to go job-hunting around the globe. As Britain withdrew, politically, from Africa, Rous was rousing a new breed of imperialist missionaries into action.

Rous is a key transitional figure in the FIFA story. Arguing for this sort of expansion from his home base, he could hardly dispute the right of the other nations to take up the challenge. Yet despite his innovations he remained trapped in an anachronistic set of values. On the occasion of his 90th birthday, BBC Radio 4 (22nd April 1985) honoured him in a documentary tribute. Rous recalls his own playing and spectating days of up to 80 years ago:

> We used to look upon it as a sport, as a recreation, we had little regard of points and league position and cup competitions. We used to play friendly matches mostly. There was always such a sporting attitude and the winners always clapped the others off the field and so on … that's all changed of course.

And despite his commitment to worldwide expansion, as early as the 1962 World Cup in Chile, at the very beginning of his Presidency, the former English FA Secretary mourned the loss of the 1930s when international tours were "free and easy affairs".

A set of crucially revealing tensions is expressed in these responses: the old world versus the new; the quiet life versus a global cosmopolitanism; a character-building participation versus win-at-all costs attitudes. Rous could be both innovatory and traditional; adventurous yet crabbily cautious; resonant of modernity yet steeped in traditional values. A world figure in sport, he carried into the sporting arena the inherent contradictions of a Britain in the middle period of a very uncertain remaking. Claimed as a modern world figure within the game, Rous could hob-nob with the Queen at Cup Finals, and publicly rebuke the Prime Minister, Harold Wilson, for posing with the victorious English team after the 1966 World Cup victory — on the basis, presumably, of bringing politics into sport.

Harry Cavan, former senior Vice-President of FIFA recalled how well prepared Rous's entry on to the world stage was: he was "probably the most travelled man in football in the world in those days. He had the right connections, he had the right influence and above all he had the ability and the skill to do the job. And of course he was clever. He was generally one or two moves ahead of most of the others". But then along came Havelange.

In 1974 Rous was clearly a great many moves behind his challenger from the Third World. When he stood for re-election as FIFA President, claiming that he wanted just a couple of years in which to push through some important schemes, he either had a confidence which was misplaced, or he miscalculated the institutional politics of FIFA. Or perhaps he was just tired, an old man from a nation in decline, sitting quietly in a corner in Frankfurt, finding himself mugged by history as Brazil dislodged Britain from the apex of world footballing politics. Ten years on Rous claimed not to have been surprised, "Because I know what activity was being practised by my successor, the appeals that he'd made to countries". Appeals! How vulgar! Clearly this was below-the-belt stuff to Rous. Appealing? Lobbying? Canvassing!! For a member of Lords/MCC (cricket), Wimbledon's All England Club (tennis) and Hurlingham (polo), this was clearly somewhat undignified. Harry Cavan recalls how Rous seemed to make little real effort to get support; somehow or other he'd lost his momentum. Havelange won in a second ballot. In conversation with Rous, sports journalist Bryon Butler recalled the moment of defeat:

> I remember just before the second ballot was taken you sat down and had an orange squash, quietly in one corner. João Havelange did so much lobbying — he was really such a blur — and that's where you lost. (BBC Radio 4, 22 April 1985)

Sir Stanley's response to this memory combined a sense of almost betrayal, even twenty years on, with his realistic perception of what was happening in the politics of world football:

> Yes, I think an Indian spoke against and I was surprised at that. People like Indonesia voted against me but I don't think they

113

... their officers have changed so much in those countries, you know. There were quite a few then who didn't really know me and they were persuaded to vote for Havelange.

So Havelange — "a very clever man, a very skilled politician", in Cavan's words — became FIFA's first non-European President. One of his campaigning commitments was to raise Third World footballing standards generally. Coaching seminars — rather grandly framed as an International Academy — were organized, in Africa, Asia and Oceania. FIFA under Havelange introduced ambitious educational projects and a World Youth Championship (hosted by Tunisia, 1977; Japan, 1979; Australia, 1971; and Mexico, 1983); and changed the rules of Olympic eligibility so that any European or South American player who had not participated in the previous World Cup could now play in the Olympics. Two developments under the influence of Havelange stand out: the expansion of the number of World Cup finalists, increased from the traditional 16 to 24 at the 1982 Finals in Spain; and the introduction of sponsorship on a large scale. Under Havelange FIFA strode into the modern world of sponsorship; Coca-Cola culture, one of the most advanced and sophisticated multi-national strategies, provided the economic base for Havelange's ambitions.

Havelange's parentage was Belgian. Havelange first studied to be a lawyer, before making several fortunes in ventures in the worlds of chemicals, insurance and transport. As an amateur sportsman — a Brazilian swimmer in the 1936 Olympics, and a member of the water polo team of the 1952 Helsinki Olympics — he had a pretty high profile in the Brazilian sports establishment. Moving into sports administration, he assumed the Presidency of the Brazilian Sports Federation. In his period as a footballing supremo in Brazil a national championship was formed out of the various regional and inter-regional championships. This championship — at times involving nearly 100 clubs — was based, in World Cup fashion, upon groups playing each other. Big clubs had to play small clubs, and all had to travel, the length and breadth of Brazil. Not surprisingly, crowds were small and club finances were also severely hit because of travelling expenses. Many Brazilian commentators have seen this development as the beginning of the end for Brazilian football.

Meanwhile, as dilemmas hit the game in Brazil itself, football officials in Argentina and Uruguay proposed that Havelange become the South American candidate for the FIFA Presidency. Accepting this, the dynamic businessman then moved fast. With the backing of most of the South American countries, Havelange spent the years 1971–1974 in worldwide canvassing. Preparing for the 1974 FIFA election, he visited 86 FIFA countries, concentrating most of all on Africa and Asia (interview in *Playboy*, Brazilian edition, 1985). No wonder Sir Stanley Rous sat quietly in a corner in Frankfurt in 1974. Clearly, he had no-one to speak to.

The effects of Havelange's dealings are highly disputed. Artemio Franchi, former President of UEFA, opposed both the expansion in the number of World Cup Finalists, and the self-projection of the celebrity President. Brian Granville reports Franchi's response to FIFA's new administrative building, opened on the 75th anniversary of the world body: "It's ostentation … and *South American* ostentation" (*World Soccer*, October 1984, p. 14). Franchi died in a car crash at the peak of his UEFA work. But some hard facts speak for themselves. At the first World Cup with expanded numbers, in Spain in 1982, an estimated £45 million was spent on putting up 17 stadia in 14 cities; and £15 million on hotels, roads and publicity (Barnes, 1982, p. 160). But the average attendance at games in Spain was the lowest since 1962 in Chile.

Parallels between Havelange's operations in Brazil and in the wider world are undeniable. An indiscriminately expanded Brazilian championship undermined the fabric of the game. Critics point out that this is precisely what is happening in the World Cup itself. In Brazil the Brazilian Football Federation recognizes no difference between amateurs and professionals; while in England there is no football league separate from the Football Association. In the Brazilian Federation each constituent unit has one vote. This means, to take an English analogy, that an amateur league club in Sussex would have the same voting power as Liverpool, Tottenham Hotspur or Manchester United. Control of the Federation will go to those who divert resources to the poor and weak — buying their support, in effect. Havelange clearly learned his lesson well in his own country. A democracy based

115

upon a premise of inequality of resources was a sound means of gaining unassailable power.

Repeated effectively on the international scale, this has given Havelange a *carte blanche* in FIFA. Rous clearly could not understand, sitting in the corner with his orange squash, the full momentum of the force which was pushing him aside. Rous' memory of his defeat indicates his lack of comprehension of the dynamics of national belongingness. The Swede Lennart Johansson's shock in Paris in June 1998 when, after years of campaigning for the FIFA Presidency culminated in a 111–80 defeat, at the hands of Havelange's protegé Joseph 'Sepp' Blatter, echoed the rout of Rous. For a quarter of a century Havelange and his insiders used the pseudo-democracy of FIFA to divide and rule world football.

The globalization at the centre of the FIFA story can only adequately be understood as one aspect of the shifting relations of international status, if not power. All nations, as Benedict Anderson (1983) has so eloquently argued, have at some stage indulged in some form of imagining. The nation, he suggests, is imagined on three levels: as limited, as having boundaries; as free, under the sovereign state; and as a community, "conceived as deep, horizontal comradeship". In this final level of imagining — that of the fraternal community — it is forms of symbolic action which state the case for the country itself. FIFA may have expressed, at various stages in its development, principles of world citizenship, or international understanding; but its major function has remained pretty much unchanged. It has offered, on the level of popular consciousness, a forum for the expression of different forms of national belonging and superiority. Adherents of and apologists for football in various countries have spoken this rhetoric of collective national identity and ambition, whilst playing into the hands of some global operators such as Havalenge.

As Havelange emerged from the Third World to give FIFA a ring of modernity, perhaps the main point to remember is that he achieved this as a skilled exploiter of others. Rous' tribute was framed in terms of service. As Bryon Butler put it, service to football, to sport, to youth and to charity. After Brazil had won the 'Jules Rimet' trophy outright in 1970, that nation asked Rous to lend his name to a new gold cup to be called the 'Stanley Rous Cup'. Rous refused the honour. Any tribute to Havelange would be unlikely to stress service. Dynamism, yes, but not service. Maybe Havelange did not drink between ballots in the 1974 election. But if he did it's unlikely that he'd have stuck to orange squash — something a little stronger would fit the image better. Rous recalls having a cold bath every morning of his life — Havelange's style would much more likely indicate a plunge into the Jacuzzi. Rous was a teacher, sent to lead the world; Havelange is much more the smooth-talking international wheeler-dealer. And this remains the final irony in the FIFA story. The challenge of the new world to the old has been led by a ritzy figure resonant of the modern, and one who at the age of 82 on the confirmation of his successor, gave no real indication that he was going to disappear from the world of football. As FIFA has gone global in the twentieth century, Havelange epitomized an opportunism that could exploit the post-colonial aspirations of nations in a time dominated by the end of empires. Sugden and Tomlinson (1998), in a fuller version of the FIFA story, relate in detail how FIFA and Havelange impacted on twentieth-century history.

Acknowledgements

I would like to thank David Barber, Press Officer of the (English) Football Association; John Humphrey, for spare-time detective work in Brazil; and Myrene McFee. ·

Details of World Cup history and incidents have been culled from two enormously useful sources which I have not cited directly in the chapter: Brian Glanville, *The History of the World Cup*, Faber and Faber, 1980; and Jack Rollin's *Complete World Cup Guide* (1982 Edition) Sphere Books, 1982. Detail of the English FA's deliberations and decisions concerning FIFA in the 1900s and the 1920s has been taken directly from FA minute books.

7 Tuck Up Tight Lads: Structures of Control within Football Culture

When I first came last season I got the feeling there was a little unhappiness at the club. One or two people had ideas of their own. But this year, irrespective of results, it is a very, very happy club. (Ian Bowyer, Captain of Nottingham Forest: quoted in Atkin, 1982: p. 43)

It seems that a succession of players, including Colin Barrett, Frank Clark, John McGovern, Justin Fashanu and Willie Young have left Forest within three months of becoming the PFA shop steward. (Robert Armstrong, in *The Guardian*, 17 September 1983: p. 14)

I

Ian Bowyer, talking of the revival of his club's fortunes, equates 'happiness' in club life with the subordination of individual views to the group. A happy club is, presumably, one in which not too many opinions — if any at all — clash with the opinion of the 'boss'. Happiness, or group harmony, is maintained by strategies of exclusion as well as strategies of inclusion. Brian Clough — the boss, in this case — actually called the police in, during the early winter of 1982, to eject the one million pound misfit Justin Fashanu when the player ignored Clough's orders that he must not come to the ground. Although Clough's ban on the young striker was overruled by the League's governing body, this would have no effect whatsoever on the structures of control within the club. The Fashanu affair encapsulated in dramatic

119

form the tight, rigid and sometimes oppressive circumstances in which professional footballer's lives are led. Fashanu was described as a million pound albatross draped around Clough's neck, in a feud which "has reached the absurd level where had Gilbert and Sullivan still been among us, it would swiftly have been set to music and put on the stage" (Atkin, 1982: p. 43). This light operatic scenario was superseded by dark tragedy a decade and a half on when Fashanu took his own life in the seedy setting of a South London rented garage. In a moving television documentary it was made clear that the Clough-Fashanu feud was based in no small part upon the former's homophobic response to the fact of Fashanu's homosexuality. This chapter comprises an attempt to account for the existence of such internal structures of control, structures which are both imposed formally from above and reinforced informally on the level of group culture.

It is no easy task to do this, for football clubs are jealously guarded worlds. Like governments, clubs are interested in good publicity or no publicity at all. They are, therefore, quite suspicious of social researchers, and of press and broadcasting journalists whose interests lie in anything other than the straight report or the novelty item. Sometimes, of course, the club might be caught out by circumstances or naiveté or a little bit of both. It was fortuitous for Granada Television that its schedule for the making of a documentary on Manchester City coincided with the stormy departure from the club of Malcolm Allison, and the arrival of John Bond (*City!*, Granada Television, 1981). It was also a slice of good luck for Hunter Davies that the Chairman of Tottenham Hotspur was so easily impressed by the prospect of extensive coverage for the club in the glossy supplement of a quality Sunday paper[1]. But such investigative scoops are not easily replicated[2]. When the secret world is betrayed, it closes ranks and intensifies its secretive nature. If orthodox channels of social research are blocked off, then it is to a variety of sources that we should turn. Sources of established pedigree for the student of the past should be drawn upon to construct a critical history of the present. In the face of rebuff from players and managers[3], we should work from whatever sources are at hand. In this paper, then, I use orthodox newspaper reports, investigative features in both press and television, in-house revelations from the pens of players and managers, and some of my own interviews, in examining issues of control and discipline within club life.

I have argued elsewhere for the 'sociological utility' of sources such as these (see Chapter 3, this volume; the phrase 'sociological utility' is Charles Page's) and in many respects they are yet to be fully exploited in any consideration of the game. There are few British equivalents of the North American 'critique-from-within' by the player-turned-radical or rebel, and yet such sources are invaluable if the investigator has been denied access to the inner life of the game; as are sources such as George Plimpton's distinctive brand of empathetic sports writing.

In his book telling the tale of his time with the Detroit Lions, as a player, Plimpton describes life in the pre-season training camp. At one point, in the dining-room, the veterans of the squad began to concentrate on the rookies, the newcomers to the squad. The rookies were aware of what was in the offing: suddenly, one of the veterans motioned across the aisle. "On your feet, rookie," he was calling. "Sing":

"What's this?" I asked Friday.

"Watch", he said. "They're calling on the rookies to sing their school songs."

A rookie, his face pale, his jaw working on a vestige of food, climbed laboriously onto his chair. He put his hand over his heart and sang in a low embarrassed monotone... .

No applause greeted his rendition. He climbed down from the chair, and dug a spoon, which he had clutched in his left hand while he sang, into his deep dish of apple pie.

Friday explained that the hazing — the singing of school songs mostly — was a tradition ... . (Plimpton, 1964: pp. 21–22)

Rookies were made to perform a variety of stunts and chores which, along with the hazing, had the effect of, in Plimpton's words, 'keeping the caste system firmly in mind'. The club culture can involve '*rites de passage*' which are designed to remind everyone of the established hierarchies.

Drawing on another account, provided by a leading baseball player and cited in Paul Hoch's book on sports, we can also begin to grasp some aspects of the character of group culture in major professional sports. One of the major popular pastimes of baseball players has been, we are told, 'beaver shooting'. This involves, by drawing upon a variety of strategies, getting into a position in a hotel or a stadium so that a view can be had 'up the skirt of some female', in Major League baseball star Jim Bouton's words, in his book *Ball Four*. Good beaver shooters could become 'highly respected persons' in the world of baseball (Hoch, 1972: pp. 150–151).

The picture that emerges is one of uncompromising groupishness and assertive masculinity; an extension, in many ways, of the culture of the adolescent male. It is not my intention here to make transatlantic inferences. Soccer is not American football or baseball; Britain is not the USA; and gender and class experiences are not identical across all modern societies. So I would never suggest that these examples of an extraordinary heightened masculinist culture within sport should necessarily be found in British sport. My point is more a methodological one. If insights into how the culture of the club is lived out and repro-duced from one generation of players to another are available from sources such as these, might we not be able to find comparable sources here in Britain? The potted or ghosted biography of the player, for instance, though at times utterly mundane, can in certain cases convey the processes, dramas and conflicts of life in the professional game. In the absence of ethnographies, such complexly mediated ethnographies may be our only way into the closed world. I have implied, too, that groupishness and masculinity can be seen as extensions of male adoles-cence. This should not be seen as a suggestion that groupishness and masculinity play no part in adult male working life. On the contrary, shop-floor culture is often the reference point for the most assertively groupish and masculinist of adolescent groups[4]. But we need to distinguish means from ends. Banana-time is not the same as beaver shooting[5]. The first is clearly a strategy of potential resistance, an assertion of at least some degree of control over the work process; or, at the very least, an attempt to give meaning to a repetitive, monoto-nous, uncreative work routine. Beaver shooting is the curiosity and embryonic sexual harrassment of pubescence. It is my contention in this chapter that football culture in Britain exhibits more of the characteristics of this sort of adolescent 'play' than it does the characteristics of shop floor resistance. Both spheres of activity may be rooted in a masculinist group culture, but the actual meanings embodied in them are quite distinct. One of the reasons for this might be the intensification of modes of control within the club, and the attempt by management to exert influence over every aspect of the players' life. The 'boss' and the 'lads' are a collaborative group, a team. But they are also separated by their position in a highly specialized hierarchy.

Both manager and players are, as well, dispensable, subject to the whims of the board and/or chairman. Ken Craggs, manager of Millwall, was sacked at the end of November 1982, two days after dining out in style with his chairman and being assured that his job was safe. The chairman saw Craggs as being 'too nice' to succeed. When Brian Clough and Peter Taylor joined Derby County as its managerial team Clough is reported as reinforcing the argument for a contract by pointing out to Sam Longson the chairman that "you've got seven directors here and, inside a month, one of them will want to get rid of us" (Taylor, 1980: p. 41). Just because the 'boss' is 'in charge', then, is no guarantee of his own security. A new messiah can always be sought to bring the club the success that the board so often feels is just around the corner.

The club is therefore characterized by a revealing paradox. It stands for tradition and continuity, but it must constantly seek the new in order to stay at the top or find success. The only 'constants' in many clubs are the fans and some elements of the board. In between, the performers walk a tight-rope between success and failure. This makes for a built-in tension between the manager and the managed, a tension which cannot easily be resolved in any collective fashion. The management and the players must work as a team, as a collective unit, but the manager must be ruthless so that the players are the appropriate ones to keep him in work. Bobby Robson has put this well when faced with his annual decision on the fate of young hopefuls. His words to a group of sixteen year olds were: "if you can't show us what you can do or if you're not good enough then we don't want to know ... it's as blunt as that isn't it"[6]. Robson recognized, however much his emphasis on the importance of being an intimate family, that, in football, Darwinian principles of production prevail.

II

In his early and seminal piece on football Ian Taylor (1971) suggested that football had moved more and more away from a 'participatory democracy'. One point that he did not stress though, was that such democracies (where 'boys will be boys'[7]) rarely if ever granted the franchise to the player. Players were in many ways powerless. Take Wilf Mannion, for instance. Mannion spent twenty years at Middlesborough and was not even granted a transfer. He claims that he often wanted to leave his home-town club but that he was simply not allowed to go. Raised in the Irish, steel working-class district of Middlesborough, and developing into a folk-hero within his home community, Mannion found himself trapped within the local setting, having little say concerning his own part in the 'participatory democracy' of the club. Such a democracy was essentially illusory. Mannion could generate bonds of empathy with the supporters but his relationship to the powers within the club was based upon bonds of oppression and exploitation[8]. Mannion was not controlled in every corner of his community. Exploited as a player, at the bottom of the club hierarchy he might have been, but he never suggested that everyday personal freedoms were limited by management. They may well have been, of course, but this did not figure so large in his experience that it warranted pinpointing. Mannion resented the board in the classic manner of the impotent individual up against the powerful and impenetrable bureaucracy. Mannion can express his regrets at being trapped within the Middlesborough club, but his regrets do not develop into resentment or explicit critique. It is likely that players such as Mannion felt little reason to openly confront the prevalent forms of authority. In the club, as in the often precarious but usually consensual local culture, authority was accepted because it was long-established and familiar and it made sense. Football players' wages had not increased between 1923 and 1946, and in the post-war period when they did increase, professional players were considerably better off than were their peers of not so long ago who were still working in local factories, pits and trades. Tom Finney, as a permanent part-timer at Preston North End, was of the local culture as a plumber, yet simultaneously beyond it as a world-famous soccer player. Finney recollected the rewards for playing in his day:

> No I don't think in our day anybody could say they made a lot of money out of the game yer know but I thought at the time we were well paid ... you were getting £10- £12 a week and the average feller that was workin' in the building trade was on £3 a week ... by comparison you were a helluva lot better than he was. (BBC Television, 1978)

Finney himself was approached by the Italian club Palermo, and offered £10,000 to sign, and a two year contract, but his club chairman would not even allow him to consider the move. So Finney, like Mannion, stayed, unable to do anything whatsoever about his position. He continued to play as a part-timer at Preston, and to build up his own successful plumbing and engineering business. Hugh McIlvaney has claimed that the injustices of the maximum wage system, under which Finney played for all his career, "will never cease to rankle with him" (McIlvaney, 1983: p. 43) but in his account of his playing days Finney relayed virtually no trace of bitterness or resentment. He simply recognized that any young man fortunate enough to be paid for doing something he'd do for nothing should recognize such good fortune. Mannion and Finney were controlled to the point of being someone else's property, but their stories are usually stories of the relationship between the player and the chairman. In later periods, structures of control have developed in new ways with the increasing significance of the club manager in the culture of the club.

As football developed into a new economic climate the manager could, more than ever before, be seen as the scapegoat in the event of success eluding a club. In these circumstances, the manager needs to do more than just one specialized job within the division of labour. He must generate bonds of loyalty with players whom he may dispose of at a telephone call's notice. He must create a genuinely hegemonic relationship between himself and his players. Players must want to be led by their boss. Different managers achieve this in different ways, but all ways are means directed towards the end of consolidating a groupishness in which the player, however well-known he is, remains a subordinate member of the group. Brian Clough, for instance, once called England goalkeeper Peter Shilton over, in the presence of the press, to instruct him how to pour drinks properly. Clough's definition of democracy is interesting (and dates from 1979, during Nottingham Forest's great years of success):

> We are a small family circle and we have the best democracy here that you will find in any football club. No one is above doing something for somebody else. (McIlvaney, 1979: p. 30)

Yet Clough could fine, suspend and turn on players at will. Jock Wallace, who managed the Glasgow club Rangers to two trophy-winning trebles in his time there, sometimes reverted to more direct forms of coercion. Having been a jungle-fighter in Malaya for two years Wallace was trained in a tough school of man-management:

> We were ambushing and being ambushed … it sharpens your instincts; teaches you survival. I never stood cowards and lazy bastards then, and I still don't. (Barclay, 1980: p. 25)

Not every manager gains consent in such a coercive fashion. Lawrie McMenemy (of Southampton) has expressed regret at the one time that he ever hit a player (BBC South, 1982), but he recognized, too, the need to call senior players like Alan Ball into line when they showed any sign of indiscipline or insubordination:

> It's nice to have you back but don't try to tell me what to do" I said. "You may be the manager of Philadelphia Furies but I'm the manager here. (McMenemy, 1979: p. 25)

When John Bond was interviewed for the vacant managerial seat at Manchester City, after the resignation of Malcolm Allison, he impressed the club's board by stressing that the team must learn to be "terribly disciplined", we "mustn't have players 'pissing about', playing about with "the image of Manchester City". At his first meeting with the players, as the manager, Bond stressed to the players that he was the boss and should be known as 'boss'. He also outlined the 'little forms of discipline' that he would impose upon players who did not show the right attitude (Granada Television, 1981).

It is clear from these examples just how much the manager considers it necessary to stress both the unity of the club personnel and the hierarchy of power within that personnel. The manager has become more answerable than ever before for the conduct and performance of the team, and has evolved newly rigorous structures of control to reinforce his authority on the playing side of the club. As this has happened, players have been spending more time together, at top level, in travelling and in preparing for matches. As Lawrie McMenemy has commented, the professional game can be a claustrophobic one:

> ... because you live so closely for eleven months of the year in each other's pocket and we travel around and go around the world in aeroplanes and buses and dressing rooms and you're bound to get little flare ups ... and ... you just carry on as long as you're the better for it, as long as something good's come out of it. (McMenemy, 1979)[9]

In some cases, though, 'something bad' comes out of it. Managers can lose control, players can withhold consent and the structure of control can be (albeit temporarily) undermined. Relations of domination can suddenly appear to be vulnerable, based as they are — at least between manager and player — upon a mutual dependency. Benny Fenton lost, forever, the respect of the senior player Eamon Dunphy on 1st October 1973:

> So we started training. A bit of running to get warmed up, then we were going to have this practice match. Lawrie was handing the bibs out. And he walked past me. "That is very odd of him", I thought nothing of it; just a little bit perturbed. I looked after

127

him, and he was giving out first-team shirts. And he was giving one to Robin Wainwright ... and he gave one to Dennis ... and I looked around ... "I'm dropped! ... No! ... I am!"

I could not believe it. I could not think for a minute. And Benny was standing there as if nothing had happened. No one said anything to me.

He had given me a reserve shirt. "Play in midfield", he said. How do you react? It was like somebody had plunged a dagger in my back. I was so hurt. Not so much because I was dropped, but because they had done it like that. (Dunphy, 1977: pp. 88–89)

Dunphy's reflexive memoir shows just how fragile established relationships can be in the game. The sudden switch from apparent indispensability to potential redundancy or wastage can be experienced by the player in the most traumatic of ways. If the difficult relation between manager and managed is handled with such hamfistedness as seems to have been the case in Benny Fenton's decision to drop Dunphy, then any basis of control can be seriously threatened. Managers must retain the respect of players. If they do not, then their authority will be jeopardized. This will lead to the need for either the manager to move on, or for changes in the personnel of the playing staff. In the case of Arsenal, in the mid-1970s, this second type of change took place when, in Liam Brady's account, Terry Neill lost the respect of the players. Brady's recollections of the crisis highlight the tension, in club culture, between the player's desire to be treated as an equal and his willingness to be dependent upon a strong figure of authority. Brady (1980) expresses distaste at the "whole mad human supermarket" (p. 83), at being treated as if he's a "cog" (p. 100), a "prize heifer" (p. 104) or a "piece of furniture" (p. 106) — in general, as a "business commodity" (p. 102). But he does not want absolute independence:

When a youngster leaves his home to join a football club, he does so hoping that he is going from one family atmosphere to another. He looks for security, for warmth and trust, confidence-building discipline and basic fair-play and justice. (p. 96)

The player wants to be led by a strong figure who will generate a sense of loyalty and trust whilst, in the end, accepting all the responsibility for the performance of the team. But, Brady alleges, "just when we needed him most, Neill let us down":

I believe that one of the signs of a great manager is his ability to obtain the respect of his players, and to be able to hammer those players within the confidential walls of the club when they let him down, without letting them down or attacking them through the media. (p. 28)

Terry Neill, the Arsenal manager, did not 'hammer' the players face to face. Instead, he made his comments to the press, and the players read there that in their manager's view they "could not have beaten eleven dustbins on that display". Neill, Brady's account relates, did this several times and lost completely the trust and loyalty of his players, describing them on television as 'morons'. The soured relationship between manager and players deteriorated to the point where, on a tour of the Far East, two star players — Malcolm Macdonald and Alan Hudson — were sent home in advance of the main party, for drinking. In Brady's view the manager was panicking. Inevitably, before very long, the squad was broken up. Neill — a former Arsenal player himself — had had difficulty in being accepted in his managerial role by players alongside whom he had lined up as a player. The disintegration of his squad was in all probability a necessary basis for him to develop that combination of roles, part tyrant and part father confessor, which so many players like to find in the football manager.

The manager is boss, then. That is the most obvious aspect of the hierarchy in club culture. But there are usually, as in many groups, informal hierarchies at work too. Within the playing staff there are senior players and junior players. There is the captain, about whose foreman's role I will say a little more later. Young players, or new arrivals, do not always find it easy to slot into the culture of the club. Some structures of control — among the players themselves — are not always immediately apparent. An example of this is contained in Eamon Dunphy's book, with the arrival of a new player into the first-team squad documented in some detail. The newcomer, Gordon Hill, was "the naive inexperienced lad" who provided, unwittingly, the running joke during Millwall's pre-season tour at Bournemouth in the summer of 1973. Dunphy described the situation clearly:

> But it's always great coming away with the lads, no matter how bad things are at the club, no matter how bad relationships are. It's always the same. You stay at a luxury hotel, and everything is laid on for you. You never have to check in, your meals are all laid on; no worrying about getting a table. You just walk straight in and sit down, and the prawn cocktail is there waiting for you. And you bring your golf clubs, knowing you will be able to play a lot. And there are no responsibilities. For four days there are no bills dropping through your letterbox, no wife, no mother-in-law. And no competition, no matches to spoil things. Just the lads.
>
> When every group of footballers go away, it's always the same. And you always have the oddball or the kid; the naive inexperienced lad. And they are always prey for joke and rags.
>
> Given the limitations of our interests, you could get a bit bored. But you never do. Because the great answer to boredom is finding someone to take the mickey out of. (Dunphy, 1977: p. 26)

Gordon Hill was perfect material for the mickey takers of Millwall. Young, confident, new, slightly boastful — Hill let it be known that he'd played at Junior Wimbledon. From that moment he was doomed. One of the Millwall players posed as a pressman and rang up Hill, flattering him and getting him to talk about the other players; getting him to dress up in tennis kit to meet a 'bogus' photographer; setting him up to play imaginary games of tennis across the hotel lobby with a settee as a net; throwing buckets of water over him for fake photographic features (Dunphy, 1977: pp. 26ff; pp. 52-53 and p. 65). Dunphy comments on Hill's relation to the group:

Poor Gordon. He's a bit like Best was at Old Trafford. In another world most of the time, not really part of the group, completely detached from reality. But George was never that gullible. (p. 65)

The control within the culture of the club, then, is not just crude autocratic control from above. The manager is the key figure, but informal everyday life within the playing group is also important; and players do aspire to belong to a family-style kind of unit. It is a precarious mix of one-way domination and mutual dependency, a mix which, as football took off into a new economic climate for a decade and a half after the abolition of the maximum wage, was inevitably to lead to more and more conflicts in club culture.

III

In this section I draw upon Hunter Davies' book on a season in the life of Tottenham Hotspur Football Club (Davies, 1972)[10] and an interview of my own with Alan Mullery.

At the beginning of the 1970-71 season Tottenham Hotspur was tipped to do very well; some football experts saw the team as the obvious star team of the year, and the arrival of Ralph Coates seemed to strengthen such a conviction. Coates, the midfield general for Burnley, had also from time to time been specified as the successor to Bobby Charlton in the English side. Coates seemed to share, not just Charlton's reluctance to admit to baldness, but also his flair for industry and skilful sophistication.

But Coates' changed, elevated status soon created problems. As Coates himself conceded (Davies, 1972: Appendix 9), he enjoyed the 'act of playing football' much more when he was 15 years of age than he does as a highly paid superstar: "The higher I've got in football the less I seem to have enjoyed it. The pressures of success spoil the fruits of success" (p. 314). Again, when asked about his plans for the future, Coates commented upon the pressures of the game: "I wouldn't like to be a coach or a manager. There are too many pressures, as a spare time interest I might coach amateurs. I like winning. I don't like having to win" (p. 323). Overall, Coates had a lot of confidence in his game — he believed that if you don't believe in your own skill then there's no point in stepping out onto the pitch. But he seemed to dislike the trappings of superstardom, and when asked what his view of his life as a professional footballer is — a job of work or a career? — he answered that it's "a job. I get paid for it, so it's a job. I can do without all the glamour that goes with it" (p. 304).

Coates' first twenty-five years were spent in Hetton-le-Hole, County Durham, where his father was a miner; and in Burnley, his only club prior to Tottenham Hotspur. His arrival at a big-name club, tipped for honours, in the biggest city in the land — and the South — was bound to be a testing move, and in very personal and everyday terms Coates could not be as settled in this new environment. His luxury bungalow in Burnley gave way initially to a flat with blanketless beds, and his personal status as the star in a far from glowing setting gave way to being just one among a galaxy of stars constantly in the line of the telescope of the media and the public.

This wasn't altogether unwelcome, for at Burnley Coates had become too absorbed in the responsibilities of the club. As he observed about those day as the idol of Burnley: "The manager himself even asked me what I thought, which front runners I'd pick. But it was always the same sort of decision, an experienced player or a young lad. I never gave him any answers. I honestly didn't know. It wasn't my job. Jimmy was the manager. But I didn't envy him the task" (p. 23). So Coates was holding back from becoming too clearly identified with the management and its problems. At Spurs he was to experience no such dilemma. His problem was the opposite one, that of getting himself at all accepted by the players themselves.

The previous season Spurs had finished third in the league; Coates' purchase was seen as the final piece in the jigsaw-puzzle, as the final ingredient in the recipe for honours and the championship; as Mullery pointed out to him: "Yes, and it's all up to you, Ralph" (p. 25). The joke had an element of seriousness to it.

On the first day of the new season all the players almost queued to look at Coates, who was unfashionably dressed in narrow trousers and rather pointed shoes. As the most costly cash-bought player ever in British football, he was bound to be scrutinized, and one apprentice actually commented on his clumsiness.

Coates never really made the impact expected of him. Not settling, sustaining the first injury of his career, and scoring only two goals, both from midfield after failing as a forward, can hardly be seen as unqualified success — yet Coates won his first honour, in the European Inter-City Fairs Cup (predecessor to the UEFA Cup), and so in personal terms the season was pretty successful. There is little evidence, though, in Davies' account, that Coates was really helped in his life at the new club. He seemed to remain a figure on the outskirts; perhaps the provincial tag with which he was labelled on arrival was too firmly stuck to him, utterly appropriate for the rather modest Northerner thrown into the culture of a glamour club in the metropolis. Alan Mullery recalled Coates' problems in an interview with me in 1979:

> Coatesy had a lot of trouble getting accepted … the most expensive player ever in the country. All the lads expected him to do everything but he couldn't. The ball kept bouncing off his shins when he tried to trap it and, to tell you the truth, he became a bit of a joke. I suppose it was all a bit much for him, coming to London from the Sticks. If any of those lads here went to Manchester or Liverpool then they'd be a bit out of their depth I think. It was like that with Coatesy, coming to one of the top clubs, to a famous club like Spurs …
>
> There were some players at Spurs, though. Gilly and Chivers, and they'd had Greavesy. The first year or so I'd watch Greavesy score goals and I'd pat him on the back and I'd say 'you jammy little bastard'. He just seemed to walk goals in; after a couple of seasons of tapping them in I saw it was genius. Well, Ralph had to come and follow this lot and it just wasn't on really, was it?

Another example of group-outsider was the England centre-forward Martin Chivers. He perhaps never became the butt of group jokes (Coates' goal in a practice match was in the later part of the season the main joke at player Mike England's party), but he remained rather outside the group, often singled out for criticism, too, by the management.

Chivers was, academically, by far the best qualified of the first-team squad, with 5 G.C.E. 'O' Levels; although at the same time he stated that he never followed current affairs: "I only read the sports pages. I've never read a book in my life ... I'm just not interested" (Davies, 1972: p. 317). Chivers, for a big strong centre-forward, was, surprisingly, physically scared of being alone:

> I really am scared. I don't know why. I don't like the dark and going to bed on my own. I worry if I've locked everything up. I never read books and I don't like TV and I can't cook or anything so I go to pieces on my own. I must have company. I must be doing something all the time and have other people around me. (Davis, 1972: p. 122)

Ironically, in a famous victory in a two-leg cup tie (a 1–1 draw against AC Milan) Chivers was almost an isolate in an all-round team victory. His reluctance to commit himself totally all of the time made him a stranger in this particular crowd — as Davies observed, "the rest of the players left him alone with his thoughts, carefully walking around him" (p. 273). Here is Chivers' own self assessment: "Despite all my success, I'd always been a timid player" (p. 120). A group battling for success in a harshly competitive world is not going to accept totally someone like this.

The collective culture of the professional footballer does not inevitably draw every player into it. Some do not find themselves as readily accepted as others. Even Bill Nicholson's attempt to, in Davies' words, 'bring out the aggressive side to his nature', took some time to have any real effect on Chivers' style of play.

Alan Mullery's story shows how individual adaptation to the group can be very difficult. The club-captain at the beginning of the season, Mullery sustained a serious groin-strain and was then loaned to Fulham. The season ended 'happily' for him in that he was recalled to lead the team to its European triumph, scoring the vital goal at Milan in the semi-final tie. Mullery missed Mike England's party because he had been playing for Fulham at Hull. Mullery had to be in on the action, so to speak, and this explained his loan period. He could not exist on the sidelines. Thus it was not convincing when he said that once his playing days were over, then that would be it. He would not want to become another Bill Nicholson: "Nobody would want to be like that. I don't know how he stands it. I'd be in the loony bin" (p. 176). Mullery in fact went on to manage Brighton and Hove Albion, Charlton and Crystal Palace — three loony bins perhaps! But he was always the one in this particular group who seemed most likely to bridge the gap between play and management, despite his trenchantly stated intention to the contrary. In his playing days, though, it was the figure of the Tottenham manager, Bill Nicholson, which he was determined never to emulate. This is how Mullery put it to me in 1979:

> I said I'd never become a manager because Bill Nick was what I knew best and I never wanted to be like him. He worked a sixteen hour day seven days a week and he wouldn't trust anybody. He'd check the bloody turnstiles and he'd check the groundsmen's job. He's been out there early on some afternoons mowing the pitch himself. When I went back to Fulham though I saw lots of managers who did sweet fuck all and I thought to myself that if I couldn't do better than most of that then I'm a monkey's uncle.

But most players do not exhibit such assertive self-confidence, for the professional football club promotes in its players an attitude of general impotence, and structurally delimits any potential that the group of players might have for expansion or growth. The group of sportsmen is in this sense essentially a stagnating group with no capacity for development.

The players are frequently treated as children rather than adults, and sometimes as robots rather than people. Bill Nicholson, the Spurs manager, showed this in some of his dealings with players. Before a match against Leeds, three players were waiting to see who would be substitute. A few minutes before the match Nicholson gave the position to Coates saying nothing to the other two (Davies, 1972: pp. 251-252). When Mullery returned to the club towards the end of his month's spell on loan with Fulham, Bill Nicholson recalled him out of the blue, just after Mullery had been expressing, in the press, his disappointment at the treatment that he'd received from Spurs.

This is how Mullery recollected the affair when I talked to him about it:

> It was when John (Pratt) got injured that Bill came to see me and said 'I hear you've been playing well'. 'Yes', I said. Bill then said 'Well, get your boots, you're in on Saturday'. In the dressing room before that match nobody said anything until just before we were ready to go out when Bill was asked 'Who's captain, boss?'. 'Alan, who do you think' he said, and that did more than anything else could have done to get me back.

But Mullery did not forgive Nicholson for his treatment. From being captain (a very important position; Mullery stated during his injury in 1970-1971 that he would not want to stay at the club if he did not hold down the captaincy — see Davies, 1972: p. 177). Mullery was simply put to one side.

From being the main link between manager and players he became a peripheral figure. This is how he described his experience to me:

> I got this injury and for two months Cyril and Eddie said 'run on it, and it'll get better.' They said it was my groin and they gave me a bit of heat. I could hardly walk some days, though, and Bill wasn't interested. I couldn't play and if you couldn't play then that was it — I'd become a useless commodity. I didn't see much of the lads because I was in early in the morning ... So I was out on my own and nobody bothered with me at all. When I went to see a lad in Harley Street ... he said that everything I'd been doing could only make the injury worse. He said that it was the pelvis and said that I had to rest. To do nothing at all. So I did, and one morning after a month or two it was suddenly o.k.

After his return from Fulham Mullery helped Spurs to win a European trophy, scoring in the final:

> That was my last match for the club. I never played for them again because I'd resented what they'd done to me so much. I could never forgive them for the way they treated me and I said to Bill that I'd never play again for the club even if it meant I'd never play the game again.

Mullery experienced a double rejection. His manager dealt with him callously and insensitively, and in injury he was excluded from the everyday life of the players. Coates suffered from the responses of his peers in day-to-day life. Chivers was constantly 'got at' by the management, which implied that he did not always do all he could for the team. Mullery suffered from both sides. As the displaced intermediary in the club hierarchy, Mullery became an embarrassment when injured. So he was, to repeat his own words, 'out on his own'. Nicholson certainly could, in Mullery's own words again, "be ruthless". Despite the working relationship of more than seven years between Mullery and Nicholson, the former, in the circumstances of injury, became to the latter as replaceable as a light bulb. Despite the intimacy that might develop within club culture, this remains a dominant characteristic of life in football. Nicholson, it seems, like other managers in the game, chose to ignore more sensitive ways of handling personal problems. The kind of treatment Mullery got was a reminder that 'life is hard', 'it's a tough game', and that the fate of the player is in the hands of the 'boss'.

IV

Brian Clough described his successful Nottingham Forest Club as the 'best democracy' you'd find in football. But it was a one-party democracy. The tales of Clough's autocratic rule are legion. One of the elements in his success has been his capacity to remind and remind again citizens in his 'democracy' just who the ruler actually is. If this does not happen in football, if the structure of domination is openly challenged, then the culture of the club as a whole can be put under severe strain.

At Newcastle United during the season 1976-1977 the club had its most successful year in the First Division for more than a quarter of a century. At the end of the 1977-1978 season Newcastle was relegated to the Second Division. During the summer in between those two seasons the Newcastle board faced a mass transfer demand from its playing staff; and early on in the 1978-1979 season, following on from the club's relegation, a group of shareholders planned to take the club to court, in an attempt to get some directors to stand down. In the middle of the successful 1976-1977 season the manager Gordon Lee had resigned, alleging that his job was made impossibly difficult because of "intolerable" boardroom interference. Within a couple of weeks the board signed a new player without reference to the man in charge of playing affairs, Lee's erstwhile deputy Richard Dinnis, who learned of the signing through the newspapers. The players supported Dinnis and expressed no confidence in the board; police warned that fans were near to rioting; and Dinnis was then appointed, at the chairman's home late one night, as 'acting manager' until the summer (Hughes, 1977: pp. 30–31). By October, 1977, when Newcastle were bottom of the First Division, the club captain Geoff Nulty stated, in a regional television programme, that "if for whatever reason, circumstantial or friction with the board, Dinnis cannot deliver for me and for the rest of Newcastle United, then he should leave and try his hand elsewhere. I, Geoff Nulty, want to be a success with United" (Armstrong, 1977: p. 20). In mid-November Richard Dinnis, who was now on a two year contract, was sacked following a board meeting at which the decision was a unanimous one. At the same time the court case against the club was dropped. Clearly, the established structures of control were not operating during this period of what was dubbed, in the sporting world, as 'player power'. Within a matter of days a new manager, Bill McGarry, was appointed, without a contract, and with a reputation as a tough disciplinarian. These were the words with which he introduced himself to his new challenge: "There are players of quality at this club … but they seem to have done more talking than playing lately. I believe professional footballers are well paid to do a job. If any decide not to do a job for me they will get their backsides kicked" (quoted in Barclay, 1977a: p. 18).

The questions of most interest here are: how could such grassroots protest develop? How was it sustained? What were its effects on football culture? Were the structures of control fundamentally altered? Throughout these events Richard Dinnis assumed consistently a somewhat fatalistic tone. Even in the summer following the season of success he was not making the most optimistic noises. The players were dissatisfied not just with the running of the club but also with their own average wage of £175 a week, which did not compare favourably with other less successful First and even some Second Division clubs. Also, what seemed to really trigger the mass transfer request by ten players in July 1977 was the Board's denial that a sponsorship deal with Bukta would bring the players more money in the following season. Dinnis' response to rumours that the Board saw three star players as ringleaders, and would be happy to see them leave the club, was a resigned one:

> I don't know about that. All I know is that I look like losing a
> very promising team...
> I thought that at this stage of the season I was going to be
> preparing a team capable of challenging for the championship.
> Now it looks as if it could be a case of getting one together to
> stave off the threat of relegation. (Barclay, 1977b: p. 18)

Dinnis was proved to be a pretty good soothsayer, although he himself departed before the restless players did. Newcastle's team in the match which confirmed their relegation included six of the restless rebels of the previous summer, and a couple of others were still with the club but inactive through injury.

In some ways the collective response of the Newcastle players to the crisis was an extension of their strong 'esprit de corps' which had developed since the point at which the superstar, Malcolm MacDonald, had been sold by Gordon Lee to Arsenal. One player, when I interviewed him, alleged that MacDonald had become known, at Newcastle, as:

> ... the traffic policeman — directing all the rest ... He'd wave
> his arms in disgust if a ball was a couple of yards away —
> wouldn't make the effort.[11]

MacDonald also earned twice as much as did all of his team-mates, and was said to need more money still because of some commercial dealing in which he was involved. His departure was therefore, I was told, "the best thing for everybody; Malcolm could get incentives at Arsenal and we could play as a team at Newcastle. Gordon got off to a good start with the board over this; it suited everybody." Even the fanatical Newcastle fans could see the sense in this. A follower of the club for half a century, Jimmy Nicholl had twice lost asphalting jobs as a result of 'watching' United, but even he agreed with the departure of MacDonald:

> MacDonald was a wonderful sight — oh, dear me, he was — but they were right to get rid. It's the team that counts. (quoted in Hughes, 1977: p. 31)

The departure of MacDonald, then, heralded a new sense of collective strength[12].

As one of my sources recalled: "Gordon really got us going when Supermac went." It was claimed, too, that three players — Mick Burns, Alan Gowling and Geoff Nulty — "a bit more intelligent and articulate than the lads" — generated a keen response from the rest of the team. These were the three players seen by the club as ringleaders. They were also the three players in the squad who had some background in higher education. Gowling was a university graduate; Burns a qualified schoolteacher; and Nulty was doing Open University courses. These three got almost total support from the players in the battle against the board. These players saw themselves as rational reasonable employees controlled by an authoritarian board. It took, interestingly, a trio with a higher educational background to co-ordinate the protest. And, in the end, it got nowhere. Soon after the club was relegated most of the protesters moved on from the club, and Lord Westwood, the chairman with the family motto of 'Deeds Not Words' was firmly in control again.

One player went to see McGarry soon after the new manager arrived. He recollected to me that:

McGarry was just a hard-liner and I suppose he was there to restore order. He'd been warned about us by the board I suppose ... He said to me, 'Do you know, I've got a poster — huh, huh, huh, huh', he's always laughing like this whilst speaking — 'and on it there's this feller pointing at you saying — huh huh huh huh — Everybody's got a right to my own opinion'.

It was also said to me that:

> ... things can't change or improve without action like ours at Newcastle. Footballers aren't allowed to criticize anything at the moment and if that carries on then things can never improve.

But what did the action lead to? In the end, not very much that was different to what had gone before. The established hierarchies, momentarily challenged, were soon re-established. A form of industrial militance or workers' democracy which stemmed from an a-typical sub-group of players with a background in higher education had little effect, in the long run, upon the culture of the club. When the court action threatened by shareholders never in fact materialized, the details of the conflicts in the club never came out fully into the open. Alan Gowling offers a relatively detailed account of the troubles at the club in the middle of the successful season, but concludes that "the only people with real power in football are directors, the men with the power to hire and fire. But players do have influence, and that's how it should be" (Gowling, 1977: p. 88). But such influence — which got Richard Dinnis a short term and then a two year contract — can, as Dinnis himself so painfully found out, be very short-lived. The Newcastle story shows just how easily structures of control in football culture can be reconstituted. Perhaps it was never a particularly strong protest anyway. As one of the alleged ringleaders of the protest has asserted: "I'm not a bolshy. I'm very conservative generally" (Ball, 1977)[13]. The club administration stands condemned by a comment such as this. As one of the players reported to me:

We'd done a lot at Newcastle. We'd been out on Sports Forums and not asked for fees — though an arrangement was made in the end with local radio giving us a bit for the work[14]. The board was very suspicious of anything like this, though, wondering what players could be up to. The board was so used to being criticized that it didn't seem able to trust anyone.

Again, we come back to the question of trust. Players want to feel that they can trust, and be trusted by, their employers. But the demands of the game and its very unpredictability militate against the development of such a relation. Investments demand results. In the end, the capacity to decide upon the structures of control lies in the hands of the management. The Newcastle case is an instructive one because of its very a-typicality; for the collectivist dimensions of the players' lives so rarely develop in the essentially political way in which they did in this case. More often, club culture is experienced as the camaraderie of the classroom.

V

Like many groups situated in inflexible authoritarian structures, groups of players might respond by generating their own informal controls and interactions. Gordon Hill was the butt of a group joke at Millwall. And there are many examples of what Alan Gowling calls 'getting a laugh out of life'.

Gowling devotes a whole chapter to this, and tells of the Phantom who used to strike when Huddersfield Football Club was away for the night before its away fixtures. If a player happened to leave his hotel room key with the reception, he would find that all the bristles on his toothbrush had been burned, his toothpaste tube was punctured, and boot polish was on his shaving brush. At Newcastle the players ran a Noshers' league, in which points were gained for consuming a 'meal in quick time'. On tour in Majorca one time, four players who were playing table tennis had bucketfuls of water thrown down on them by Malcolm MacDonald and the club goalkeeper Mahoney.

Sociologists of education have noted that one response of some school children to boredom and to authoritarian classroom regimes is to 'have a laugh': "laughter has a central place either as a natural product or as a life saving response to the exigencies of the institution — bored, ritual, routine, regulations, oppressive authority" (Woods, 1976: p. 185). Such writers have tended to idealize the 'laugh', to see in it an "ingenuity, creativity, brilliance and joie de vivre", almost a form of Bakhtinian carnivalesque (Bakhtin, 1998); from this point of view the laugh is a raw, inchoate form of subversion or rebellion. But 'having a laugh' in football is rather different, because it is usually focused within the players' group itself. Players cannot afford to 'have a laugh' at the expense of their manager and employers. Their 'mucking about' must be directed inwards. Very senior players might be an exception to this. Jimmy Greaves recollects that the regulars in the West Ham United drinking school included himself, Bobby Moore, and half a dozen others. Once, travelling to New York for an exhibition game, one of Bobby Moore's business friends 'spiked' the manager Ron Greenwood's coke with a bacardi — half a dozen times in all. Moore and Greaves did nothing to stop the 'mischievous' Freddie from doing this, and Greaves admitted to "having a juvenile giggle" (Greaves, 1979: p. 80).

Much of the culture of the player is given over to having such juvenile giggles. Time might be spent resenting the structure of authority, but little time is spent opposing it. The player is dominated and knows it; but he is also dependent upon the shared success of manager and managed.

Brian Clough's definition of democracy approximates a description of the working life of a capitalist entrepreneur who has experienced the work of which he later becomes a supervisor:

Furthermore, the personal leadership and appeal — the charisma, to use Max Weber's word — of the capitalist himself served to cultivate workers ... this success depended on his ability to get work out of his workers, whether by harsh discipline or by inspiration, undoubtedly, most attempted to use both. Successful entrepreneurs understood the possibilities (and limits) of such personal motivation and to some extent realised its benefits. Workers undoubtedly were oppressed and exploited

143

by such employers, but they also became enmeshed in a whole network of personal relations. They had someone with whom to identify. (Edwards, 1979: p. 26)

Edwards could have been describing the management style of Brian Clough here quite as much as the style of, say, any enlightened Quaker employer. This is the real paradox of the culture of the game. The nature of the labour process in soccer might have changed (new forms of training, coaching, and preparation and a constant search for the most successful tactical formula) but the manager as dictator of the workers is often comparable to the early capitalist entrepreneur, or at the least to the managerial agent of the entrepreneur. This is further complicated by the modern working techniques of managers who themselves introduce new types of scientific management into the game.

Boys will be boys in football culture because the structures of control allow them to be little else. First, structures of control in the club position the player rigidly at the bottom of the hierarchy. Second, the playing group is unpredictably fluid; the bulk of a team can disappear within weeks, for various reasons, to be replaced by a new crop. And third, the collectivist dimensions of the culture of the player are directed, on the whole, towards essentially harmless laughs and jokes.

Chas Critcher's player-typology refers to "incorporated players" (Critcher, 1979: pp. 162 ff). The supreme irony in the culture of the club might be that as the increasingly affluent and mobile player is breaking his links with the culture of his origin, he is simultaneously bounded in unprecedentedly rigid ways in the culture of the club. Jovial Joe Mercer has said that "compared with our day, when I see the boys running out of the tunnel nowadays they all look as if they are on their way to Vietnam" (Green, 1974: p. 8)[15]. And this is not just a Saturday afternoon experience. When Don Revie's Leeds team was at its peak the influence of Revie on the everyday life of his players was extreme. Hunter Davies writes that:

Just before ten o'clock, two of the Leeds stars, Eddie Gray and Peter Lorimer, popped their heads into the lounge on their way to bed. 'We stay here every Friday night before a home match,' said Eddie Gray. 'Room 303, always the same one. We've both got young babies who keep us awake. Don rings us at ten to make sure we're in bed... (Davies, 1972: p. 287)

Tuck up tight lads, Don is on the prowl, making sure that his boys will stay boys in the culture of the club.

Notes

1   The book which emerged, Hunter Davies, *The Glory Game*, Weidenfeld and Nicholson, 1972, was not what the chairman anticipated.

2   When I first interviewed Alan Mullery about his time at Spurs, one of his first points, now that he was manager of Brighton and Hove Albion Football Club, was that he would not consider granting the kind of access to the life of a club which Davies was granted by Spurs.

3   I wrote personally to three other members of the Spurs squad as well as to Mullery, requesting an interview. None of them replied. I also received only a few replies to letters I wrote to several Newcastle United players.

4   As Paul Willis has demonstrated in his ethnographic studies — see Willis, 1977.

5   The classic study of 'banana time', of shop-floor 'talking, fun and fooling', is that of Donald Roy. See his 'Banana-time: job satisfaction and informal interaction' (1960), excerpted in Salaman and Thompson (eds) (1973): pp. 205-222. For a similar argument concerning 'games' at work and further forms (and in the language of neo-Marxism) see Burawoy (1979).

6   For evidence of his committed involvement with those players who do 'make it' see *The First 90 Minutes: Bobby Robson ex Ipswich*, Channel 4 (Pelicula Films, 1983, produced by Mike Alexander and Mark Littlewood).

7   This is the title I gave to my initial floating of these issues at a BSA/LSA Workshop at Sheffield Hallam University, in 1983.

8   See *Wilf Mannion*, BBC North East, 1978, written and produced by John Mappledeck. This is not to say that intimate relations of mutual respect did not develop between 'managed' and 'managing'. Herbert Chapman's death when manager of Arsenal, recalled by his daughter Molly Alsop, reduced big tough professional

footballers to tears. See *Britain in the 30s: Arsenal*, BBC 2, 1983, directed by Victoria Wegg-Prosser. Bert Chapman, like many visionaries, was a pretty a-typical figure of his time.

9　See *The Ian Wooldridge Interview*: Lawrie McMenemy (BBC South, 1982). McMenemy really does see himself as the head of a family. In an interview, talking about the crisis that occurred at the club when two players were charged with rape on a pre-season Swedish tour, and when several senior players left the club, he had this to say: "You shut the doors and pull the family all together ... we had many good chats about it ... there was no rubbish talked then ... it was about life, and livin and learnin and growin up" ('Football Focus', BBC1, 2 May, 1983).

10　Hunter Davies, *The Glory Game*, London: Weidenfeld and Nicholson, 1972. Page numbers cited in the rest of this section refer to this text.

11　Where quotes are not acknowledged, they are from my own interviews with Newcastle personnel. I leave the sources anonymous because of the provenly vindictive nature of the Newcastle hierarchy, and because of the draconian punitive sanctions which the Football Association can still impose upon players (and managers) who are said to 'bring the game into disrepute'.

12　Interestingly enough, a key player at Arsenal has commented on the same problem. Liam Brady wrote of his delight at Macdonald's 29-goal first season in London, but also commented that Macdonald's 'single-minded' selfishness restricted the way in which the team could play. Consequently, "when Malcolm dried up ... the whole team suddenly appeared to function on three cylinders". See Brady, 1980: pp. 79 and 88.

13　The penultimate chapter in Gowling's book is entitled 'We're not bolshy'.

14　This is testified to, as well, in Gowling, 1977: pp. 30-31, and 87.

15　Hunter Davies (1972: p. 287) also refers to Mercer's point.

8 North and South: The Rivalry of the Football League and the Football Association

The Football League was founded in 1888, the oldest professional soccer league in the world. In the Spring of 1991 the Football Association, an older body by a quarter of a century, published plans to recruit the top 18 clubs from the Barclays English Football League and set up its own Superleague. Incensed — especially given that the Chief Executive of the Football Association, the man behind this irreverent challenge to the League's 103 year-old authority, was a former Secretary of the League itself — many League representatives appealed to history, tradition and paternalism to justify the status quo for the League's structure. Tensions between the Football Association and the League were certainly nothing new, although at the beginning of the 1990s there had been increasing talk of fuller collaboration between, even the merger of, the two bodies. The genesis of these tensions over the last century will be the main focus of this chapter, followed by some comments upon case-studies of two types of club: the member of an embryonic European élite, Tottenham Hotspur; and two of the most unsuccessful clubs in the season 1991-92, Aldershot and Halifax Town. Common themes explaining the crises in these two very different clubs/organizations will highlight the major shifts in the fortunes of football in the dawn of its second century of openly professionalized organization.

A major interpretive strand to this chapter will be the traumas encountered by the League in its reluctant embrace of the new, its inelegant stumble towards modernity. In this, the League shares a dilemma with other cultural institutions which were born of the new industrial society, which have given pleasure to millions in traditional forms, but which have begun to look anachronistic in an age — which some would no doubt call a post-modern one — of cosmopolitan innovation, cultural experimentation and bland consumer sovereignty. In the same week in which news of the Football Association's initiative broke, the phased closure of London Zoo was leaked to the press. Sentimentalists called for the protection and retention of an institution dating from the 1820s; progressives pointed to the outdatedness of the London Zoo concept; the British love of pets and caged wildlife was appealed to by animal lovers.

To progressive critics of the established cultural institution such as the football ground and the zoological gardens, a different model of the future beckoned: the modern purpose-built leisure environment, the consumer-friendly multi-experience facility — the Disneyesque theme park. Big money would be needed for mega-complexes such as these, the need for and arrival of which would make the traditional nineteenth-century cultural facility less acceptable to new more discriminating and McDonalds-fed publics.

But traditions of an authentically lived kind are not inventions or fictions. Traditional values might well stand for generations of stoutly defended beliefs, principles and practices. It is these principles and the influences upon them which this chapter sets out to examine and account for, by looking at what key individuals in the making of the football culture have stood for.

Football has always been characterized by a fascinating set of dynamics: North versus South; working class versus middle class and middle class versus upper class; new money versus old status. Professional players in the hundred years of the league's history have been predominantly working-class; administrators of the League have been predominantly first-generation middle-class; administrators on the level of the Football Association have been more upper middle and middle-class. This has led to many clashes of values, of a classically patrician-plebeian kind, in which the old amateur/professional tensions have been relived. To understand the source of such clashes it is necessary to look at the specific origins of the two rival organizations which have dominated English football.

The Football Association (FA)

The FA was formed in 1863. It was formed as an association of clubs, on the basis of an agreement between the representatives of a few clubs [mostly southern English ones] to play each other regularly according to a shared set of rules of play. By 1868 the FA had 30 member clubs; by 1870, 39 clubs. Revealingly, though, only 4 of these 39 clubs were still in existence by 1900. In the 1870s an increasing number of city and county-based associations was established throughout England, but as Tony Mason has noted "after the speed of this expansion the other most important fact to notice was that all these associations looked to the FA itself and wished to affiliate with it" (Mason, 1980: p. 15). By the mid-1880s, then, the Football Association was a kind of umbrella body, an administrative catalyst for the county and district associations which were springing up throughout the country.

The FA's most celebrated initiative — beyond the standardization of the rules of the game — was the setting up of the FA Cup. This was first competed for in 1871-72, based on the public school competition at Harrow, and inspired by the youthful experiences of the Football Association's Secretary of the time, Charles Alcock. At the age of 22, he had been one of the influences upon the formation of the Wanderers FC, one of the 15 teams to contest the FA Cup in its inaugural season. The list of all 15 of these entrants makes fascinating reading:

1. Wanderers
2. Harrow Chequers
3. Clapham Rovers
4. Upton Park
5. Crystal Palace
6. Hitchin
7. Maidenhead
8. Great Marlow
9. Queens Park (Glasgow)
10. Donington School (Spalding)
11. Royal Engineers
12. Reigate Priory
13. Hampstead Heathens

14. Barnes
15. Civil Service

The winner of this inaugural tournament was Wanderers, a team including "four Harrow graduates, three Etonians, and one representative each from Westminster, Charterhouse, Oxford and Cambridge" (Tischler, 1981: p. 26). The Association itself had been founded by representatives of Harrow, Eton, Winchester, Rugby and Westminster Schools, and in its early days recruited exclusively from the upper-classes and the public schools. Only Donington School (East Midlands/ East Anglia) and Queens Park Glasgow represented any part of the United Kingdom outside of Greater London and the Home Counties of South-East England. It was not until 1882 that this essentially Southern and upper class domination of the FA Cup was challenged, when Blackburn Rovers reached the Final, to be followed in 1883 by Blackburn Olympic's historic defeat of Old Etonians. Blackburn Rovers themselves then won the Cup in 1884 and 1885 and after the 1884 victory a disapproving commentator in the capital wrote that London had witnessed:

> An incursion of Northern barbarians on Saturday — hot-blooded Lancastrians, sharp of tongue, rough and ready, of uncouth garb and speech. A tribe of Sudanese Arabs let loose in the Strand would not excite more amusement and curiosity. (*Pall Mall Gazette*, 31 March 1884, cited in Tischler, 1981: p. 124)

The Football League

Founded in 1888, the League was an inevitable outcome of the FA's legalization of professionalism in the summer of 1885. Once professionalism was accepted, the expanding football industry needed to be put on a sound business footing, with regular fixtures, standardized procedures, rigorous monitoring of professional standards and enforceability of accepted rules and regulations. The strongest teams which had moved towards a professional footing were in the industrial commu-

152

nities of the North of England and the Midlands. The founder members of the Football League were:

1. Preston North End
2. Aston Villa
3. Wolverhampton Wanderers
4. Blackburn Rovers
5. Bolton Wanderers
6. West Bromwich Albion
7. Accrington
8. Everton
9. Burnley
10. Derby County
11. Notts County
12. Stoke

Lancashire and the Midlands were the dominant geographical strongholds of the pioneers of the League. William McGregor of Aston Villa was the prime mover — inspired, it is sometimes said, by the innovative new National Basketball League in the United States, but in his own expressed view modelling the League on the County Championship in cricket. McGregor himself was a self-employed smalltime shopkeeper selling linen. He also had a passion for football and a sense of its potential contribution to sport. Social conscience and municipal pride mingled with a passionate Liberal politics and a Methodist non-conformist conscience. McGregor was "a dedicated Methodist, at a time when Christianity, combined with a concern for social welfare, often manifested itself in the promotion of sport" (Inglis, 1988: p. 2). Along with McGregor, 6 individuals met on the eve of the 1888 Cup Final. The Blackburn Rovers representative was a factory inspector. Burnley's representative was an auctioneer. The West Bromwich representative was a former player turned club secretary who had initially worked in a spring and scale manufacturing plant. Wolverhampton Wanderers were represented by a local boot and shoe maker. Stoke sent a local printer, soon to become the league's first secretary. Only one "gentleman" attended that meeting, a solicitor and former Rugby schoolboy who was there on behalf of Notts County.

So the socio-economic and cultural roots of the Football League are very clear: Northern and skilled working-class cum self-employed. The Football League was not a separatist initiative — McGregor was a faithful adherent to the FA as the ruling body — but it represented a very different set of sporting principles to those of the founding members of the FA itself. In the years immediately prior to the formation of the League, the commercial imperative had come more and more to the fore in the industrial areas where the game was flourishing. Clubs were recognizing that players must be paid. As a committee man at Burnley said in 1885: "The fact of it is, the public will not go to see inferior players. During the first year we did not pay a single player, and nobody came to see us" (cited in Tischler, 1981: p. 47).

The FA's roots lie in the professional class' need for therapeutic exercise of a morally uplifting kind, and in certain circumstances the patrician's messianic zeal to convert the less civilized; whereas the Football League's roots lie in a vigorously assertive localized culture, and an alliance of the interests of the (often self-made) local elite and those of the predominantly working-class player and spectator.

In the following section on Football League personnel, typical prominent figures are examined to see just how deep-rooted some of these differences have been.

Football League Personnel

The Presidency of the Football League is a position which has remained dominated by representatives of Northern and Midland clubs, and delegates from Lancashire clubs in particular. The following table shows this, along with the occupational background of the incumbents. (Details in the table are adapted from the text and Appendix 2 of Simon Inglis's [1988] indispensable study).

There have been 13 Presidents of the Football League, 6 of them from Lancashire clubs, 1 from Yorkshire, 4 from the Midlands/East Midlands, 1 from the North-East and 1 from the East Coast of Central England.

Presidents of the Football League, 1892-1991

1892–94	W. McGregor	Aston Villa	Shopkeeper
1894–1910	J.J. Bentley	Bolton	Railway clerk
1910–36	J. McKenna	Liverpool	Grocer's boy / vaccination officer
1936–39	C. E. Sutcliffe	Burnley	Solicitor
1939–49	W. C. Cuff	Everton	Solicitor
1949–54	A. Drewey	Grimsby	Fish-processing business
1955–57	A. H. Oakley	Wolves	Coal merchant
1957–66	J. Richards	Barnsley	Self-made manager / businessman
1966–74	L. T. Shipman	Leicester	Wholesale fruit/road haulage business
1974–81	Lord Westwood	Newcastle	Railway clerk/ manager/ businessman
1981–86	J. J. Dunnett	Notts County	Solicitor/Labour Member of Parliament
1986–1989	P. D. Carter	Everton	Managing Director, Littlewoods Pools
1989–(August)	W. Fox	Blackburn	Fruit/vegetable wholesaler, managing director (vehicle company)

Early domination was in the hands of Lancashire men, and the troubled years of the late 1980s, have seen the leadership back in the same hands. It is undeniable, then, that the leadership of the League has had these Northern roots, and that as an institution the League is rooted in strongly felt regional loyalties and identities. Although by its Centenary year the League's 86 committee men from 45 different clubs did not show an obvious bias to North-West England — Everton, West Bromwich, Birmingham, Arsenal and Newcastle had provided most members of the Committee — the leadership had certainly had a Lancastrian brand. The location of the League's headquarters — up until 1946 in modest office accommodation rented by the League Secretary in Preston, then in a modest terraced house bought by the League itself in Preston, and then from 1959 (and controversially) in a converted hotel in the retirement coastal resort of Lytham St. Annes — stubbornly reinforced this regional emphasis, in stark contrast to the ostentatious headquarters of the FA around the corner from Marble Arch in the country's capital.

Simon Inglis has claimed that two single individuals more than any others have affected the structure and character of the League in its 100-year history. These are the "little lawyer from Lancashire", Charles Sutcliffe; and Alan Hardaker, the League's Secretary from 1957 for 22 critically stormy years.

The Lancashire Legacy

Charles Sutcliffe did not assume the Presidency of the League until 1936, but he was a Committee man from 1898 through to 1939, the year of his death, with just one year of non-membership (1902-3). Sutcliffe was born in Burnley in 1864, the son of a local well-established solicitor, and raised in a strictly Methodist household which did not allow any games on Sunday, or even newspapers in the house. As a young man he played rugby for Burnley Rovers, a club which converted to soccer in 1882 and changed its name to Burnley FC. Qualifying as a solicitor in 1886, around the time he actually stopped playing for Burnley, he then became a nationally prominent referee and became one of Burnley's directors in 1897. On giving up refereeing in 1898 Sutcliffe was immediately elected onto the Management Committee of the League, and joined a group of men steeped in non-conformist respectable Liberal values. In his politics and religion, Inglis observes, he continued to stand for the core values of the League's founder, William McGregor. He was an active Liberal, and a "devout Methodist":

156

Sutcliffe ... campaigned ardently for the Temperance Movement ... as a youth Charles was a leading member of the Curzon Street Mission's minstrel troupe in Burnley. He taught in Sunday School, once gave evidence to a Royal commission on the problem of alcoholism, and ... became a much sought after speaker on religion, the Temperance Movement and, of course, football. (Inglis, 1988: p. 108)

Sutcliffe was the brains behind four key phases of expansion of the League, in 1898, 1905, 1919 and 1920-3, moves which increased the number of clubs from 32 to 88, and made the League a truly national body across England and Wales. He was also the spirit behind the League's survival, indeed strengthening, during the years of the First World War. He prosecuted corrupt players in the courts; organized refereeing appointments; and drew up League fixture lists. He worked too for the FA, on committees concerned with referees, international selection and the revision of rules; and sat on the International League Board and the Anglo-Irish League Board. He was President of the Lancashire FA, and of the Northern Counties Amateur Championship; served on Appeals Committees for twenty other leagues; and was Chairman and then Vice-President of Rossendale United — all on top of his devotion to Burnley Football Club and his conscientiousness as a practising solicitor. In the world of football Sutcliffe was branded the "football dictator" and acknowledged as the "brains of football". He had his failures in his lifetime of involvement, as well as his achievements. He failed to get approval for a two-referee system in 1935, and fought and lost the League's battles with the Pools companies in 1936. But for 40 years he cajoled, bullied, disciplined and developed the League into the modern era. Indeed, Inglis identifies Sutcliffe's as the single most influential contribution to the development of the League in its entire history:

His exhaustive mind took in fixtures, insurance schemes, wages, transfers, refereeing, the jubilee celebrations and the jubilee history. (Inglis, 1988: p. 163)

Sutcliffe also embodied an extremely important philosophy of mutual protection. For him the expanding League was like a prolifically multiplying extended family network. As he presided over this growth, he combined his adversarial skills with those of the compromising legalistic mind, and blended this with patriarchal and paternalistic concern for the well-being of all the family. Two examples illustrate extremely clearly how his specific skills could be put to work in defence of this philosophy.

First, in the 1890s when Charles Clegg of the FA was making a strong anti-professional case for reform of the retain and transfer system, Sutcliffe defended the system on the basis of a League in which the better-off members would have shared interests with the less well-off members. Similarly, in the Kingaby case in 1912 the same issue arose, with the same principle at stake. One of Aston Villa's former players — Kingaby — was supported by the Player's Union in a court case in which it was argued that an overvaluation of the player by Villa had restricted his work possibilities. Sutcliffe himself briefed the lawyer representing Aston Villa and convinced him that the retain and transfer system was legally watertight. Kingaby's case was not supported by the judge, and League controls were reasserted. The principle behind this was not just anti-unionism — though Sutcliffe is on record as saying that "the League could not be dictated to by any organization" — but, again, the power of all clubs to control their players equally. A free-for-all in the playing market would no doubt strengthen the rich at the expense of the aspirations of the poorer clubs. Charles Sutcliffe ruled with a rod of tradition, but wielded a protective rod. His anxieties were certainly prophetic. A freer movement of sporting talent in a commercially intensified climate would create an elite group of clubs.

The second example of Sutcliffe defending this central principle was in the immediate years after the Great War. Players were demanding a doubling of expenses to £2 per week. Having ordered out the press and the players, the Management Committee handed over to Sutcliffe. He offered an evaluation of the economic state of the clubs and then made a classically conciliatory proposal:

If every club paid each player £2, as ... proposed, ten of the well supported clubs would have to subsidise seventeen of the others. The remaining thirteen would neither pay out nor receive help. It was the typical Sutcliffe formula: the rich helping the poor, to keep the family strong. (Inglis, 1988: p. 112)

Charles Sutcliffe's Lancastrian legacy has been a fascinating one: to argue for an authoritarian grip on the functioning of the League, in the interests of the minnows as well as the mighty.

In Sutcliffe's day the longest-serving Secretary of the League was Tom Charnley, who held the position from 1902-33. He worked from four different rented offices in Preston during his 31 years in the job. Tom Charnley was the same Lancastrian type as Sutcliffe — together they traversed the country, Sutcliffe and Charnley, with the ring of a respectable but unglamorous legal partnership. Sutcliffe saw him as the perfect Secretary, and he ruled the roost at the League headquarters until the age of 73, ensuring a succession by bringing in his son-in-law and next-door-neighbour, Fred Howarth, as assistant in 1921. Howarth himself became Secretary in 1933 and was to appoint Charnley's grandson as Assistant Secretary in 1946. Fred Howarth had spent a short spell as a teacher before serving in the First World War and then joining what in retrospect would look like a 71-year-long "family business". Fred Howarth, Secretary himself until 1956, could not guarantee the succession, though: Charnley's grandson only lasted 5 years and Fred's nephew Eric would stay with the League until 1973, but never in one of the big jobs. Clearly, the world was changing. A young man called Alan Hardaker had been standing in the wings since 1951, and was well aware of the need for initiatives needed to usher the League into the contemporary world of communications and cosmopolitanism.

But Tom Charnley supported Sutcliffe in the first three decades of the century. They were similar types — both Liberals and committed Christians; and none remembers Charnley making a racket or consuming alcohol, whether at work or at play, his main relaxation being the game of bowls. Retiring in 1933, he received from the League a £350 annual pension, and a £200 cheque, along with an engraved silver tray.

The following year, retiring as Secretary of the FA, Sir Frederick Wall was given a golden handshake of £10,000.

The metaphors of the family and the friendly society — lifelong obligation to shared values, and support for the infirm or unfortunate when necessary; all steeped in a rigidly paternalistic discipline defended with a zealousness akin to a moral crusade — these metaphors best describe the Lancashire legacy of the League.

Go West Young Man — from Preston to Lytham

Alan Hardaker joined the Football League as Assistant Secretary when the League felt compelled to advertise the post for the first time ever in 1951. After a high-profile working life as a Senior Naval Officer during the war and then as Lord Mayor's Secretary in two big towns — Portsmouth and Hull — he arrived at Preston to be greeted by a graceless resentment of his meritocratic worldliness and potential. Fred Howarth would not even give this high-flying 39 year-old a desk; and Hardaker was snubbed extraordinarily in his first few years, unconfirmed even in his post as Assistant Secretary until 1955. A day in the life of the League was an unhurried day, and Hardaker began to diagnose the condition of the organization, tagging it "a machine covered with rust and cobwebs":

> Pressure was almost non-existent and a day at League head-quarters was slow, uncluttered, peaceful. It often reminded me of an endless patrol at sea — boredom sometimes strangled you. Nobody really had enough to do, but Fred Howarth loved it this way. He was against change of any sort, particularly if it meant more work for him or threatened the familiar, traditional flow of life at headquarters: I was a salaried outcast, I was given no responsibility. I was not allowed to talk to anyone. I was told nothing. I was not even allowed to go to Inter-League matches and the only football I saw was at Preston — but even here I knew nobody and nobody apparently, wanted to know me. (cited in Inglis, 1988: p. 188)

Fred Howarth's endless patrol in a calm sea was ignoring meteorological forecasts, as Hardaker was well-aware. Football could not keep plodding cosily into a secure future in an unchanging world. A post-war period of austerity ensured a period of peak popularity for the professional game, but many alternatives for the consumer gate-money were emerging, and expectations of players themselves were certainly increasing. Hardaker sat in isolation but not idleness in his early years at the League, observing the consistently downward trend in the graphs of Football League attendances after the record-breaking figures of 1949.

Howarth had a style, that of the strict Methodist headmaster that he initially set out in life to become; he held strong views on the undesirability of betting, the sanctity of the maximum wage, and the absurdity as he saw it of player power or collective organization by the players. He ambled through his administrative responsibilities, in Hardaker's eyes, doing only the bare minimum necessary. He also covered whatever tracks he might have left in his leisurely stride through League business, by ignoring the press; not filing material; cutting out selected Minutes/Items from Management Committee meetings, including Members' resolutions; collecting all written notes at meetings so that no personal notes could be taken away by members; and getting Committee members to sign blank cheques so that he could pay the bills. In the 1950s relatively low-profile and acquiescent Presidents had allowed Howarth to go his own unchallenged and unchallenging way. "If Fred Howarth did not like an idea it was never implemented — or even recorded", recalled Hardaker. The new team of 1957 — Hardaker at the helm, and Joe Richards of Barnsley in the President's position — recognized the challenges of the day. Its response was to meet the challenge, but without sacrificing long-established core values.

Hardaker and Richards made up an ecumenical team. Hardaker himself was from a Hull family committed to Liberalism and Methodism; Richards was a Barnsley boy, a freemason, a practising Christian and an independent politician. Both were born into white-collar "management" worlds of work, where respectable careers in management, business and administration were promised as a reward for hard work. Both played football in their youth, Hardaker for Hull reserves, so becoming the first League Secretary ever to have been "on the books" of a League club (as an amateur, as — ever pragmatic — he turned down the opportunity of signing up for an always precarious professional future). Richards suffered an industrial injury which curtailed his playing aspirations, but was a fanatical Barnsley follower and at the age of 46 became Chairman of Barnsley Football Club, a position which he held for 32 years.

Richards was born in 1888, the year the League was founded. He stood down as President in 1966, the year England won the World Cup (with a team of players made up entirely of players from League clubs: five players from Lancashire clubs, four players from London clubs, one from the East Midlands and one from Yorkshire: with boys from the South that old Northern/Midlands combination had now conquered the world. The Second Division of the League also provided some of the winning side). And this was no ordinary Joe bowing out after a long and dedicated career in the game. It was Sir Joe — the "Soccer Knight with the common touch" as the popular press gleefully labelled him, knighted the month before the World Cup Final, ennobled by a Huddersfield Town fan and famous professional Yorkshireman who was the country's then Prime Minister. Look back at the clips — Sir Joe and Harold Wilson were seated there at Wembley, in the limelight at the peak of both of their careers in public life.

Joe Richards was also a citizen with a conscience. He always showed a great interest in the welfare of young people, sat as a Governor of Barnsley Grammar school, chaired the juvenile court and spent 20 years sitting on the local probation committee. His sense of regional pride was legendary, with him even stating that he got more pleasure out of Barnsley winning the Third Division than from England winning the World Cup.

Together Hardaker and Richards confronted the problems of the modern period. They introduced the League Cup in 1960, a tournament that was to emerge as a major one as soon as it was established as a gateway to Europe; though the metamorphoses of sponsorship might have confused them from 1981 onwards, when the sponsorship meant that the trophy was known as the Milk Cup, then the Littlewoods Challenge Cup, the Rumbelows Cup, the Coca-Cola Cup and the Worthington Cup. At the 1991 Final at Wembley the players were presented not to some haughty member of an anachronistic royal clan, but to a person of the moment — Tracy from Edgbaston, Rumbelows Employee of the Year. Perhaps this was too much for the out-of-sorts aristocrats of the game, Manchester United, who looked a little put out for the following 90 minutes of play. It was the Second Division Yorkshire side Sheffield Wednesday which added some class to the game, with the graceful Sheridan providing the drama for Wednesday's restoration, striking the only goal of the game. Whether Sir Joe would have approved of the image of the moment is hard to tell. Tracy certainly seemed to enjoy herself, as of course did Sheridan. As for the League — in such a deal it gained a lot of money but lost its identity, bundled out of the limelight by Rumbelows: new generations of television-football fan in the late 1980s and the 1990s would not know what the *League* Cup was.

Joe Richards was also determined. In 1952, in his earlier years on the League Management Committee, he had proposed that the League establish a youth cup among its member clubs, but there was no support for his idea. He immediately took the idea to the FA, and within a few months the FA Youth Cup began. As this indifferent response by the League to one of its own stalwart members shows, the blinkered thinking of the League itself has on occasion pushed it towards forms of parochialism when it had the chance to pursue a policy of enlightened patronage. Episodes such as this show how a fuller remit for the good of the game generally might be more openly fostered in FA rather than League quarters.

Joe Richards and Alan Hardaker worked together to adapt an old dream to the demands of a new age. The philosophy behind their dream stressed continuity of core principles. This led them inexorably towards some very public defeats over issues which had gained an unstoppable momentum, and over which they lost much public credibility. The maximum wage had been a yoke around the talented individual player's neck for generations; the retain and transfer system had looked like an infringement of labour rights for the bulk of the League's history. They were principles fundamental to the formative values of the League's founders. Their survival in the age of affluence and a climate of the "You've never had it so good" rhetoric looked almost ludicrous. A fluent, confident irreverent figure emerged to speak for the players in the form of the bearded Fulham inside-forward, Jimmy Hill. With television and the popular press focusing in on the League's business in unprecedentedly intense and sustained ways there was an unanswerable case for overall reform of the League's structure and administration.

The maximum wage was abolished in January 1961, after the players' union was geared up to strike, backed publicly now even by larger-than-life traditional figures such as Stanley Matthews. Hardaker had sensed the need for reform, but when Richards asked the clubs to grant the Management Committee full powers with which to negotiate, this was refused. Hardaker showed a progressive pragmatism here, but was not empowered to act upon it.

Two years later the famous George Eastham case in the High Court adjudged the rule in the "retain and transfer" system which allowed clubs to retain a player, to be "an undue restraint of trade". Some of the core principles which Charles Sutcliffe had stood for were now looking close to redundant, overtaken by history.

Hardaker had been fully aware of this, and drew upon his intimate knowledge of the inner workings of the "machine covered with rust and cobwebs" to develop a radical plan for the modernizing and restructuring of the game. He did this as early as the 1960-61 season, early on in his partnership with Joe Richards. The League Cup proposal which surfaced in this plan was only one part of an overall package for the development of the game. The plan was called "Pattern for Football", and proposed:

- 5 Divisions of 20 clubs (two of them making up an expanded region-ally based fourth division).

- 4 promoted, 4 relegated each year, to sustain public interest.

- A League Cup competition, played at the beginning of the season, in regional groups.

- Automatic expulsion for a club seeking re-election two years in a row.

- An amendment of the voting system at League meetings, scrapping the 75% "majority" rule.

Hardaker employed a market research consultancy to analyse the public-player relation, and got the Management Committee to revive the debate on reconstruction. The club ignored most of the ideas first time round, backing just the League Cup on its own, but the debate was sustained until a decisive vote in 1963 rejected all innovative plans and opted for an unreflecting adherence to the tried, tested and the familiar. The "Pattern for Football" would have been adopted if at the Annual Meeting of June 1963 it had attracted 37 votes, so securing the necessary three quarters majority. The plan received 29 votes in favour; the 20 or so delegates who did not back this plan increased the resentment of non-league clubs which were looking for fairer means of winning entry into the League; and of the FA, which was interested in creating conditions more conducive to the cultivation of a national side (the World Cup was only three seasons away), and creaming off an elite network of clubs into a Super League in preparation for an eventual European League that the former FA Secretary Stanley Rous believed to be inevitable. Hardaker's plan was a beautiful balancing act, extending the concept of the League and opening it up more, but streamlining it simultaneously. Under his proposals 100 League clubs were playing 2028 matches. The new League Cup would add more matches, excitement and revenue. Hardaker recalls that some club chairmen, though, even refused to recognize the precision and correctness of this calculation. Hardaker has sometimes suffered from an image of him as a rigid battle-axe, an authoritarian dictator; but he was powerless in the face of the traditional obstinacies of the club chairmen:

> We were wasting our time. It was defeated by selfishness and shallow thinking. It was rejected because, myopically, too many clubs could see no farther than their own little worlds. They were not interested in the future of the game as a whole. Their own concern was self-preservation. They closed their eyes and minds to anything which even remotely threatened their status and lifestyle. (cited in Inglis, 1988: p. 230)

So spoke St. Alan of St. Anne's, as he was cruelly called by critics of his style, in sad recollection of his doomed attempts to act as the Saviour of Soccer. But he claimed to have brought in £12 million for the League, and a rather more adequate system of accounting of such sums than his predecessor Fred Howarth had provided. In his time the League headquarters were moved to Lytham St. Annes, a half hour's drive west of Preston, so, for whatever motive, staying faithful to the League's Lancastrian roots (Lytham is a few bracing miles' walk down the coast from Blackpool). He recognized that entry into European competitions would have advantages. In 1959 he masterminded the League's legal victory which secured it big money for the Pools companies' use of the League fixture list. In the early 1960s he flushed out the rigging and betting scandals that had involved a large number of players, mostly in the lower divisions, but rumours of which were harming the game's image. In his time at the helm, first with Richards and then with Len Shipman of Leicester and Lord Westwood of Newcastle, he gave the League a chance, 'coaxing, dragging and bullying' it "from its dusty, tradition-bound state in the mid-1950s into a tough, commercially-minded giant which stood a chance (but only a chance) of surviving the even harsher, tougher days which loomed ahead" (Inglis, 1988: p. 291).

Hardaker was single-minded, ruthless and often abrasive. He had no time for the hauteur of the FA, and was even sent to Coventry for a period of six months by the diplomat supreme, Sir Stanley Rous. Rous' cosmopolitan aspirations, his public school moralities, his hob-nobbing with Jules Rimet, his Presidency of FIFA — all these urbane characteristics would cut no ice in Lytham. For in the end, for all his revisionist progressivism, Hardaker was defending long-established structures. He never sought, in Simon Inglis' words, "to trim the numbers or create an elite" (p. 288).

Thirty years on from the thinking behind the "Pattern for Football" the dispute continued to rage as to the relative claims and merits of the League, the individual clubs and the national interest. Much had changed. Many of the communities for which football was a vital form of cultural expression have very different profiles; new generations of soccer fans buy franchised strips of big-city clubs on the basis of their television viewing patterns and a glimpse at the top First Division (soon to be, of course, Premier League) positions on Ceefax or Oracle — the cost of their strip might have a good part of the way to a season ticket for their local club. The League could never have hoped simply to survive in its traditional form, with television and sponsor money directed at glamour clubs, and those clubs becoming increasingly hostile to any policy of mutual benefit. For such clubs, the metaphor of the benefit society or the extended family was giving way to that of the League as highwayman. Something had to give, and one spark was the Heysel Tragedy and the exclusion of English clubs from European competition. This led to immediate threats of breakaway and Super Leagues, with the Big Five, Everton, Liverpool, Tottenham Hotspur, Arsenal and Manchester United — London and Lancashire in league at last — planning to invite another 13 to 15 clubs to form a new autonomous Super League with them, free to set up its own television and limitless sponsorship deals. The marketing possibilities of such a small group were irresistible to these clubs.

Compromises were struck in the 1980s and the League staggered out of the decade shaken to its core yet bonded by the crises of hooliganism and the tragedies of the Bradford fire and the Hillsborough disaster. By the autumn of 1990 there was optimistic talk of unification of the two bodies, especially as Alan Hardaker's protégé and eventual successor Graham Kelly (League Secretary 1979-88) was now in the top job at the FA. But things reverted to form by the early Summer of 1991, when FA plans to form its own Super League were revealed. The new Europe of post-1992 free-trade was beckoning and the big clubs were not likely to object to a change of stewardship. Lytham was beginning to look undeniably antediluvian; with superb irony the sounds from the FA in Lancaster Gate were sounding unambiguously contemporary, and the gatekeepers of the game's wider values were speaking the language of the modern.

Scenario 1 — Superleaguers and League Saviours

David Dent, Football League Secretary since the defection of Graham Kelly to Lancaster Gate in 1988, knows his League. He was club secretary at Carlisle for 18 years, and at Coventry for half a decade. When the news of the FA proposal to recruit top clubs for its own Super

167

League broke, the old FA /League tensions dominated the sporting press. Asked by the *Daily Mirror* whether a Super League would mean the end of League football, Dent replied: "Yes, if it goes through the ramifications to the League will be far-reaching". Bill Fox, the Blackburn fruiterer, called up the spirit of Joe Richards, alleging that ordinary fans would be "absolutely appalled": "They are interested in their own team, whether it is Wolves, Crewe or Tottenham Hotspur, not the England team. We can ride along on the crest of a successful England team, but people want to put their own team first" (*Daily Mirror*, Tuesday April 9 1991: p. 28). Gordon Taylor, Chief Executive of the Professional Footballers' Association, defended the League: "I am proud of having 92 clubs and 2,000 full-time professionals and 1,200 on youth-training programmes. Our contacts and commitment is with the League. We hear a lot of criticism about the way our football is run, but the control of the players and clubs is better in this country than virtually any other country in the world" (*The Independent*, Monday 9 April 1991: p. 28). Graham Kelly's "Blueprint for Football" received strong support from some sports writers. Jeff Powell praised the man who had once been "perceived as the puppet of the ego-mongers at the League", and went on to endorse the plan: "The FA Super League is the future. The Football League is the monolith of the past and their bluff has been called. Their attempts to inveigle themselves into excessive power have little to do with their propaganda about representing the good of the game at large. The grass roots of the game are tended by the Football Association, through the junior, local and county levels of their administration, and not by one League, however overbearing ... 'What's got into Graham?', you could almost hear them asking between the squeals of protest. Perhaps it was their own self-importance when he was trying in vain to run a rational game" ('Kelly coup has League running for cover', *Daily Mail*, Tuesday 9 April 1991: p. 39). The League had developed its own proposals for reform the previous Autumn, in *One Game, One Team, One Voice*, but this was rejected outright by the FA Council and the FA's proposals immediately put in jeopardy three and a half million pounds worth of deals which the League was working on. Trevor Phillips, the League's commercial director, accused the FA of plagiarism, its proposals being "essentially a rehash of *One Game, One Team, One Voice*. From a commercial point of view, every single item is the same — and I mean every single item. There are no new ideas — what is different is the structure in which to develop those ideas" (cited in Russell Thomas, 'League anger at FA "hi-jack"', *The Guardian*, Tuesday 9 April 1991: p. 14). The *Independent* gave one of its two editorial leaders over to the issue. Here it is in full:

In football's best interests
For anyone who does not follow English football — and perhaps for many who do — how the game is run in the country of its birth must seem baffling. Contrary to practice elsewhere, responsibility is divided between two competing organizations. The Football Association is responsible for the rules and laws of the game, for promoting it at grass-roots level, for running the England team and for the FA Cup. The Football League runs the four divisions into which England's 92 senior professional football clubs are divided according to their cumulative performance in League matches. It is from the players in the First Division of the League that the England team is mainly drawn.

The interests of the two organizations inevitably conflict. The FA is primarily interested in quality. The Football League, being composed of member clubs, is also concerned with quantity: clubs have to pay players and have heavy capital and running costs. Notionally, the more fixtures, the more revenue. The FA, by contrast, argues that too many games make for lower quality: the more First Division fixtures and additional competitions there are, the more lack-lustre the performance of the England XI is likely to be.

The conflict is encapsulated in the Football League's decision to put the number of teams in the First Division back up next season from 20 to 22; and in the contradictory proposal, endorsed yesterday by the FA's councillors, to create a Premier League of just 18 clubs. To that the Football League has given a venomous response — not surprisingly, since the proposed

Super League would be run by the FA and would drastically undermine the prestige and revenue of the Football League. The Football League's counter-proposal, that it should have equal representation on the FA's executive board of directors, was thrown out yesterday by the FA. The Football League is in no mood to sign a suicide note and the FA is not about to share its responsibilities for its Super League brainchild with the Football League.

The FA argues that a successful national side is the key ingredient in generating interest in the game and that fewer fixtures would tend to produce a better England XI. If top division standards were raised, they believe, more people would make the effort to attend. The Premier League's higher profile would moreover, attract better sponsorship and television revenue. The most successful clubs favour the proposal, since it is likely to give them a larger slice of a larger cake.

The question at the heart of all this is: what form of structure of English football would produce the best results for the maximum number of people? Football is different from most sports in that it arouses fierce local loyalties. It would be sad if the existence of a Premier League had a demoralizing effect on teams that remained in the Football League. But the game has to fight for its place in the competitive world of the leisure industry, in which public interest tends to focus on stars or star teams. In such a world a continental-style Premier League makes sense.

The logical way to solve the conflict would be for the Football League and the FA to merge. Such a move has been mooted, but each party is, inevitably, afraid of being eclipsed in the merged body. Pending such an outbreak of unselfish good sense, the Super League concept deserves encouragement. (*Independent*, Tuesday 9 April 1991: p. 16)

The targeted figure of the contemporary consumer dominates this analysis: the discriminating consumer, not the traditional fan; the leisure industry, not the local culture — these are the considerations

170

that sway the argument towards an element of support for the FA proposal.

The League's long-standing reluctance to reform, and so guarantee continuity within change, had made it vulnerable. It had not so much been criticized as vilified at times in previous years, nowhere more bitingly than in the words of Robert Maxwell. The media magnate had nicknamed the Management Committee the Mismanagement Committee, after the "Football League ... called an extraordinary general meeting in January 1988 to stop the Maxwell family extending its influence" (Haines, 1988: p. 447). Maxwell had rescued Oxford financially in 1982, Derby in 1984, and had dabbled in shareholdings at Reading; reports in 1984 also linked him with bids to buy Birmingham City and Manchester United. In late 1987 the rock singer Elton John, chair of Watford Football Club, offered Maxwell his majority share in the club for £2 million, and this precipitated the League's refusal to approve such transactions. Maxwell mobilized his media against the League: "the Football League is now being run by small men with even smaller minds" (cited in Inglis, 1988: p. 357). And he continued to speak out personally: "anything that the League's Mismanagement Committee takes the initiative about has a kiss of death about it. Nobody should pay any attention. These are the people that have allowed the game to be run into the ground. They're just nothing" (BBC 1 Television, 'Sportsnight', 21 November 1990). Whitewashing or simply overlooking his own involvement in notoriously unproductive television negotiations on behalf of the League in the mid-1980s, Maxwell continued to postulate and pontificate on the shortcomings of the League, and even called for the Football League to apologize "for questioning his motives in seeking a £13 million stake at White Hart Lane" (Lovejoy, 1990: p. 32). He evidently lent Irving Scholar, the Tottenham Hotspur chairman, £1.1 million for one of his companies, a sum then loaned on to Tottenham/Spurs to pay Barcelona the final instalment of Gary Lineker's transfer fee. Asked whether fans of the club of which he had become chairman in 1987, Derby, might consider the £1.1 million to have been better spent on their/his own club, Maxwell responded: "If a supporter asked me about that I would tell him to get stuffed. What I do with my money is my business. Have

I not done enough already for Derby? They were in the knackers yard when I was invited to help them" (Lovejoy, 1990: p. 32). That same season Derby fell into a steep decline culminating in relegation to the second Division in 1991. In his discussion of Maxwell's entry into League affairs and club management, Simon Inglis quotes the warning words of the League's founder, William McGregor: "Beware of the clever sharp men who are creeping into the game" (Inglis, 1988: p. 301). During the Spurs affair a League spokesman responded to Maxwell as follows: "Regrettably, Robert Maxwell mirrors one of the unfortunate traits of the modern game — he can afford the entrance fee, but he doesn't seem to appreciate the value of decorum" (Lovejoy,1990: p. 32). For all its obstinacy, intransigence and procrastinations the League has represented a clear set of values. But more and more the type of magnanimous messiah to whom more clubs were turning would be revealed as a maverick or a monster.

Scenario 2 — Spurs, Shots and the Shay

The Football Association is the highest parliament in English football ... Though an autonomous body with its own regulations, the Football League acts only under the licence of the FA. The relationship of the FA and the Football League is a delicate one, indeed. Yet by patience and the understanding of each other's objects, friendly relations have been maintained across the years, for all the occasional difference of opinion. (Green, 1960: p. 47 and p. 55)

By the last decade of the twentieth century this delicate relationship had become stormy; the "occasional difference of opinion" looked like deep-rooted irresolvable tensions. And it is the traditionalists of the League who have usually been blamed for this. But as the FA looked to a lucrative future as an entrepreneurial promoter of money-spinning Super Leagues, it is worth looking at the fragility of a faith based almost exclusively upon the notion of financial salvation. Tottenham among the elite and Aldershot at the bottom of the League in 1991 were sobering case-studies. Halifax at the bottom of the League represented an alternative model. Between these extremes lie the values of regional pride, mutual support and local loyalty which have been at the centre of Football League philosophy.

Spurs

Tottenham Hotspur provided the biggest recurrent news story in football throughout the 1990-91 season, as its debts of £13 million or more were revealed to burst the post-World Cup Italia '90 bubble. Spurs had been £3 million in debt in 1982 when Irving Scholar and Paul Bobroff, businessmen and long-time Spurs fans, bought up a controlling interest in the club by initially buying up the shares held by widows and daughters of deceased male fans. Bobroff and Scholar set up a rights issue to existing shareholders in 1983, and followed this up by making Spurs the first football club with a Stock Exchange listing. This wiped out the clubs debts of £3,287,952, with shares oversubscribed at 4.5 to 1. "Football clubs are an Aladdin's cave but the riches inside are untapped", Scholar told Neil Wilson (Wilson, 1988: p. 120). Scholar spoke the language of economic regeneration and enterprise. He was "in the vanguard of the Thatcherite entrepreneurial revolution: commercialization, diversification, aggressive marketing and merchandising were the solutions to the game's problems" (Manning, 1990: p. 10) Some solutions! By 1990-91 Scholar had risked criminal prosecution for his "dealings with Robert Maxwell on behalf of Spurs" (Jason Nisse, 'Ex-Tottenham Chairman ran risk of breaking law', *The Independent* [Business & City], Tuesday 13 November 1990, p. 26); the sports equipment subsidiary of Tottenham Hotspur PLC (Hummel UK Ltd) had proved an economic disaster, despite claims that it had been making profits after only one year; the club manager Terry Venables was trying to establish a consortium to both buy the company and bale it out of debt; and the club was having to consider selling its top players to cope with its level of debt. The Spurs story in the early 1990s was one of the entrepreneurial dream turned sour. Would an FA Super League safeguard Spurs from the consequences of the Scholar initiatives?

Shots

Aldershot Football Club — the Shots — were also in trouble in 1990, facing a winding-up order at the end of July. Saddled with debts the club ceased to trade after 64 wholly undistinguished years in the Football League. One week later they were back in business. A 19 year-old property tycoon called Spencer Trethewy had come forward claiming to be able to pour £200,000 into the ailing Shots. Within days the young saviour was on the board; within two weeks he was a guest on the national network "Wogan" chat show on BBC TV, introduced as the central figure in a "fairy story". His answers in the Wogan interview were naive and evasive in the extreme:

Wogan: What business are you in? Speculation …

Trethewy: Not really…I think that's a little too risky…Occasionally I do buy a few houses and then I sell them on. (Wogan, 13 August 1990)

But such waffle didn't seem to matter. Trethewy claimed to have it made, so he was acceptable: he flew around in helicopters, seemed to be chauffeured in big cars, and the Shots appeared to be saved. It was in a Sunday tabloid paper, the *News of the World*, that it was revealed that the "Soccer Saviour is a Fraud" (4 November, 1990). Trethewy had actually been working, up to the point of Aldershot's winding-up order, as a copy-machine salesman on £7,500 per annum. He was soon off the board, and Aldershot was actually saved by sources from elsewhere, including the club doctor and other associates ('Shots in the Dark', BBC2 'Southern Eye', 3 November 1990).

   The then chairman of Aldershot, Colin Hancock — a television crew's dream subject at the time, in the working setting of his dental surgery — reminded enquiring journalists and broadcasters that "those of us who involve ourselves at this level are crazy". Local businessmen in football, he said, forget that they're businessmen, 'just to buy a pair of legs'. In a business sense they actually act illogically, irrationally: "you do it because it's football, and that's part of the romance of football" (BBC 1, 'Sportsnight', 21 November 1990).

Crazy, irrational and illogical they might be, in terms of entrepreneurial criteria. But such eccentrics have a pedigree in the philosophy of the Football League, a cultural rootedness and genuine community base which guarantees a stability of sorts — unlike the wafer-thin guarantees of the economic messiah and the popular capitalist parvenu. Alas, all Mr. Hancock's surgery and the rallying of the local community were not enough to bolster the club, which finished bottom of the league and so lost its league status in 1991.

The Shay

Halifax Town play at The Shay. In the season 1990-91 they tussled with Aldershot themselves and the Welsh border club Wrexham for bottom spot in the League's bottom division. But the club is unique in the Football League. Whilst Birmingham Football Club was looking to strike deals with McDonalds in developing new facilities in multi-leisure complexes, Halifax was owned by the local authority, Calderdale Council, which had the majority shareholding and also owned the ground. David Helliwell, Leader of the Council, speaks soberly and respectfully of the contribution of professional football to local cultural life: "Professional football is not about making profits, just as opera is not, just as ballet is not, just as orchestral concerts are not. The sooner we recognize that what's good enough for opera — that is subsidy, subsidized tickets — is good enough for football, the better. I have no doubt that as we approach the end of the century our model will spread, and in ten years from now people will not see it as odd. We've had a problem making people understand that it's normal ... The commercial model of football — what I always term the butcher, baker, candlestick maker model — has we believe failed miserably. Probably even now 80 of the 92 League clubs are insolvent and probably technically trading illegally. I'm glad to say that whilst we may be 92nd in the Football League we're one of the 12 that is solvent" (BBC 'Sportsnight', 21 November 1990).

Helliwell criticizes traditional styles of management of League clubs; yet his vision and Halifax's experiment place football firmly within the local culture. Professional football has been too bounded by tradition at key moments in its history — a game with too inflexibly framed frontiers — but if modernization is to mean marginalisation for the majority, under the supposedly caring embrace of an FA initiative, then the cultural values at the core of the professional game in Britain will have been abused. Halifax weathered some difficult years when losing its league status in 1993, but in 1998 regained this status and demonstrated the solidity of the club's base.

Concluding Comment

All six League Secretaries who held the position from 1888-1991 were born in the North of England. The Football Association's first three and its fifth Secretaries were Southerners, the fourth one having been Derbyshire-born. When the League's fifth Secretary became the Football Association's first Chief Executive in February 1989, it looked like the relationship between the League and the Association would be closer than at any previous time. Graham Kelly had learned his trade well at the League, where he had leapfrogged into the primary post on merit. Men of the moment swim with the tide, and in the Thatcher years the League had many problems of image, credibility and continuity. It is interesting that the first League Secretary to take a top job at the parent body turned so punitively on his mentor. The success of what became the Sky television-funded English Premier League — populated widely with world stars offered millions on contracts as foreign player registrations were lifted in the mid 1990s— has been undeniable. But, as Leicester City's group chief executive Barrie Pierpoint has put it, it is an ambiguous success, with many clubs desperate merely to survive. Talk of European Super Leagues and media-owned football PLCs has tolled the death knell for the older league values of mutuality and open competition, as resources more and more move towards the centre. The legacy of the Football League was based on the formation of "companies only to protect themselves ... companies in structure, but clubs in style ... a game, not a means of making money" (Conn, 1997: p. 158).

The Premier League broke with this ethos, supported by a compliant Football Association, and English football rushed headlong into the money years of the 1990s, driven by money men, city flotations and the profit projections of business advisers. All the big money from television revenue would stay with the big boys: "I don't think there was any intention to take a proportion of their revenue", Graham Kelly conceded (Conn, 1997: p. 283), insisting too that the Brightons, Exeters and Darlingtons "haven't necessarily been disadvantaged by the Premier League". But it was Kelly's financial dealings, in tandem with one of the new Premier League money men, FA Chairman Keith Wiseman of Southampton Football Club, that was to lead to his own sudden downfall. In setting up million pound deals with the Wales Football Association, linked to wider FIFA politics and manoeuvring around the England 2006 World Cup bid, Kelly and Wiseman came down to earth with a nasty bump. In December 1998, the FA Council registered a vote of no confidence in its Chief Executive and Chairman. Kelly, honourably, resigned on the spot. Without doubt, some Football League members of that Council would have relished this opportunity to bring the upstarts down. A century of rivalry would not dissolve overnight, and the politics and future of English football would continue to be framed by the feuds and tensions characterizing the dynamic between the FA and the League.

Acknowledgements

I feel an enormous debt to Simon Inglis for a great deal of the material which I have used in this chapter. His history of the Football League is an exemplary blend of social history, cultural analysis and sporting gossip, moulded into a highly accessible popular history. The book is 'the official centenary history of the Football League', but it is also an objective piece of scholarship; official here does not mean whitewashed. It should be required reading in all professional football clubs, at the Football Association itself and in the office, perhaps, of any latter day Robert Maxwell. I want also to thank Liz Crolley for providing me with background material on key people at the FA. I have also drawn on the writings of a number of sports journalists, and hope that I have represented fairly the positions that they were taking when I have in turn reported reporters' opinions.

9 The Sky's the Limit: Sport, Football and Media Consumption

Sport in Media Culture

Critical upon the development of contemporary football has been the increasing influence of television upon the game. This has meant that long-established local affiliations and regional rivalries have, for new generations of football followers, given way to media-generated patterns of football following and supporting.

This is not an entirely new phenomenon. W. G. Grace mobilized innovative reproductive technologies to market his image and his merchandise, ridiculing strict codes of amateurism along the way (Midwinter, 1981). And in mid-twentieth century English football the media locked into the national populist sentiment when Manchester United's outstanding side of the late 1950s was decimated in the Munich air disaster (Dunphy, 1991). This created a basis for the emergence of Manchester United as a national institution. Affecting in more and more ways the culture and the political economy of modern professional sport, the media have embodied an increasingly generative rather than reflective role in relation to sport. At the same time, the place and profile of active sport within contemporary leisure changed markedly in the shifting climate of the consumerism and expanding leisure culture of the second half of the century.

In a conference in Vienna in 1992, Bero Rigauer has posed a very important question (Rigauer, 1992). In response to a question posed by Gunter Gebauer, he asked 'will the media contribute to the disappearance of sport?'. Now, this is a very easy question for Rigauer to put, for his own theoretical framework is premised upon a notion of the immanence of sport which gives to sport an almost trans-historical and supra-social purity: in this model the 'immanent values' of sport burst into history, society or culture untainted, an immaculate conception of the corporeal spirit. 'Sport', in such an approach, is constantly threatened by a series of social/political/economic determinants. At a certain point one could, on the basis of such a model, conceive of sport as disappearing: corrupted away, to put it provocatively, by the eroding forces of capitalism, consumerism, corporatism or whatever. Gebauer himself pointed out, in responding to Rigauer, that the media do not in any simple way contribute to sport's disappearance. Rather, they generate a media-specific aesthetics of sport.

Nevertheless, Bero Rigauer is right to ask such a question, provoking as it does a reappraisal of sport's place in and changing contribution to wider leisure cultures and cultural relations. Clarifying the relation between forms of participation in sport (participation in spectating at live events, or in actual sporting activity), and modes of consuming media representations of sport, is the central analytical challenge for the cultural analysis of contemporary sport.

Sport's place within the contemporary leisure culture of modern Britain is often misrepresented, as figures are too often conflated around the most generalized conception of physical activity and active participation. As already cited in Chapter 1 above, The Sports Council (London) can claim that "By 1990, some two-thirds of adults regularly participated in some form of sport: 29 million adults in total" (Hart and McInnes, 1992: p. 123). But such a claim (based upon the General Household Survey national data for England and Wales) includes 'walking' as one of "the ten most popular sports in Britain ... In the most popular quarter in 1990, over 20 million adults reported walks of over 2 miles, more than twice as many participants as in any sport" (Sports Council, 1992, p. 27). Individuals who might walk only moderate distances, and maybe even only once a year, are included in these figures. In fact, active sports enthusiasts/participants are actually minorities, and recent trends in participation have continued to be bounded by key persisting influences such as class and gender.

Women's participation in sports activities reached 36% in 1986, rising from a figure of 32% in 1980. But women's involvement in outdoor activities (including walking) did not rise very much — having risen from 21% in 1977 to 25% in 1980, it levelled out at 24% in 1983 and 1986. But in indoor activities women's participation rates rose much more dramatically, from around 12% in 1977 to 15% in 1980, to around 18% in 1983, and to 21% in 1986. Through this period, almost twice as many men (in proportionate terms) participated regularly in a sporting activity (Philips and Tomlinson, 1992, p. 19).

Influential commentators note that: "During the 1980s, there was a relative increase in many physically active leisure pursuits" (Henley Centre, 1992: p. 20), and evidence data on significant rises in participation in individual sports between 1985/86 and 1990/91. The most notable increases were among 16-19 year olds, 20-24 year olds and people aged 60+. The Henley Centre presents the findings as shown in Figure 1.

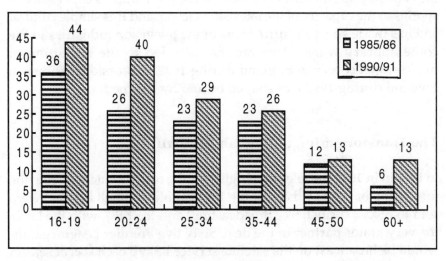

Figure 1:   The growth of active leisure. Percentage participating in individual sports by age group
[*Source:* **Henley Centre Time-Use Survey**]

On closer inspection, though, what is of most interest here is the deep-rootedness of some of the cultural inequalities clearly characteristic of patterns of sport participation. The upward trend in female participation is dictated by domestic obligations — an hour at bingo, or keep-fit, and swimming with the children are manageable within the constraints of traditional domestic and familial obligations and responsibilities. Apart from the youth and younger adult age ranges, the "public leisure culture of evening and weekend remains a male domain — pubs, clubs, sports leagues and other associational leisure forms continue to cater predominantly for men" (Philips and Tomlinson, 1992: p. 20). In an increasingly privatized and individualized context of consuming (Tomlinson, 1990), sport's profile is more and more based upon the representation of sports in the media. It is within this wider context of broad trends in sport and leisure cultures that sports consumption in its media forms must be understood. This provided the perfect basis for the transformation of football as media and consumer product, as television's and sponsors' income revitalized it after the crisis years of the game in the 1970s and the catastrophe-ridden 1980s. Most of the population's experience of sport is in the capacity of the television viewer, and this simple cultural fact has made sport a central focus of the television industries in the contemporary world. This fact has also led to the reshaping of professional soccer in England during 1992. Professional soccer in England during 1992 was shaped by and for the media.

The Transformation of English Football

In Britain in 1992 the television rights for the new Premier League (the former top or First Division of the 104 year old Football League) were sold to BSkyB (British Sky Broadcasting) and the BBC, with the latter the very junior partner in the deal. Sixty live Premier League games would be broadcast on the satellite service BSkyB each soccer season for the next five years. The national service, the BBC, would offer late-evening highlights of some Premier League games. ITV (the Independent Television Company) had been boldly outbid. ITV —

which had held the rights for several years — had offered £200 million over four years, or £262 million over five (Henry, Thorpe and Mullin, 1992: p. 1). This offer had been made on Monday May 18, to the meeting of the Premier League chairmen in a London hotel. This meeting was adjourned for half an hour to allow for the reading of the offer. In that half hour more went on than just the careful reading of the ITV offer. One of the club chairmen, Alan Sugar of Tottenham Hotspur Football Club, went to a telephone and rang BSkyB. His phone call is said to have been overhead by Trevor East, executive director of ITV football, the man who had just submitted the revised ITV bid. Mr. Sugar's call "included details of ITV's new bid. Mr. Sugar was said to have ended with the words 'Blow them out of the water'" (Mullin, Henry and Thorpe, 1992: p. 3).

And so the satellite company BSkyB did, and England's national sport was taken from the screens of all television owners in Britain, destined for the screens of those already owning or willing to go out and buy a satellite dish. With this huge outlay of over £60 million a year, too, it was more than likely that BSkyB would seek to recover some of its outlay by introducing financial charges for big special matches — generating large 'pay-per-view' revenues. Soon rumours abounded that BSkyB had its eye on other jewels in the sports broadcasting crown: "BSkyB is planning to buy the exclusive rights of the Wimbledon tennis tournament as well as Premier League soccer, forcing television viewers to pay hundreds of pounds a year to see top live sport. 'The TV sports couch potato has had it too good for too long in this country', said a BSkyB executive this weekend" (Brooks, 1992: p. 1).

What was this 'too good, too long'? In Britain, evidently, the viewer was being over-protected and cosseted, from the point of view at least of the BSkyB type of executive. For in West Germany, for instance, most television viewers could not watch Boris Becker and Steffi Graf win their 1989 Wimbledon titles. The European Broadcasting Union had been outbid for the Wimbledon rights, which had been sold by the All England Club to Bertelsmann, a German-based media conglomerate. Bertelsmann then sold on the rights to television companies across Europe. In Germany itself these rights were "passed to Bertelsmann's own subsidiary, the satellite-delivered and subscription-based private channel RTL Plus" (Barnett, 1990: p. 119). In Britain, for over thirty-five years television viewers have been guaranteed the opportunity to see 'important sporting events' as an established right, after debates concerning the broadcasting of 'sporting or other events of national interest', in the words of the Postmaster General, led to a mutual agreement by ITV (the commercially funded channel comprising regional companies) and the BBC (the licence-fee funded channel carrying no commercials or advertising) that ten events would always be covered by the 'national service', the BBC, and so be available to all the viewing public; a 1984 Act continued to protect the viewers' access to 'events of national importance', whosoever bought the rights. But the 1991 Broadcasting Act ended this restriction on competitive bidding. The Guardian journalist Matthew Engel's words of 1989 were romantic, a mite jingoistic but prophetically precise: "In Britain we can probably kiss good-bye to the pattern of televised sport we have grown to know and mostly love. Watching the best presented sport in the world on national television has been a reason for living here. The advent of satellite TV is likely to change all that, as sports choose to sell their major events to smaller audiences for more money" (cited in Barnett, 1990: p. 205)[1].

The ascendancy of the auction of the rights to the highest bidder and the culture of consumer choice and market fragmentation, and the abnegation of any notion of sport as part of a cultural inheritance or national heritage — these factors played into the hands of a cast of players at whom it is interesting to look that bit more closely. Dominant ideologies do not fall down from the sky; they are the accomplishments of specific human agents. Who was actually gaining the upper hand in this media power struggle? And who was losing out in the outcome?

Suffice to say, for the purposes of my argument here, that although there is no doubt whatsoever that both the Football Association and the Football League have been rigid, autocratic and authoritarian, the Football League often stood for traditional, sometimes strongly regional, values and mutual forms of support. The top clubs believed in the support of the whole league, for a number of reasons including the 'safety in numbers' argument, in which the strong supported the weak, and because the smaller clubs provided for generations a supply of groomed talent which was bought up by the larger clubs. On the eve of the foundation of the new F. A. Premier League, Aldershot Town Football Club left the league, bankrupt and unable to meet its fixture commitments. At the very beginning of the 1992-93 soccer season, in the dawn of the new Premier League, another Football League club folded — Maidstone United Football Club. There may not be any obvious cause and effect here, but it is symbolically revealing that two clubs should collapse at such a moment, when no club since Accrington Stanley in the early 1960s had folded in this way. To the twenty members of the F. A. Premier League, though, with eyes on the metropolitan centres of Europe rather than the far corners of distant regions or the obscure commuting suburbs beyond the city, the demise of such minnows was no longer any cause for concern.

Earlier threats had come from the fraudulent tycoon Robert Maxwell, by now dead and exposed, a bitter memory in the history of football clubs such as Derby County, Oxford United, Reading and, for a short while, Tottenham Hotspur. Maxwell had attempted to gain control of Tottenham Hotspur, with typically bellicose attacks upon the club manager Terry Venables' attempts to mount a successful bid with the entrepreneur/tycoon Alan Sugar: "As for Mr. Venables, Mr. Sugar is the fifth pair of knickers he has tried on. And none of them seem to fit" (cited in Fynn and Guest, 1991, p. 357). But even though Maxwell's Nemesis was imminent, other parties would emerge: parties willing (in true Maxwell style) to turn their backs on the old model of the Football League, and giving the Football Association expansive new ambitions, particularly in terms of the astronomical rise in remuneration for the sale of television rights, and concomitant levels of sponsorship. Alan Sugar and Rupert Murdoch emerged in this context as pivotal figures in the story. One of the coups achieved by BSkyB was to ally with the BBC in its bid. Marmaduke Hussey, then chairman of the BBC, was a former employee of Rupert Murdoch, boss of BSkyB, at *The Times* newspaper. The stakes for these players were high, their alliances formed in the networks of big business, their deals struck outside of the conscience of history, tradition or cultural affiliation.

Alan Sugar was not a new player in this game. His company, Amstrad (abbreviation of **Alan Michael Sugar Trad**ing), had bid unsuccessfully to become the first sponsor of the Tottenham club back in 1984. Amstrad knew the Tottenham manager of old too, for Terry Venables had "appeared in a testimonial advertisement for Amstrad, extolling the virtues of the company's hi-fi range" (Fynn and Guest, 1991: p. 355). In March of 1991 Sugar had cashed in some of his personal shares in his company, and after much wrangling within the club it was he and Venables whose bid was accepted, not least it seems because "nobody here wanted to work for Maxwell" (Fynn and Guest, 1991: p. 359). When Sugar rang the satellite television company BSkyB and urged it to blow the Independent Television company offer 'out of the water', it seems that he was not driven by the most disinterested of motives. His entrepreneurial background had been, on leaving school early, in "boiling beetroot and then selling car aerials" (Mullin, Henry and Thorpe, 1992: p. 3). By the mid-1980s he was said to be worth around £600 million, although in 1987 the stock market crash wiped out £400 million of his personal wealth. In backing so energetically the BSkyB bid he was acting more as the entrepreneur than the Football Club Chairman, for if the bid were to succeed, then it was anticipated that millions of households in Britain would then purchase a satellite dish, to guarantee access to the top level of football in England. And the country's major supplier of dishes was Amstrad. *The Independent* newspaper was stimulated to comment upon the matter, as follows:

'A tilted playing field'
Earlier this week, football fans were distressed to find that they would be obliged to buy a satellite dish if they wanted to watch live coverage of the new Premier League's matches from August. For the past four years, League matches have been shown live only on ITV, under a deal costing a mere £55m; the BBC's Saturday night Match of the Day, a cherished feature, lost its regular slot. Under the new deal, the contract for live coverage of the new League has been won by BSkyB in conjunction with the BBC — at a cost of £304m for the next five years. The

deal has generally been seen as a remarkable coup for BSkyB, as it will force football fans to go to the expense of buying a BSkyB aerial. The result can only be a massive shot in the arm for BSkyB and its advertising revenue. The BBC meanwhile will regain the right to broadcast recorded highlights. If the BBC had not supported the BSkyB bid, it is unlikely the bid would have been accepted. As Rick Parry, chief executive of the Premier League, put it: 'The BBC's position was critical [sic] because there was no way I would have recommended a satellite-only bid'. Why the national, centrally funded broadcasting service decided to throw in its lot with a satellite company half-owned by Rupert Murdoch, rather than with its main competitor, is a separate but interesting issue.

The story was given an altogether different twist yesterday when it became evident that ITV and BSkyB were bidding on far from equal terms. In short, BSkyB was at the last minute informed of the size of ITV's offer and enabled to improve on it. No such information was extended to ITV, whose negotiator not unreasonably imagined that both bids were confidential and final. He had further, and no doubt correctly, assumed even if BSkyB's bid had been higher than ITV's (as it was, though not by much), preference would have been given to a terrestrial station.

One of the players in this drama was Alan Sugar, who had a vote as chairman of Tottenham Hotspur Football Club, and an interest as chairman of Amstrad Consumer Electronics, the principal maker of satellite dishes. It seems that when he told BSkyB about ITV's offer, he was not the first to do so. Why BSkyB and the BBC were allowed to come back with another bid remains unexplained. The impression given is that the rules were being made up as the meeting went along. There was a vote, after concern had been expressed, on whether Mr. Sugar should have a say in the final decision. It was decided that he should, by 20 votes to one. In the light of the closeness of the eventual vote, that decision takes on a new importance.

The Premier League has ended up with significantly more money. That was the object of the exercise, and if judiciously used, the revenue could help the game in many ways. Equally, it could be frittered away. But the manner in which the deal appears to have been done is damaging to the league's infant reputation. The independent television companies are entirely justified in demanding that the bidding be reopened. When the agreement was first announced, it looked as if ITV had simply been beaten at its own game, albeit with a result certain to irritate millions of the game's followers. In the light of yesterday's revelations, the playing field is seen to have been very far from level. It is time to begin again. (*The Independent*, Friday 22 May 1992: p. 20).

It is a fascinating story of intrigue and mixed motives. And BSkyB's success pushed its rivals towards interesting counter-initiatives. Channel 4 television broadcasts live the Serie A matches from Italy; and regional television companies broadcast live games of interest to audiences within their own regions. More live football emerged on English television than would have seemed possible just a few years before, and competition became cut-throat: for the first time ever in England, three different football matches were simultaneously available to some viewers. And the new Premier League soon exhibited internal conflicts with squabbling over sponsorship deals and "threats of a breakaway from the breakaway" (Haylett, 1992: p. 34). And all of the build up and all of the hype ('A whole new ball game', the billboards and the television advertisements barked at the English public, in trans-Atlantic come-ons) was soon followed by some stark statistics: an 11.7% drop in live attendances at Premier League matches, in comparison with the First Division of the previous year, for the first six weeks of the season.

The story continues, then. And elements of it are far from new. The Football League's founder, William McGregor, had warned that the League should "Beware of the clever sharp men who are creeping into the game" (Inglis, 1988: p. 301). A new breed of an old type got into late 1980s and 1990s football, with less localized business/sport connections, and more to lose and gain.

Selling the Soul of English Football

In the early 1990s the cultural consumption of football in England entered a new phase of media-driven uncertainty. It is media capital and metropolitan exclusivity that led this initiative. Early on in the first season, the newcomer Blackburn Rovers sat atop of the Premier League, revitalized by the philanthropy of Jack Walker, a locally born tax-exiled businessman. And of course the Rovers club is not such a newcomer after all. An original founder of the Football League, it was one of the pioneers of the newly professionalized working-class game which undermined the dominance of the amateur public-school model of football. Blackburn did not stay there in that season, but won the title in the 1994–95 season, prompting young people nation-wide to buy the blue and white shirts of the club for Christmas morning, and for birthdays throughout the season. For one thing is beyond doubt. Televised football and its products are at the centre of football culture now, and it is football as media sport which constitutes most people's introduction to and regular experience of the game.

BSkyB talks a slick marketing line. Its Australian director claims that business is good: "We are selling satellite dishes. Satellite dishes are selling at about 20,000 a week in this country ... which is an awful lot of product to move in a very deep recession. We're absolutely delighted with the way business is going" (Bonnet, 1992). In fact, more people in the country were watching Italian Serie A Football on the terrestrial Channel 4 than were watching the hyped-up 'whole new ball game' claimed by the new F. A. Premier League; and some highly influential figures in football were far from ecstatic about the early days of the new structure. David Dein, chairman of Arsenal Football Club, expressed this concern: "We are concerned that there are six clubs including ourselves who voted against the BSkyB deal on the base that we were worried about the lack of terrestrial coverage, and the fact that the bulk of the population will not be able to watch Premier League Football ... and was this the right way forward?" (Bonnet, 1992). Dein was questioning the effectiveness of the promotional strategy of the new Premier League, when "we've allowed Italian football and Football League football to take preference and really go into the shop window'".

In September 1992 a meeting of the Chairmen of the Premier League clubs broke up in fury, over disagreements concerning sponsorship deals. The Chairmen had not, by mid-November, regrouped. As Bonnet put it (Bonnet, 1992) what was behind the row was "the fundamental issue of commercial revenue — whether to share for the common good or whether to let the rich get richer and the poor poorer". Bonnet was able to title his radio essay 'The Missed Opportunity'.

Similar tensions and rivalries were to resurface a half-decade later when after the France '98 World Cup the European football scene reverberated with threats and counter-threats concerning the prospect of a European Super League. The last decade of the century ushered in a wholesale transformation of the culture and economic base of the professional game in England. Based upon undreamt of levels of television money — £670 million pounds from 1997–2001 from Sky to the twenty Premier League companies (Conn, 1997: p. 158) — and, for the giants of this elite, huge swathes of merchandising and sponsorship income, football would become a target for the vultures of the city and marketing gurus. The early 1990s saw the new breed of business chairman and television mogul bidding for the soul of English football. Its cosmopolitan profile and spiralling, self-generating inflation was evidence, to such parties, of the revitalization and buoyancy of the football culture. Harold Macmillan's clarion call to gentrification comes to mind here: 'You've never had it so good', he pontificated in the late 1950s to the people of Britain, on the eve of the explosion of the affluent, consumer society. Yet issues of social exclusion and inequality dominate the political landscape forty years on. Beware false prophets, especially the get-rich-quick parvenus and the yuppified barrow-boys of English football's end of millennium political economy.

Concluding Comments: Analytical and Interpretive Themes

It is only possible to understand this transformation on the basis of an adequately developed social-historical grasp of process; and to appreciate fully the effects of such a transformation would need some careful formal/discursive analysis of the competing media forms of the game. I have demonstrated the point about process with reference to the legacy of the traditional League, and the nexus of actors instrumental in the new Premier League's dealings. Sustained work needs to be done on the various forms of media coverage of football, which would also be cognisant of the different ways in which the media forms are consumed.

The analysis of shifts in the power to define and control popular cultural forms, and of the changing features of the forms through which the popular is consumed, does not proceed according to some preset formula. And a sensitivity to the cultural legacies of socio-historical process is not automatically some form of collectivist romanticism. The cultural analysis of football's transformation outlined in this chapter is not a simple search for any oppressive dominant class or for instances of resistance to the dominant order; nor is it a manipulation of concepts to revivify some notion of contestation of hegemony. But the story as I have presented it is one revolving around the interrelationship of several processes: the intensification of the process of commodification of the popular, albeit in the context of a deeply divided and quite complex set of capitalist relations; the painful rupturing of a cultural past which, for all its faults, seemed to serve a wide range of interests; the increased direct competition within the television industry for the armchair sports fan; and the responses of the football enthusiast to the impact of these processes[2]. The key questions posed by British cultural studies — around cultural reproduction, cultural contestation, domination and ideology — do not delimit the interpretive possibilities around these processes. Indeed, they open up such possibilities, and enable a framework to be developed which recognizes the complexity of the cultural — not in any idealist or reductionist extreme, but in terms of the relation between various levels of the cultural, and the relations of domination, subordination and change. A fully developed case-study of contemporary professional football in England awaits more work, detailed textual analysis and audience research in particular[3]. But frameworks for such work are available in the tradition of British cultural studies — not blueprints for predictable theorizations, but innovative frameworks promising integrated levels of understanding of the cultural phenomenon as a whole, and its relation to the wider context of which it is a part.

To conclude, the nature of the relation between sport in its non-media and its media forms can be understood only on the basis of an integrated analytical framework, in which social history and sociology are co-terminous; ethnography and discourse analysis are equal partners; and broader trends in our contemporary leisure cultures are interrelated. Case-studies of key moments — of practices in transition, of dominant forms being challenged, of residual forms struggling to survive, of emergent forms' expansionist thrusts (I add here the cultural categories of Williams 1977a and 1977b, to my cultural studies debts) — are essential if we are to understand fully the story of sport in our more localized cultures and, increasingly, in the contemporary world order. Only then, on the basis of such a developed understanding, will we really know whether the dash for the cash by football's new masters has been in the interests of those for whom those money-men claim to speak; or no more than a piece of naked financial opportunism.

Notes

1 The debate on the national networking of broadcast events in the UK has rumbled on throughout the 1990s. By the end of 1998 the situation was as follows, with the 'A' list referring to sports which must be guaranteed live coverage on non-fee-charging terrestrial television, and the 'B' list assuring at least 'satisfactory' coverage on terrestrial.

> 'A' Olympic Games
> FIFA World Cup Final
> FA Cup (football) Final
> Wimbledon Finals
> European (football) Championship
> Rugby League Challenge Cup Final
> Rugby Union World Cup Final

> 'B' Cricket test matches in England
> Other Rugby Union World Cup matches
> 5 Nations Rugby Union
> World Athletics Championships
> Home Counties matches in Cricket World Cup Finals
> Ryder Cup
> Open Golf Championship
> Non-Finals play at Wimbledon

2 It is not necessarily the case that a 'cultural studies' led-analysis fits the caricature presented by one commentator on cultural studies, for whom CCCS (and Open University) writers are rigidly Gramscian: "... those who use selected concepts, based on a reading of Gramsci, to develop a definite 'mobility', to be able to manipulate these concepts, define them flexibly, and make them refer to a wide range of phenomena, or use them to endlessly generate a sense of newness, relevance and beginning" (Harris, 1992: p. 3).

3 The work of Anthony King (1995; 1998) has blended such concerns to good effect.

III

Observing the Olympic Story

10 From Myth to Tradition: Pierre de Coubertin and the First Modern Olympic Games

Introduction

The rebirth of the Olympic Games was not a restoration. Ancient Greece, where the classical Olympics flourished for a thousand years, was a very different world from the modern nineteenth and twentieth century world. And yet, for some, the ancient world operated as a set of idealized standards, as an embodiment of all that could be seen as excellent in a civilized society. In ancient Greece, though, the Olympic Games were an integral part of a wider world of religion. In our world the Olympic Games have been something different; secular in character, they have been bound up with the political and economic tensions of their own time.

The formative period of the modern Olympics was the late nineteenth century. The first Olympic Games, in international terms at least, was held in Athens, in the spring of 1896. Social historians have documented a number of earlier initiatives which laid claim to reviving the Olympics. There is, for instance, some evidence that a kind of sporting festival was held in Wenlock (Shropshire) England in the nineteenth century (Hill, 1992: pp. 9–15) An annual 'Olympick Games' also took place in the seventeenth century, when a Catholic landowner organized an event at Whitsun, as a way of registering his dissent from Puritan codes of conduct which saw play as sinful. These Games had an obvious religious or political meaning to them, reminding us that play activities do not belong to some independent realm of the pleasurable.

In modern Greece too, Olympic Games seem to have come and gone. An Athens Olympics took place in 1859 and drew large numbers of spectators. Further games were held in 1870, 1875, and 1888. But these did not occur regularly; and they were, in world terms, highly regionalized. 1896 is the date of birth of the modern Olympics, for in Athens that year athletic contests took place between teams representing different nations; and the Olympic Games have taken place every four years (or Olympiad) since then, barring world wars. If history can ever be said to be made by any individual, then it is to Baron Pierre de Coubertin that most of the credit must go for this achievement.

Of course history is never the product of single individuals. As Marx put it, "men make their own history, but they do not make it under circumstances chosen by themselves, but under circumstances directly encountered, given and transmitted from the past". De Coubertin it was who argued for, strove for and eventually achieved a revival of the ancient Olympics. But he did so for reasons which were historically specific to the France of the last quarter of the nineteenth century. In this chapter I want to unravel the rhetoric that has often obscured the actual roots of the modern Olympics. Marx also talks of how in periods of revolutionary crisis men [sic] 'anxiously conjure up the roots of the past', borrowing 'names, battle cries and costumes' from that past 'in order to present the new scene of world-history' in 'time-honoured disguise' and 'borrowed language'. The so-called revival of the Olympic Games must be understood in these terms, as the project of an increasingly displaced or dis-located aristocrat who looked towards both the model of athleticism pioneered by the contemporary British upper-classes, and a world of mind-body harmony in ancient Greece, in order to breed a new generation of men to rule the modern world.

The first Olympic Games in Athens was an experiment in international relations. The 1984 Olympic Games in Los Angeles are a particular kind of experiment in global capitalist relations. In comparing the two it is hard to show that they are the same thing at all. As the early Games developed arguments were put forward for, among other things, the introduction of the Winter Olympics and the expansion of the arts contests. Nowadays, when the image conjured up by the Olympics is one of a celebration of the body, a fetishism of the physical, it is hard not to smile at this excerpt from an entry in the 1912 Stockholm literature competition, authored by Georg Hohrod and Martin Eschbach, made up of nine stanzas, and entitled 'Ode to Sport':

O Sport, delight of the Gods, distillation of life! In the grey dingle of modern existence, restless with barren toil, you suddenly appeared like the shining messenger of vanished ages, those ages when humanity could smile. And to the mountain tops came dawn's first glimmer, and sunbeams dappled the forest's gloomy floor.

O Sport, you are Beauty! ...

There can be no beauty without poise and proportion, and you are the incomparable master of both, for you create harmony, you fill movement with rhythm, you make strength gracious, and you lend power to supple things ...
(cited in Killanin and Rodda, 1976: p. 161)

In this encomium to sport, in its seven other stanzas, sport is said also to be justice, daring, honour, joy, fecundity, progress and peace. What was the context out of which such a declaration could emerge?

The Context: A Nation and Class in Crisis

The time in which the Olympics took root, the late nineteenth century, was a major period in the formation of the nation-state. The period of post-Civil War Reconstruction in the United States has always been known as the gilded age, when capitalist entrepreneurs led a process of massive transformation of that nation's economic base. New generations of American youth were going to college, where strength and physicality were often stressed at the expense of intellectual pursuits. It was in the United States that de Coubertin found some of his earliest collaborators in his Olympic project. In Britain, new generations of military, economic, political and cultural elites were being bred in the nineteenth-century public schools. Britain is the only country to have entered teams at every Winter and Summer Olympic Games.

Economic and political developments took place alongside technological breakthroughs in mass-communications and travel, producing a sense that the world was both in the making and directly makeable. By this I mean that in a period when new ways of looking at and knowing the world were becoming widely accepted, persons in power could believe that this was a period not just of progress, but of transition toward perfection. This is what Queen Victoria's husband Prince Albert said the year before the Great Exhibition of 1851, the first truly international exhibition of the modern world:

> Nobody ... who had paid any attention to the peculiar features of our present era, will doubt for a moment that we are living at a period of most wonderful transition, which tends rapidly to accomplish that great end, to which, history points — *the realisation of the unity of mankind.* (quoted in MacAloon, 1981: p. 129)

Those of us raised in the British educational system and served up maps of the world smeared in the red of the British empire may like to ask at what cost Albert's unity was, even partially, achieved. But the point is this — that to some nations the world seemed to be within their grasp; to them mankind was potentially united because they began to see the nation and the whole of mankind as synonymous.

In the last decades of the nineteenth century such idealistic conceptions of unity were shattered, for the likes of de Coubertin at least, by the Franco-Prussian war of 1870, in which it was shown that the development of nation-states was hardly the soundest base for the achievement of any sort of global unity. It was after this defeat that the French Third Republic was founded. Industrially, the new Germany rapidly left France far behind. And the new Germans bred well, producing an expanding population, and thus a younger one. France, not surprisingly, was worried about not just its place in the world, but on the mainland of Europe too. In a way, France attempted to make up for these shortcomings of people and machines by offering itself as the centre of the cultural universe.

One sports historian has suggested that "the lavishness of the French world's fairs can be seen as compensation for France's diplomatic isolation and relative economic stagnation" (Mandell, 1976: p. 42). In 1878 an exposition in Paris attracted 16 million visitors, more than twice as many as had attended one in 1867. Paris' exhibition of 1889 attracted 40 million visitors. And in 1900 the Paris world fair, on the edge of which the second modern Olympics balanced precariously, attracted 100 million people.

This then was the context in which de Coubertin developed his vision. As a new world sought to show off its cultural wares in the global marketplace, the Baron — drawing upon a sense of the physicality of the ancient Greeks which was being increasingly developed by, above all, German scholars at the ancient site of Olympia — argued more and more publicly and persuasively for the development of an international culture of the body.

The Man: Towards World Patronage

Baron de Coubertin was thirty-five years old when the Athens Games were staged in 1896. When the Greeks took on the task of staging those first modern international games, though, they seem to have done their best to ignore de Coubertin, to play down his influence, and to make the Games into a statement of the distinctive national quality of the Greeks. In the very early history of the modern Games, it is worth noting this central tension — the founder of modern 'Olympism' was eclipsed by the nationalist aspirations of the first host nation. Some commentators have even suggested that it was on the crest of a jingoistic wave whipped up by the 1896 Olympics that the Greeks went disastrously to war in the following year.

De Coubertin was born into a quite wealthy, rather distinguished and loyalist family. His father painted and exhibited his paintings in the Salons of the Second Empire, particularly throughout the 1860s. Most of these paintings were characterized by themes of the church, the family, and nobility, combining into a 'classical heritage', as one writer has put it, of 'La France'. Pierre de Coubertin grew up in such surroundings, then, but he also knew that, after France's defeat at the hands of Prussia and its move towards another republican constitution, such a period of classicism was all but over.

Pierre was the third son of his family, and received a conventional aristocratic upbringing, learning how to live the leisured life of the affluent. He learnt how to fence, row and box. His schooling took place in a highly conservative Jesuit institution. At the age of 17 he entered St.-Cyr, the French military academy, but resigned without committing himself to any military career. He then spent some time in England, where, over a period of several weeks in 1883, he visited the famous public-schools of Harrow, Eton and Rugby, and the Universities of Oxford and Cambridge. He returned to England in 1886, again in 1887, and then quite regularly in the following years. His knowledge of the public-schools in Britain increased with each visit.

In England, de Coubertin visited a number of schools, chatted with masters and pupils, toured grounds, observed games and lessons, and worshipped alongside and dined with the schoolboys. He had read Thomas Hughes' *Tom Brown's Schooldays* in 1875, in his early adolescence, and much of his study of the English public-school was intended to give him direct experience of an ideal that he had taken from Hughes' novel. Pierre read the novel at the age of 12. In his twenties, on his English visits, he always carried his English-language copy with him, "on all my peregrinations ... the better to help me bring to life again, in order to understand it, the powerful figure of Thomas Arnold and the glorious contour of his incomparable work" (quoted in MacAloon, 1981: p. 53).

The trips to England were a way of reassuring the young Baron that the ideal of Muscular Christianity, of the building of intellect and body (Holt, 1989: pp. 1 and 94–95), was alive and well in England. His sense of the importance of physical education for an adequate all-round educational upbringing derived almost exclusively from his interpretation of the athleticism bred in the English public-school system.

After his first trip to England the young de Coubertin enrolled, under his father's influence, at the University of Paris' Faculty of Law. But he rarely attended classes, and found legal studies 'horribly repelling'. Soon he enrolled in the Ecole Libre (Free School of Political

Sciences), which, a few years later, he compared with 'that purely scientific and sacred character of the Athenian gymnasiums'. Here, in the mid-1880s, the atmosphere of enquiry was a liberal republican one. This liberalism, though, should not be exaggerated, and one eminent French historian of the twentieth century referred to the Ecole Libre of the 1880s as 'the spiritual home of the scions of rich and powerful families'. But a lot of the thinking and work going on there was very innovative indeed.

At the Ecole Libre de Coubertin was encouraged to pursue his adolescent obsession with the 'other culture' of the English public-school, and with civilizations of the past, as respectable enquiry. The young aristocrat never actually took a diploma there, for, not seeking any government position, he felt no need for one. He spent two years or so soaking up its atmosphere, and then for the following ten years laboured with little success to reform the French education system. Most of all, though, he worked on a kind of freelancing international organization and administration, increasingly geared towards the revival of the Olympic Games.

The atmosphere at the Ecole Libre, was, to Pierre's family, repellently liberal. For the young man it was the perfect setting for developing his ideas on how new educational systems might reconstitute French greatness in a world of peace. For the young Baron was, in his own way, putting into practice a very traditional principle of the French aristocracy. This is the principle that some writers have called *prouesse* (MacAloon, 1981).

Prouesse refers to the instinct for making the grand gesture, and to the honour which such a gesture can bring. An aristocrat is rooted in a position of privilege and status, yet such a position is often under threat, not least from classes on the ascendancy, be this a working-class or a bourgeoisie. In reaffirming his precarious status, the aristocrat, in France, has often made some sort of grand declaration of his and therefore the nation's quality and greatness. It is in this sense that Pierre's father Charles evoked a particular image of France. And it is in this sense too that Pierre, in drawing upon the past ideals of ancient Greece, and the current upper-class ideology of athleticism in the English public-schools, was striving towards a form of *prouesse* by relocating France at the centre of the world stage. Just as France sought world recognition by staging unprecedentedly grand exhibitions, so the young Pierre, last in his own line of aristocrats, sought through an emphasis on the training of new elites, to find a new and relevant place for his own social group. In a period christened by historians as one featuring 'the end of the notables', de Coubertin's projective vision was an eloquent statement of the crisis of a declining social group.

We are, to echo Marx, makers of our own history, but our raw materials do not spring from nowhere. Pierre de Coubertin worked with materials that were already there — the relatively recent knowledge gained from the excavations at Olympia, the English public-school system, the emerging emphasis on College athletics in the United States — and moulded them into an incredibly romantic ideal. The world might be reformed, he thought, if new generations of (exclusively male) youth could compete together, every four years, in different parts of the (civilized) world.

Prouesse sought in this way is inherently romantic. It has little to do with rational decision-making or with routine organizational life. It is a grand statement of patronage. Indeed, if the revival of the Olympics had been dependent upon the day-to-day workings of bureaucracies, there is little chance that they would have got off the ground at all.

Pierre de Coubertin was, as are most romantics and dreamers, overtaken by his dreams. He died in 1937 comparatively penniless, supported by Olympic charities, alone on a park-bench in Geneva. He had spent his not inconsiderable fortune on developing his dream, but his last public appearance had been in the previous year at the Berlin Olympics, where, in one of the biggest events yet staged by the media anywhere in the world, he had announced that 'the important thing in the Olympic Games is not winning but taking part. Just as in life, the aim is not to conquer but to struggle well'. The Nazis had a different message.

Coubertin himself died in solitude but his death was followed by a bizarre ceremony. He was buried, privately, in a graveyard close to the present IOC headquarters. But his heart was not buried there. In March 1938 Crown Prince Paul of Greece officiated at a ceremony held at Archaic Olympia. Pierre de Coubertin had requested in his will that his heart be cut out of his corpse, and then sent to Greece in a wooden box lined with white satin. At the ceremony the Crown Prince, honorary President of the Hellenic Olympic Committee, officiated as prayers were said and the heart was blessed by a Greek priest. The Crown Prince then lifted the heart from the altar and placed it in a marble pillar. The French Baron's last gesture was his grandest, a fittingly dramatic conclusion to the glory-seeking project of a dis-placed aristocracy.

De Coubertin's greatest qualities in getting the Olympic Games off the ground were organizational. Not in any orthodox way, though. For much of its early life de Coubertin's International Olympic Committee was little more than a phantom organization, given some flesh on letter-heads of de Coubertin's note paper, but little substance in reality. But the young aristocrat was extremely adept at making international contacts, and at staging elaborate congresses at which the value of athletic education could be extolled. Two of these, in 1889 and 1894, were of particular importance.

De Coubertin moved in influential circles in the Paris of the 1880s. This enabled him to put on functions at which illustrious and prestigious guests from the political and academic worlds lent credibility to his venture. At the 1889 Universal Exhibition there were many exhibits. In one, 182 Asian and African natives were imported to recreate their daily lives for audiences of their oppressors. Something called Garnier's History of Human Habitations featured live actors, serving native refreshments, in a range of settings from Renaissance palaces to Russian peasant villages. At Buffalo Bill's Wild West Show, Buffalo Bill's troupe played its first European show, featuring real Indians playing themselves. Those themes, preserved still in the River Caves and other remarkable rides at, for instance, Blackpool Pleasure Beach and Disneyland, formed the centre of a strong colonial emphasis at this exhibition. However interesting de Coubertin may have found such side-shows, it was not these which gripped his imagination.

He was very impressed by the ceremonial rituals, including an entry procession by politicians and soldiers, featuring flag-raising and national anthems. Much of this was to be replicated in the opening and closing ceremonies of the Olympic Games.

At the Universal Exposition de Coubertin proposed and staged a 'congress on physical exercises'. This was one of 69 congresses to take place at the Exposition. De Coubertin's congress included five sessions on different aspects of physical exercise, and an address by the Baron himself on innovative forms of physical education in the English-speaking world.

De Coubertin had, through his aristocratic position, managed to lobby politicians in such a way that ministerial decrees were made in late 1888 and early 1889, providing for the Congress for Physical Exercise. The Olympic project, at this stage, was still in formation. Exhibits from ancient Olympia, and *jeux olympiques* held in the Exposition itself, were staged. But de Coubertin did not yet give full voice to his Olympic project.

Before the end of the Universal Exhibition, de Coubertin managed to get himself designated as an 'official' representative of France and set off on his first visit to America. There he made some important alliances within the sports establishments of the universities and colleges. Returning to France, he worked at bringing together national sports associations, and continued to hold sports events with festive trappings. He was particularly adept at getting distinguished personalities — a Russian Grand Duke here, a French diplomat there — along to his sporting jubilees. At the session which concluded one of these gatherings in 1892, de Coubertin hired the great amphitheatre of the Sorbonne. Three speakers spoke on the historical significance of sport in the evolution of civilizations. De Coubertin himself spoke on 'physical exercise in the modern world', and argued that athletics, along with the telegraph, railroads, the telephone, and universal exhibitions could contribute towards 'the progressive diminution of the chances of war'. He then made his first public statement on the framework within which sport could be truly internationalized:

> Let us export our rowers, our runners and our fencers: that will be the free trade of the future. What I mean is that, on a basis conforming to modern life, we re-establish a great and magnificent institution, the Olympic Games.

Not taken too seriously at this time, de Coubertin nevertheless continued to work to convince international audiences of the viability of his project. By 1894, after another trip to America, he had hustled enough support to organize his 'Sorbonne Congress' at which the rebirth of the Olympic Games could be formally discussed. There were 2,000 people at the opening banquet in June. These included 79 official delegates, and representatives of 49 athletic societies from 12 countries. A poem on athleticism, speeches praising the classical world, champagne banquets and a musical rendition of a recently discovered lyric ode set the tone for the Congress. The Congress then divided into two to discuss amateurism in sport and the Olympic Games. Most of the chairmen were personally chosen by de Coubertin himself. 'Almost without debate', in the Baron's own words, the main principles of Olympism were approved — four year intervals between Games, modern sports, no children's contests, a stable IOC, and respective sites for the Games.

Throughout the Congress de Coubertin staged fete after fete, including foot races and fencing matches in a Parisian playing field illuminated by a thousand torches. Trumpet fanfares, military music and a fireworks display rounded off such an event.

At the final ceremonies of the Congress delegates voted unanimously for the restoration of the Olympic Games, and for the staging of the modern world's first International Olympic Games within two years, in Athens. In de Coubertin's own words, it was a vote for the "men of antiquity" for whom "character is not formed by the mind, but primarily by the body". Here, in this almost anti-intellectual primitivism, we see another simplistic principle of Olympism which could easily be exploited in future political contexts.

But the Baron's dreams did materialize. Marginalized in Athens in 1896, he knew nonetheless that he had at least laid the foundations for the further development of his project. The Olympic engine spluttered at first, for in 1900, 1904 and 1908 the Games were a mere appendage to grander exhibitions. But by 1912, in Stockholm, the Games were cruising smoothly rather than spluttering. The declassé French aristocrat, soaked in the internationalism of pan-Hellenic enthusiasm, increasingly marginalized in an Empire in crisis, and resorting to an athleticism-based culture of the body for a source of inspiration, achieved his goal. Four years later his project for international peace was reduced to the sidelines as the Great War reduced sport to a more peripheral role.

The Spectacle: Athens in 1896

The road from the Sorbonne Congress to the Athens Games was a far from smooth one. The barely kindled Olympic torch did not burn brightly very easily. At one stage, in order to prompt Greece to commit itself to the Games, de Coubertin began to put into action a contingency plan to stage the first games in Hungary. But he also, accomplished hustler that he was whenever necessary, made an influential trip to Greece itself. He spent several weeks in Athens, speaking to various audiences about the world history of sport, and complimenting the Greeks on being the inventors of sport. De Coubertin referred to a 'moral disorder' produced in people's minds 'by the discoveries of modern science', and suggested that a conception of athletics rooted in democracy and internationalism would be a strong enough moral force to keep athletics from 'sinking into the slough of commercialism'.

Not everyone in Greece was convinced by the young French zealot. His low projection of the cost was seen as verging on the fraudulent. But with internal governmental changes, the example of royal patronage, and the philanthropic gift of one million drachmas from a wealthy Alexandrian, the Games did get off the ground, and took place. In the build up to the Games de Coubertin himself withdrew into an intense period of labour in which he produced a history of the French Third Republic, a study which met with lukewarm reviews. Any fame that was to come to him was not based upon the two or three thousand pages of historical and educational writing which he produced throughout his life, but upon his role as rénovateur, restorer of the ancient Games.

For the Athens Games a new stadium was built in Olympia, produced by a work force of 500 men on day and night shifts for over twelve months. In some ways Athens offered one of the biggest non-military pageants yet staged in the modern world. In the great exhibitions of the nineteenth century millions came, at one time or another, but not usually in mass gatherings. At these Games, staged during a triple holiday period of Easter, Independence Day and the Games themselves, mass crowds were encouraged to respond to pageant, ritual and ceremony on, for modern Greece, a previously unrivalled scale. One young English observer wrote that in the most animated crowds 'the most perfect order never ceased to reign' and contrasted them with the less 'organized' behaviour of an English 'north-country crowd' at a soccer match.

Estimates have put the crowd assembled outside the stadium on the opening day at 40,000 to 70,000, and the crowd gathered on the surrounding hillsides at between 80,000 and 120,000. For the Marathon, four days later, the largest crowd of the whole Games assembled to see the Greek Spiridon Loues, running a race the more leisured athletes of ancient Greece would have seen as an act of gross distaste, win for Greece in the Marathon. At the time, Athens had a population of some 130,000. Virtually the whole of a city was drafted in as extras on the Olympic set.

On the whole what they were watching was the privileged at play. Most of the teams were made up of people with enough time and money available to get to Athens in the first place. Britain did not at this stage manage a co-ordinated response to an invitation to participate. De Coubertin even bungled the invitations, sending them out in French and German and only at the last minute in English. And the Games coincided with the University holiday for the Oxford and Cambridge athletic elites. So the British 'team' in Athens was made up of six athletes. The hurdler was someone with competitive experience in South Africa. The renowned 'British' runner was an Australian living in London. Britain's tennis representative — and Olympic champion — was an Oxford man who just happened to be in Athens at the time. The two British cyclists were employees at the British Embassy in Athens. Other British competitors, offended by the cyclists' non-amateur status because they worked as servants, made unsuccessful efforts to exclude the two boys.

The American team, made up of a dozen or so young men, was recruited mostly from the Princeton and Harvard University athletic communities. A team of eight Hungarians was in Athens to compete, but also to make the case for Hungary's independence within the Hapsburg empire. From France, the nation which de Coubertin wished to reform on the basis of his philosophy of physical education, came two cyclists, some fencers, a runner and a couple of tourists who, like the English tennis player, just happened to be in Athens at that time. Rivalries within gymnastic and sporting circles threatened to leave Germany with no representatives; eventually three track and field athletes and ten 'turners' (gymnasts) were rustled up and shipped off to Athens. The Americans swept up most of the prizes. They won the hop-skip-and-jump, the discus, the long jump, the 400 metres, and the shot-put.

French and Greeks shared honours in fencing. Weight-lifting competitions were won by a Dane and an Englishman. An Australian won the 1500 metres and the 800 metres. Greeks won the rifle shooting and a cycle race, but these were too distant from the stadium to produce a real crowd response. Germans, Swiss and Greeks won gymnastics competitions. The Greek spectators, seeing their flag raised for victory for the first time in the stadium, had their chance to practice for the great moment that was to come when a Greek won the marathon. Americans also won the marksmanship competitions, the 100-metre dash, the 100-metre hurdles and the pole vault.

Not all activities generated enthusiastic responses, particularly those at sites scattered around Athens. It is indicative of the lack of intense competition in some of these events that the Englishman who 'happened along', a Mr. Bland, became Britain's first Olympic champion — twice over — winning the tennis singles and sharing the doubles title with a German, the only documented case in Olympic history of a mixed-national winning partnership or unit. So the competition was, on the whole, monopolized by the Americans and the Greeks. The contests themselves live on, for the most part, as historical curiosities. But what makes the Athens Games so much more important than a relic is its significance as spectacle.

For it is in the ceremonies, the staged pageants, that the first modern Olympics was so important. The Games opened with a royal procession, led by King George of Greece in military uniform. His procession entered Olympia with the Greek national anthem and the roar of the crowd combining to give him the most popular reception he had ever had. In the stadium the King and Queen sat on marble thrones, with the Greek cabinet, orthodox bishops, the court, foreign diplomats and representatives of foreign athletic commissions alongside them. The Greek Prince Constantine then spoke, invoking God to ensure that 'the celebration of the Olympic Games' would 're-animate bodily exercise and national sentiment and contribute to forming a new generation of Greeks worthy of their ancestors'. Sitting at the back of the 'foreign delegations', de Coubertin had notice here that his hopes for global harmony might produce forms of jingoism hardly compatible with such hopes. The Greek King rose and then declared the Games open. Canons fired in recognition of this moment, and thousands of pigeons were released in the stadium.

Throughout the week of the Games other events were featured. New gas and electric street lights in Athens were illuminated on the night of the first day and for every night thereafter. And fireworks displays lit up the Acropolis on the second night. Military parades, and a King's breakfast and many other banquets were major side-shows in the Olympic programme. There were no arts competitions but several dramatic performances took place. A music competition had been planned, but no foreign entries had been received. The pageantry continued through to the closing ceremony, when again the royal family and the national anthem prefaced the proceedings.

An Oxford student, G. S. Robertson, read a Pindaric ode, celebrating the Olympic Games, to start-off the ceremony. The King then began the presentation of awards. Victors received an olive branch, a silver medal, and a large certificate. Runners up received laurel branches and bronze medals. The prizes were kept at deliberately low values — no gold — to emphasize the amateur spirit of the event. National flags had been raised at the time of victory. The closing ceremony ended with a procession of all the athletes around the stadium, led by Spiridon Loues.

It was Loues who generated the most fanatical response from the crowds. The race — with its echoes of heroic sacrifice in the story of the Athenian Pheidippides running forty kilometres from Marathon

211

to announce 'Rejoice, we have won' before dying — had been suggested to de Coubertin by a distinguished classical scholar. An entirely modern invention — foot races in the ancient Olympics never exceeded 5000 metres — by 1896 it had gripped the Greeks', if not yet the world's, imagination. And it was in the Marathon that a somewhat disconnected series of events was bound together as a public spectacle rooted in a mass nationalism.

In the build-up to the Games Athenian businessmen of all kinds offered all sorts of prizes (openly flouting the principles of amateurism) to any Greek who could triumph in the Marathon. The momentum which was built-up is an interesting case of how, in one sense, history can be invented. The new or the novel can be soaked in tradition to re-affirm values from the past, values which in some cases are wholly fictitious, but which are seen to be desirable in the present. Nobody can be sure who Spiridon Loues actually was. This structured ambiguity in the retelling of his tale has been highly convenient as the everyday events in the Athens Game have been turned into powerful legend.

Many trial races were held over the Marathon distance. The eventual winner, Spiridon Loues, was offered money and goods of all kinds. It seems that Loues turned down all such offers. De Coubertin himself put this down to 'the sense of honour which is very strong in the Greek peasant'. But the first Olympian Marathon champion may not have been a simple peasant, a simple primitive. He was, it seems, 24 years old, but he has been described as a poor shepherd, a well-to-do farmer, a well-owner, a goatherd and a village postman. No single account appears to be definitive.

But this does not really matter. In spectacle it is the spectacle itself and the emphasis of the moment that count. Loues was *seen to be* a peasant and that was enough for people to see in him all the apparent strengths — of simplicity, pure strength, muscular innocence — of a pre-industrial order. The presentation to Loues was the highlight of the closing ceremony, when the crowd was at its loudest and most demonstrative, and when doves decked out in the national colours of Greece were released from the grandstands.

Greece had eventually welcomed the Games as a way of diverting attention away from its economic and social crises, as a way of emphasizing the deep-rooted qualities of Greek culture. A year after the Olympic Games were staged, Turkey in response to an increasingly jingoistic and aggressive Greek presence in Crete, declared war on Greece. The thirty-day Cretan War led to humiliation at the hands of the German-trained Turks. De Coubertin's dream had been realized for one week in 1896. In 30 days in 1897 an emergent Greek nationalism, fostered if not initially created by the Olympic revival, led to national disaster.

The Man, the Moment and the Myth

Pierre de Coubertin was a reformist educational campaigner, emerging out of a traditional aristocratic background. He wanted to rebuild the greatness of France, but he was also a confirmed pacifist throughout his life. This meant that his project was clearly susceptible to corruption by forces beyond his control. He was a republican, a declared egalitarian, but his vision was premised on a notion of amateurism rooted in privilege and patronage. It depended upon the existence of elites of potential leaders, and the exclusion of women. He had a global vision but he saw the world through the eyes of an imperialist. And the dream of an anti-industrialist romantic provided the foundation for a sport production process based upon the most sophisticated and at times surreptitious applied science.

De Coubertin was always aware that international sport could create tensions between nations quite as much as harmony. Yet he persisted in his belief that an international athleticism could tip the balance towards peace. The five rings of the Olympic symbol were meant to represent the unity of the five continents. But such a notion of unity was born in inequality, for the Baron himself was born into a fading elite looking for a new role at a time when the imperialist powers still had their fingers on the pulse of world history.

His moment was soon to fade. But the myth of an Olympic ideal took hold, to be reworked, as myths so often are, in new times and places.

De Coubertin had hoped to rebuild the youth of the world:

I shall burnish a flabby and cramped youth, its body and its character, by sport, its risks and even its excesses. I shall enlarge its vision and its hearing by showing it with wide horizons, heavenly, planetary, historical, horizons of universal history which, in engendering mutual respect, will bring about a ferment of international peace. All this is to be for everyone, with no discrimination on account of birth, caste, wealth, situation or occupation.

As long as you were amateur or male. At the 1912 Olympic Games after which Jim Thorpe was stripped of his great victories for competing professionally, it was de Coubertin who won the prize for literature with his 'Ode to Sport'. It was not Hohrod and Eschbach who wrote the winning Ode: these were aliases assumed by the Baron himself. Who judged the contest? Perhaps de Coubertin did, under yet another name.

We do not know. The man created a powerful myth in a particular moment. He himself became part of that myth. But the complexion which international sport took on under his influence became itself a 'name, battle-cry or costume', as Marx put it, which would be borrowed and reworked again and again by future generations of Olympic ideologues. In such reworkings, the myth would be remade time and time again in the name of tradition.

In a series of spectacles symbolic of the economic and political tensions of the respective times, there would be less and less scope for the grand gesture of *prouesse* out of which the modern Olympic Movement was, in all its contradictions, born. It did not take long, right from the beginning, for the Olympics to take on political and economic meanings undreamt of by de Coubertin. Unwittingly, the dislocated aristocrat's legacy to the modern world has been its biggest non-military propaganda machine.

Acknowledgement

Much of the detail upon which this chapter is based draws upon the splendid study by John MacAloon, (1981) *This Great Symbol*. Mandell's (1976) study *The First Modern Olympics*, and Lord Killanin and J. Rodda's volume *The Olympic Games (1976)* have also been valuable sources.

11 Standing on Ceremony: Representation, Ideology and the Olympic Games

What would the founder of the modern Olympics de Coubertin have made of the opening and closing ceremonies of the 1984 Olympic Games, witnessed by 2.5 billion citizens of the world? Would he have recoiled from the sight as from some gross deformity of the human body and soul — or would he have recognized them as a celebration of physical perfection, grace and beauty? Perhaps he was more at home at the 1936 Berlin Olympics, where Leni Riefenstahl laid the emphasis on the good and the pure and the Nazi fixation upon pageantry and mass spectacle. At which event, then, were the true 'Olympic ideals' perfectly expressed? Surely the answer is "In neither place". For the Olympic ideal has been contested and remade throughout the Games' modern history.

The Olympic movement, from its very inception in the modern historical period, has always been wracked by tensions and contradictions. The Olympic Ideal has survived a succession of reformations, usurpations and, in a very real sense, a necessary series of arrogations. What I mean by this is simple enough: the allegedly pure Olympic ideal has always been moulded in the image of the time and place of the particular Olympiad or Games, rendering all claims to the representation or protection of some set of pure Olympic ideals unjustifiable. That is a legacy of the historical period in which the modern Olympic movement was both conceived and born: the period of the emergence and consolidation of first-world nation-states.

The realization of De Coubertin's dream was from the very beginning a betrayal of an ideal: a version — like amateurism in sport for much of this century — of what the American sociologist Robin

217

Williams called a 'cultural fiction', in which lip-service is paid to values which do not match with or prescribe the limits of everyday action[1]. It is no less a cultural fiction today. In the song to round-off the 1984 Opening Ceremonies (both pre-Opening and once the Games were officially open), the stadium swayed to the tune of "Reach Out and Touch" with adapted lyrics stressing international friendship:

"Reach out and touch somebody's hand,
Make the world a better place if you can;
Come join the celebration as we salute the unity of every nation ... ;
That we all care and it's love and people everywhere ...
We can change things if we start giving;
Why don't you ... Reach out and touch?"

In terms of the United States' presence in the world, a much more plausible set of values is to be found in its declarations of foreign policy. But cut-throat international companies will happily fund the perpetuation of the cultural fiction as long as attractive bodies and star personalities people its events.

The survival of the Olympic ideal has been dependent, then, upon necessary arrogations of, often unjust claims about, that ideal. A nod of consent towards shared Olympic values has usually been forged with a particular cultural or nationalist version of those values. And, from the 1936 Berlin Olympics onwards, the significance of the mass media has inexorably increased, in terms of both how the *meaning* of the Games has been framed and, more recently, how they are staged and funded. In this essay I offer some general thoughts on this process, and a description of and some critical comments upon how British television viewers were bid welcome and farewell to the 1984 Games.

It has become obvious to many commentators on modern sport that physicality, bodily culture and sport are being given more and more space at the heart of the commodity relations of consumer capitalism[2]. Not many people actually engage in sport, but many watch it and increasing numbers *look* as if they do it. We can enter the sports culture now by donning our trainers and our jogging-suits and watching or reading about the latest record attempts or contests in which our nouveau-riche sporting heroes play their dramatic roles. This is a fundamental transformation of the underlying experience of most of us, compared with that of our parents, in the cultural relations of sport. Tom Causer, a London boxer in the late 19th century, was a very different figure to Barry McGuigan[3]. The top sports person is now a national celebrity — a media figure rather than a local character. I am not romanticizing the past here, but recognizing that the impact of the explosion of sponsorship in competitive sport on the economics of the media has led to a re-making of sport as a social phenomenon (Whannel, 1986a).

Sport has featured significantly in the history of technological experimentation in communications. Its dramatic nature (the contest) and its elemental side (human beings putting themselves on the line against other human beings or against nature) are inherently visual and captive of audiences. In Britain in the 1930s the challenge of the Welsh heavy weight boxer Tommy Farr for the world heavyweight crown, relayed trans-Atlantically, was a breakthrough for radio technology. In 1985, Britain's largest ever after-midnight television audience was spell-bound by the climax of the World Snooker Championship final, in which Dennis Taylor went ahead for the first and winning time on the last ball of the final frame (Burn, 1986). There is certainly a gripping element in the agonistic narratives provided by sport. But when *nationalism* is the major context in which the international sports event is presented, it is the *spectacle* which is given most prominence. Asked, a few years on, what they could recall of the 1984 Olympic Games, it is more than likely that most television viewers would mention 84 grand pianos and singer Lionel Ritchie, rather than Carl Lewis or Daly Thompson. For the Olympics on television are just another show-biz challenge. The sandwiching of the actual Games (which, remember, are not 'officially' begun until after the opening extravaganza, and are officially closed before the closing night party) between quasi-traditional ceremonies (torches, flag changes and flag troopings, team parades, the taking of oaths) and extravagant nationalistic displays, positions the Games in a supporting role. And here the balance of presentation has changed. The sporting event becomes the occasion for nationalist histrionics.

And the mass media have been harnessed, at different stages in the development of modern sport, to particular nationalist ideologies. Leni Riefenstahl, in her film of the 1936 Berlin Olympics (*Olympia*) presented to the world a technologically innovative and brilliant encomium to the aesthetics of the body. She also produced political propaganda. In an earlier film of the 1930s (a mountain film, clearly consonant with the primitivist Wandervogel element in early Nazi ideology), Riefenstahl, in Susan Sontag's words, "devised for herself" the role of "a primitive creature who has a unique relation to a destructive power" (Sontag, 1983: p. 77). In retrospective accounts of the making of her 3.5 hour Olympic film, Riefenstahl has often been presented as the individualist genius, the romantic artist, unimplicated in any crude political process. She herself has further vivified this interpretation; as related by Sontag:

> Riefenstahl has maintained in interviews since the 1950s that *Olympia* was commissioned by the International Olympic Committee, produced by her own company and made over Goebbels' protests. The truth is that *Olympia* was commissioned and entirely financed by the Nazi government (a dummy company was set up in Riefenstahl's name because it was thought unwise for the government to appear as the producer) and facilitated by Goebbels' ministry at every stage of the shooting. (Sontag, 1983: pp. 79-80)

Riefenstahl's film reworked Olympic icons — statues, ruins, physical grace — to fit an elitist politics of racist superiority. The image of Germany, in both her film of the Nuremburg Rally (*Triumph of the Will*) and the Olympic work, was unashamedly ideological: the medieval spires and the outdoor camaraderie of the body in political camp or sporting village shrouding the facts of modern Germany, in which modern industrial production was geared to ambitions of world conquest. The innocence of the bucolic fronted the most ruthless and tyrannical political regime of modern times.

It would be meaningless to seek to understand the relationship between this example of representation of the Olympics to the process of arrogation of Olympic ideals with no reference to either the film-maker's other works or the political context in which the work was done. Similarly, the Los Angeles Games must be seen as a social production, staged by professional experts groomed in Hollywood and the entertainment industry, in one of the most powerful capitalist societies on earth, and in the context of the height of the Cold War.

The workings of ideology can mask core or alternative meanings, reshaping values and meaning to suit the purposes of particular groups and interests[4]. In a society in which the mass media have become a major agent of socialization, the ideological dimensions of media practices, conventions and products are the object of vital debate. As the osmosis of sport and the mass media has intensified, the analysis of the ideological workings of television is a critical element in the study of sports cultures.

On some very obvious levels, sport can be changed by the media: in its television form it might well become unrecognisable. In Britain, some of the Channel 4 experiments to liven-up swimming virtually transformed the swimming pool into a water-filled discotheque. Many Olympic sports resist this kind of transformation: the distinctiveness of the occasion, the global profile of the event help to preserve the sport's form (if not a sensible or sensitive sense of scheduling). But on the edges of the event, yet crucial in framing the Games themselves, the 'tradition' of the host nation's own Olympic ceremonies has virtually nothing at all to do with sport. They might as well be the interval show at the Superbowl[5].

The 1984 Opening Ceremony marked the beginning of the Games with a deep, resonant and melodramatic voice from the heavens bidding the world welcome to a "wedding of image and sound". In the view of award-winning film and TV producer David Wolper (the designer of the designer-Olympics): " The world expects more from Hollywood". Thus the showbiz spectacle pre-empted the sports festival right from the start. This prefaced what the British BBC commentator David Coleman referred to as one of the Olympic traditions: "It has become a tradition for the host nation to display" its history, music, dances and culture before other traditional Olympic Ceremonials. Coleman had little choice but to say this. To wonder why such spectacle might be permitted at the Olympics at all would be to raise questions about the distinction between showbiz/entertainment, and sport/contest. Coleman then negotiated things quite skilfully as he welcomed us to the Coliseum:

> ...where in the sunshine of this Californian afternoon, ancient Greek rites, Hollywood fantasy and the reality of life in 1984 will find common ground ... The two faces of the Olympic Games have become unreal. Here, in the Olympic Stadium the pageantry and festivity designed to present the Olympic family of nations as unified and living in harmony, whilst everywhere in this Olympic city there are thousands of police and hundreds of secret service agents prepared for anything to protect the lives of Olympic athletes and officials, prepared for nuclear attack or germ warfare, suicide pilots or suicide drivers of bomb-filled cars ... hard to relate the joyous extravaganza we're going to see with the facts of modern Olympic celebration.

But, Coleman had to concede, here in L. A. there were more nations, more competitors than ever before (despite Soviet bloc boycotts) to be welcomed by a showbiz style of "pure Hollywood extravaganza on a gigantic scale". There was a note of reflection for a while in David Coleman's voice, even of incredulity, and all he could utter was that "the show must go on". Yet in having talked about nationalistic chest-swelling as having *become* a tradition, he firmly located David Wolper's production within the audience's expectation for Olympic events.

What was it that we actually got in this display of pure Americana? A huge cast of regimented extras included 1000 vocalists, 800 marching musicians, 1500 dancers. The ugly urban landscape receded as the voiceover (God-tone) was joined by the Rocket Man (a black man in a silver suit) flying into the stadium. A launch of huge balloons made way for marching bands with a repertoire of well-known USA tunes. The scene was then set for a pre-school illustrated history of American Culture. God-tone prefaced this with the claim that we were about to be told of the making of one nation out of many.

The stadium was overrun by covered wagons "thundering across a map of America from west to east" (Banks-Smith, 1984) with designer cowboys performing dextrous tricks of acrobatics and musicianship, dancing away the conquest of the frontier with wholesome looking young women. Even David Coleman was a bit lost for words here, but he found some: " … as they pushed onward across the continent- relying on music for relaxation and fun." Desperate stuff indeed, in the face of these fiddling pioneers. But his task, unless it were to be critical and myth-exploding or intertextual (references, say, to *Seven Brides for Seven Brothers*) in a truly contextualizing way, was simply impossible. What is there to say about a caricature of a caricature, prepared as mass spectacle for 2.5 billion viewers worldwide? Particularly if that caricature is a B movie cowboy figure (an antiseptic version of the Marlboro man), and the country's own President is one of those caricatures himself.

The designer cowboys were followed by a concession to black culture: the paddle steam boat of the South being traced out in formation by the marching bands, and that most indigenous of cultural legacies — jazz — brought on to the stage. But it did not take long to refocus on the mainstream (in God-tone's terms): "And from under two headless bronze statues queues of blue clad black female dancers emerged to the music of George Gershwin, to be followed by 84 grand pianos". (Coleman had just about held on here, though even he had warned us that we wouldn't believe what was coming next.)

The voice from the heavens then reminded us of the cultural sources of all this: the world of movies and the musical — "the stage is the world of entertainment. Let's play the music and dance". Closeups of celebrated individuals in the stadium audience, after the Reagans, were of Hollywood heroes — Gene Kelly and Cary Grant — not stars of the sporting world.

Finally, the stage filled out with white-clad males and females in flowing evening attire, with the stadium audience joining in the singing of "God Bless America", and the performers producing, in Coleman's words, "a glittering climax to the theme of the twenty-third Olympiad — within a human outline of the map of America". This was accomplished with the help of 12,000 extras/performers, and prefaced, again in Coleman's words, "the biggest piece of audience participation in Olympic history, if it works". All the spectators in the stadium stood

223

up at the command of God-tone, held up coloured cards and produced a salute to the world, a human display of the flags of all the countries competing in the games. A couple of countdowns later (God-tone commanding this like a space-centre operation), and it was over to the athletes: two female swimmers of the USA women's diving team at the 1920 Games in Antwerp were led in to feature in the flag-exchanging, part of the official Opening Ceremony — human relics, reminders of the USA link with the first occasion on which the "flag ceremony" had taken place.

More dramatic than the Opening (illuminations work better in the dark), and more self-congratulatory (the Games had succeeded, L. A. had shown the world), the Closing Ceremony had an understandable air of smugness about it in both presentation and in the response of the British commentator. "We had the privilege of looking on ...", intoned Desmond Lynam. The Closing Ceremony contributed more marching bands, a further parade of flags, a fireworks display and Lionel Ritchie singing "All Night Long". A man from outer space, summoned by a laser-beam light show and emerging from his spaceship to the theme music from Stanley Kubrick's science fiction epic *2001*, drawled this profound message to the waiting world:

> I have come a long way because I like what I have seen — a family of men involved in the limitless possibilities of human achievement. For almost 100 years you have celebrated the best that humanity has to offer. You call it the Olympic Games, and for that and the cities that have kept the Olympic ideal alive, I salute you.

So the Games, despite carping critics, had gone on. More than this they were accomplished as a resounding success. The movement had come through. Again, America had saved the free world and in so doing reinflated the currency of Olympism.

Yet, on examination and reflection, the ceremonies are open to a number of criticisms concerning the political, historical and cultural messages contained in them. First, these spectacles were unashamedly patriotic, to the point of crude ethnocentrism. Doubtless, too, Ronald

Reagan was enjoying this access to a glamorous and irresistible electioneering platform — despite having called off his plan to pop out of his bulletproof box to greet the U. S. team on the edge of the arena. His brief address might have been kept within a 16-word limit, under the strict terms of Olympic protocol, but simply in being 'lined up' televisually with Gene Kelly and Cary Grant, he did well enough.

Reagan's very appearance at the Games was an amplification of his pre-Olympic claims concerning the country's enthusiastic response to the processional progress to Los Angeles of the Olympic flame. The patriotic fervour aroused in Americans by the dramatic relaying of the flame extended beyond their hearts and into their pockets. Patriots were willing to *buy* participation in the carrying of the Olympic flame. At the Games, David Coleman remarked (as Greece, as always, led the 'parade of nations') that the Greeks were not too happy about the commercialization of the torch relay. The response of the International Olympic Committee was that the flame belongs to the Olympic Movement, not to Greece. But Reagan had already put this grubby dispute into perspective: "This outpouring reflects the new patriotism that has swept our land". So much for the universalism of the 'Olympic Ideal'.

And the torch relay — the ritual transportation of the 'sacred' Olympic flame from the site of the original Olympiad to the modern site of contest: an invention for the 1936 Berlin Olympics, introduced to dignify Aryan elitism — becomes in its most recent manifestation no more that a token of a carefully nurtured patriotism within the host country. Here we see the United States at its most ethnocentric: the Olympic ideal laid fully bare.

As a second criticism, the version of history offered in the opening ceremony was truly phantasmagoric — a series of shifting illusions. Some commentators in Britain were merciless in their criticism of this. For instance, the former professional soccer player Eamon Dunphy remarked:

The broader spirit of the Los Angeles Olympics ... was most accurately reflected in the Opening Ceremony, the first hour of which was little more than a maudlin Hollywood-style celebration of American history, a presentation of clichés. (*New Statesman*, 10 August 1984: p. 9)

and:

> As an opening, it lacked universality, good taste and even a passing reference to the original inhabitants of North America — the Indians.

One point here is quite simple, and deeply ironic given the prominence of black athletes in other stages of the official opening rituals, such as oath-taking and lighting of the Olympic urn. The version of history here presented was consonant with main-stream white American culture. This was as *invent*-ory of selected North American stereotypes — not a cultural history. The late journalist James Cameron commented on both the political and the cultural tones of the ceremony:

> ... a lavish occasion of quite sensational vulgarity which would have appalled the originator, De Coubertin ... the irony of the banal and fulsome show-biz commentary was matchless, certainly in a year when the Communist slice of the world publicly, and perhaps pettishly, was not there, thus making a nonsense of all this Sportsmen-Are-All-One drivel that sports commentators use in moments of drawing breath. (*The Guardian*, 31 July, 1984: p. 10)

Other reviewers (notably in *The Times* and the *Daily Telegraph*) commentated on the ceremony as a Hollywood spectacle. One response, which really did capture the cultural essence of the spectacle, compared the ceremony to Disneyland:

> What is wonderful about America is that it's the only nation founded on the principle of having fun, and fun is what America does best: hot fudge sundaes and hot pink convertibles are the real lure of the American Way. If only reality didn't intercede. The best thing would have been if Mickey Mouse

(who was always a bit of a Young Republican anyway) had come on and opened the Games. Instead we had President Reagan standing in a glass observation booth, his chin quivering with what could have been emotion but looked like senility. (Mary Harron, *New Statesman*, 3 August, 1984)

Harron captures the attractions of such ceremonies: in many respects it is the playful image that persists longest — the childlike pride at doing the trick in public; the gleeful dressing up as cowboy or rocket man; the physical exuberance; and, all embracing, the naiveté (or simple-mindedness) of the messages offered the world. The spectacle was what Gilbert Adair (1986) has called "Spielbergien" or "para-Spielbergien", mixing visions of a yet retrievable, simple and untainted past with the impact of new and sometimes alien forces, in an optimistic blend for the future, exemplified in the closing ceremony by Wolper's spaceman — the Grand-Daddy of E.T. For Adair, the Spielberg film "was predicated on a universe of infinite spiritual consciousness" and, "groping towards a literal *theology* of space", is a form of Christian Science-fiction. And the 1984 Los Angeles Olympics opening and closing ceremonies, addressing the world in an accessible language of popular entertainment, offered their own version of the miraculous route to future salvation.

After some restraint during the *official* rituals of the closing ceremony, the stadium commentator reassumed his omniscient cum prophesying tone, as, in Coleman's words, we were treated to the sight of "2000 Los Angeles citizens dressed in the costumes of their native countries". God-tone addressed the world: "Citizens of a world grown small, an island in the endless sky. We are still bound in common destiny ... join hands each to each ...". The Coliseum floor turned for a while into a fancy dress parade which parodied world culture and history. At this point, for some observers in Britain, the spectacle — more or less out of hand from the beginning — now exceeded the bounds of credulity entirely. Nancy Banks-Smith wrote: "I thought my mind had snapped"[6]. For British observers, by now, it was four a.m....

So the language of popular entertainment, as spoken in the opening and closing ceremonies of the 1984 Los Angeles Olympics and broadcast over the airwaves from the Coliseum to the rest of the world, dominated Olympic ritual — a language drawing upon a reservoir of meanings, deep wells of cultural prejudice and national solipsism. LA '84 — for all its apparent harmlessness and innocence — was one of the most fascinating "necessary arrogations" of the 'Olympic ideal'.

The commercial forces of sponsorship and the political adrenaline of the host nation form a very strong partnership against which to contend, but the Olympic Movement could seek to intervene. It could develop criteria for the pre-official Opening Ceremony; demand priority for *its own* history to be displayed in the ceremony; insist that the athletes themselves are the leading players, not support cast waiting in the wings; and require that the host country stage its own historical display, if at all, in preview. Televisual images do linger on; and those of the Los Angeles Olympics of 1984 can be said to owe more to the spirit of the Hollywood producer than to that of the founder of the modern Olympics.

Notes

[1] Robin Williams (1963). Williams points out that there are different categories of cultural fiction (see pp. 391-395). Generally, the main point is to stress that consciousness/action tensions involve gaps between beliefs and conduct: the very stuff of the ideological process.

[2] See Clarke and Critcher (1986); Hargreaves (1986); Alt (1983).

[3] See Shipley (1983); and for a comment or two on Barry McGuigan, see Tomlinson (1987).

[4] I cannot possibly rehearse here the last generation's debate on concepts and theories of ideology — even if I felt capable of doing so. Just one reference, then, to a collection of articles on ideology (including pieces by Anthony Giddens and Ernesto Laclau): *Ideology/Power, Canadian Journal of Political and Social Theory* Vol. VII Nos. 1-2, Winter/Spring 1983. Suffice to say, with Anthony Giddens, that ideology cannot "be defined in reference to truth claims", in any crude fashion, but that the "concept of ideology should be reformulated in relation to a theory of *power* and *Domination* — ideology as the mode within systems of domination, so as to sanction their continuance" (p. 19).

[5] On January 25th, 1987, the Denver Broncos played the New York Giants in the Rosebowl (Pasadena, California). The half-time interval spectacle of the body included dancers from *Flashdance*, from *Fame*, Mickey Mouse and elaborate renditions of Hollywood theme tunes such as "That's Entertainment". Mere razz-matazz? Or more than that? For my part, it portrayed a version of success and male/female positioning which amounted to a celebration of the beautiful in support of the brutal.

[6] I cannot resist reproducing in full Nancy Banks-Smith's 1984 television review of the Ceremony, from *The Guardian*, 30 July:

> I don't know if you have ever felt like a bald-headed eagle? Around 4 o clock on Sunday morning I felt a mystic unity with Bomber, a

bald-headed eagle which started to lose weight, showed signs of anxiety and embarrassingly expired while being trained to wear a toupee and sing America the Beautiful for the Opening Ceremony of the Los Angeles Olympics (BBC-1).

I am trained to a hair, a finely tuned or perhaps honed viewing machine. I survived two gruelling hours of the Olympic Games Concert (ITV) only slightly shining with sweat. Neil Diamond had "performed in Birmingham, England for the Prince Charles and Princess Diana Charity Trust" and Brooke demonstrated the indomitable human spirit by hanging from a rope — 'she thought it was impossible' — by one leg. All this and I was barely blown. No collapsing on the track with grimaces of pain. Nothing like that.

The gala was followed by a David L. Wolper ('Louder, Longer, Larger') spectacular. It began with covered wagons, thundering across the map of America from west to east, and continued with extended musical items involving 2000 dancers, a 1000- voiced choir, the Great Olympic All-American Marching Band (not counting 84 grand pianos which could not march) and "the biggest piece of audience participation in Olympic history" in which spectators formed the flags of all nations (but not of course the hammer and sickle).

Training tells. My stiff upper lip concealed the shaking of my knees. The athletes of 140 nations, give or take those who had decided to stay away and put their athlete feet up, now paraded for two hours. I quite liked this. They did not play loud concertos on grand pianos. They did not dance in top hats. Norway (and Sweden when they remembered) all raised their hats in concert like perfect gentlemen, which I thought sweet.

Australia's bush hats were supposed to be kept secret, though how you can keep several hundred bush hats and T-shirts emblazoned with koala bears quiet beats me. Lesotho, my all-time favourites, wore straw huts (or straw hats, as they would insist). Lesotho proved the truth of the rule that the smaller the nation the longer the names. Machochono Mokhutlole carried their flag (which also had a straw hat on it).

Beware, friends, the home stretch. Around 4 am I was flexing a seized-up knee. David Coleman was talking in his sleep — "As the sun sinks in, er, this California city" — when suddenly a large woman in a dressing gown with a rose on her head burst on us, followed by a man with a hearth rug on his head. Thick and fast they came in grass skirts and straw helmets, wearing gilded pagodas and 40,000 feathers and tigerskin trousers.

There was a Rasputin, a Hiawatha, assorted Gauchos, various virgins dressed for a ceremonial slaughter, and a particularly vacant-looking Dutchman. I thought my mind had snapped. They were, explained the stadium commentator "2000 citizens in the dress of their native origin entering to honour the athletes". In elevated mood he continued, "Citizens of a world grown small. An island in the endless sky. We are still bound in common destiny ... (and so forth) ... join hands each to each!"

On this cue a woman not known to me but, I trust, to the LA police department launched into "reach out and touch somebody's hand. Make this world a better world if you can", sprinkling the song with shrill injunctions. "Come on, reach! Reach for the sky! Reach out and touch it! We can make it! The world has joined in the dance!" (This being a reference to the fact that on the Great Wall of China and in the drive of Windsor Castle children were swaying to and fro, clearly believing they were in a coke commercial).

RIP Baldy, you wise old bird.

12 Images of Sport —
Situating "Chariots of Fire"

For a long time I'd been looking to do two things. One was a film that dealt in sport as metaphor: the most problematic thing with the plot of a film is if the basis is arguable, but in sport whoever wins, wins — there's no argument about that, and all other areas or issues become clear in those terms. And I'd also been looking for a subject not unlike *A Man For All Seasons*, about a man who did something quite extraordinary. I feel that we live in an age of expedience, and I wanted to do a film about a wholly unexpedient decision. (David Puttnam, Producer of *Chariots of Fire*, in interview with Clive Hodgson, cited in National Film Theatre Programme Notes)

Images of Sport and the Sport-media Complex

The media-sport relation has been a major influence upon the world of contemporary sport. There is little doubt that our modern conception of sport is as much produced by as reflected in television sport and the representation of sport in other media forms. Images of sport are not simple chunks of evidence concerning what the sport is actually like. As Garry Whannel (1982: p. 212) puts it:

... the event is always mediated by its television coverage. One cannot simply talk of a correct representation and a false one.

'Images of sport' is then a deceptively simple phrase and focus. Images surround us, appearing in different forms — in the press, television, cinema, prose, poetry, drama, magazines, comics. The production of a social history of key points of transformation in sports image-making would be a mightily demanding but very rewarding task. And images of sport can be images of many things — of masculinity, femininity, privilege, harmony, nationalism, contained violence, physical taboos. Much careful textual analysis is needed of the ideological dimensions of images of sport in different media forms. But it is undeniable that the media-sport relation has been a central influence upon the re-making of contemporary British sport. Put crudely, just about every sport in Britain wants to get itself on television — because television is the source of most people's experience of sport. Governing bodies see sponsorship deals premised on a high television profile as their route towards long-term solvency, and the small screen in the domestic house as the major source for recruiting new generations of participants. For the majority, it is the media which makes the experience of sport — as spectators — possible.

In 1986 the Henley Centre quoted a MORI poll which "indicated that while only 25% of all respondents had attended a major sports tournament/match in the last twelve months, 90% had watched such a tournament or match on television" (Henley Centre, 1986: p. 84). Although this says nothing about the mode of watching of the television coverage/reporting, it is a hugely significant trend, as so many knew in 1985 when over 19 million people stayed up after midnight to watch the Dennis Taylor—Steve Davis snooker World Championship final cliff-hanger.

And the media are pretty precise in their marketing, in affirming and reproducing the social relations of capitalist society. Here is Bruce Kidd on this question:

The result has been coverage which heavily favours male team sports and only certain Olympic sports, and which is highly patriarchal, at times gladiatorial; nationalistic; and confirming of existing hierarchies and inequalities. (Kidd, 1987: p.10)

234

Kidd cites a number of sources which argue his case (Jhally, 1984: Whannel, 1984). To these could be added more which trace the relationship between television's interest in sport and the involvement of commercial sponsors (Whannel, 1986a). To understand the place of the media within the contemporary political economy of sport, several questions come to the fore. In what ways have the media (particularly television) reworked sporting conventions? What pressure is put upon sports by commercial sponsors, to conform to particular expectations/stereotypes? How has the *control* of sports been altered by the emergence of the agent/fixer/entrepreneur? Who owns what, in terms of symbols, values, and conventions in sporting traditions and practice?

These are some of the biggest issues of the day for modern sports, and the consolidation of the sport-media complex *as a model* for sports development generally produces a serious dilemma and crisis for many contemporary sports.

This crisis is captured in the response of one governing body (albeit a dance body) to a survey/questionnaire on pressures concerning eligibility/finance in the world of sport today. This forms the response of the Imperial Society for Teachers of Dancing (maybe that sounds as marginal as you can get, but dancing is a much more prevalent participatory activity than is sport):

(a) the cost of venues is being pushed up by sponsored events
(b) the lack of media outlet for activities that are not heavily sponsored ... may lead in the longer term to distorted development in some activities over others. (Bull and Tomlinson, 1987: p. 12)

The sport-media complex is beginning to *dictate* the terms in which sports are seen as thriving, prosperous, successful and so on — and this is developing very much in terms of the perceived televisual (therefore high-profile, advertising-easy) appeal of the sport/activity. John Hargreaves observes:

The entertainment values that underpin media sport articulate with a drift in the historical development of individualism towards promoting the family as the individual's source of well-being, and away from the ideal that individuality is promoted by extending opportunities to participate in public life. (Hargreaves, 1986: p. 159)

Put less conspiratorially, television has, in Garry Whannel's view, generated an "enormous pressure towards routine" which has involved a loss of "the aesthetic excitement of its own days of uncertainty" (Whannel, 1986b: p. 30). Images of sport are therefore constructed for us according to media conventions, and consumed by us in orderly and domesticated contexts.

And to the media, sport is above all "showbiz". Jonathan Martin, former Head of the BBC's Outside Broadcast and Events Unit, was quick to point out that his department is "in the entertainment business" (personal discussion). In victory or defeat, athlete Carl Lewis always managed to produce the most irresistible copy, with comments on the prevalence of drug-taking, on the almost para-normal performances of previously run-of-the-mill athletes. Lewis's style was captured by Frank Keating on the occasion of a press conference in Rome:

Carl Lewis, his four Olympic gold medals still metaphorically gilding his unhairy chest and razz-matazzy persona, called a news conference at Garibaldi's one-time palace, the stately Villa Miami perched on the highest of the city's seven hills.

Lewis, theatrically camp and dressed all in billowing creamy-white tracksuit, stood on the balcony taking in the ancient view. Here Garibaldi had gazed down on the Vatican and dreamed of his take-over bid. For the moment Lewis looked like the first black Pope blessing the city and the world ...

With great ceremony, a golden pen and his widest Colgate smile and interminable translations from the unending gibberish of Japanese sales managers, he signed a contract with a Tokyo manufacturer of Plimsolls. They named him their "doctor-professor of shoeology".

"I'm truly excited", he said, "these are definitely the lightest, tightest and fastest articles of footwear in the whole world and we're gonna have a wonderful relationship ....". (*Guardian*, 28 August 1987: p. 20)

In this combination of circus and selling, of sport and marketing, Lewis portrayed some of the major elements of the contemporary global sports culture — a supra-national language of the physical tied in with an international language of the market. It is an image of sport a long way removed from the image of the sprinter in the film *Chariots of Fire*. It is at first glance remarkable that just about the most commercially successful sports-movie ever could offer up an image of sport so far removed from contemporary images. Yet, as world sport stumbled from crisis to crisis, from controversy to controversy, an image of a simpler age was an attractive image. It was as if the blatant showmanship of Carl Lewis signalled the end of the amateur athleticist ideal, an ideal which in British sport had been precariously preserved, for a century or so. Lewis' public performances represented an image of sport as showbiz, the sports star as marketing tool. Yet millions flocked to the cinema and the television screen in 1981 and since to watch, in *Chariots of Fire*, a story of an earlier, simpler time.

Whose Feet in Which Time? Situating *Chariots of Fire*

Let me try and get this connection clear. Sports participation is *not* a majority activity, by any stretch of the (social survey) imagination. Live spectatorship has plummeted in Britain during the last generation. Television coverage of sport, of events around the world, has increased. Yet at this very moment of transformation a film centring upon the stories of two British sprinters in the 1920s gained huge international success. Sports films are notoriously unsuccessful in the film-making world. Historical movies are really risky ventures too, unless rooted at appropriate times in established genres such as the Western or the War Movie. *Chariots of Fire*, a movie on sport and on history, defied the conventions of blockbuster planning. In this second part of this essay

I will describe the film, comment briefly upon its narrative structure and, finally, speculate upon the reasons for its immense success in Britain and America.

Chariots of Fire runs for just under two hours and after starting with a scene of young men running by the sea, moves to a scene in a London church in the 1970s, where a congregation is gathered to pay its respects at a memorial service for Harold Abrahams. Two old men are in the congregation in the church. One is Aubrey Montague, the other Lord Andrew Lindsay. Lindsay is delivering the funeral oration on their dead friend:

> All these men were honoured in their generation and worked for glory in their day. We are here today to give thanks for the life of Harold Abrahams, to honour the legend. Now there are just two of us, young Aubrey Montague and myself, who can close our eyes and remember those few young men with hope in our hearts and wings on our heels.

The film then takes us back to the Kentish coast in 1924, where the British Olympic team is in preparation for its departure to France for the 1924 Paris games. Aubrey Montague writes to his mother, and this device takes us back to 1919, to the new Michaelmas Term at Gonville and Cais College, Cambridge, where Harold Abrahams is arriving. Harold Abrahams is then the focus of the narrative. He achieves the 'impossible' feat of running round the College quad (with Lindsay as his hare) within the time it takes the bell to peal twelve times. He joins the Gilbert and Sullivan society. He expresses resentment at the anti-Semitic tone of College employees and authorities. Running becomes a metaphor for Abrahams himself. His talent for running will be a way of "running them off their feet", not just his sporting rivals, but also those who continue to convey to him a sense of his own marginality.

Eric Liddell is introduced in the film as an established Scottish rugby international who turns to running as a form of secular preaching. For Liddell success on the track is part of his missionary vocation. His sister Jenny is highly disapproving of this. The film evolves around a rivalry between Liddell and Abrahams, and the inner tensions that both seek to resolve. For Liddell, the secular world of sport does not fit easily with his mission, and the ethical crunch comes when his 100 metre heat/event is scheduled for a Sunday. Hearing this as he boards the ferry for France, Liddell is plunged into a massive dilemma of loyalty. For Abrahams, the tension resolves around his committed, determined approach to preparation for competition, frowned upon by the College masters at his University, but prominent and effective in the figure of Sam Mussabini, the Arab-Italian Newcastle-brown swigging Geordie whom Abrahams employs as his trainer/coach. At the Paris games Liddell takes Lindsay's place in the 400 metres and wins the gold medal. Abrahams loses in the 200 metres but wins the gold in the 100 metres. The major rivals, the Americans Charles Paddock and Jackson Scholz, have been shown engaging in much more rigorous, scientific forms of preparation, but for all this Eric Liddell's animal talent and Harold Abrahams' coach-aided determination see them through.

The film ends with the two old men walking away from the church, and Aubrey Montague providing Harold's epitaph — "Well he did it Andy ... he ran them off their feet"; and the final visual images of, again, the group of young male athletes running along the beach, almost non-human as they merge into an anonymous mass within the natural landscape of sand, sea and sky. At both the beginning and end of the film only one of the runners is smiling, laughing or expressing anything that could be described as joy — Lord Lindsay. Three anthems dominate the soundtrack of the movie — Vangelis' rousing theme-music in the opening and closing sequences and at many points when the film focuses upon running and physical exertion; the congregation's singing of Jerusalem (in "England's green and pleasant land"), the source of the movie's rather obscure title; and 'To Be an Englishman', the Gilbert and Sullivan number which Abrahams performs.

The narrative structure of the film works effectively on the level of holding the viewer/audience. Sport is a guarantor of this anyway, in that there will be a winner and at the outset of the race or contest it can never be certain who this will be. This dramatic element is compounded by the inner tensions which operate on the two main protagonists. 'Will they win' becomes further complicated by the question 'Will they run?' The fact that they do run, though not against each other, resolves the narrative tension so that in the end they not only run but they also win — for the nation, as well as for themselves. As an enabling agent within the narrative, Lord Lindsay plays a key role. He encourages Harold, drives him on, befriends him at Cambridge. And he volunteers to stand down to enable Liddell to run in a different event. Lindsay, within the narrative, is vital. He is rich, confident, talented, and happy — he can afford to make concessions. In the end, the tensions within the narrative are resolved on the basis of a noble aristocratic gesture which enables the outsiders to both win races (they could of course not have both won if Liddell had remained in the same event as Abrahams). A story of marginality, identity crises, of post-World War One youthful striving, becomes an encomium to the nation, and a celebration of established values. Released in the Spring of 1981 the film was an enormous success on several levels. A year later, in April 1982, the film had won four Oscars, for the Best Original Screenplay, the Best Original Score, the Best Costume Design and, to top it all, Best Film. After the film had received its Oscar nominations the BBC paid £1 million for the rights to show the film in 1984 (year of the Los Angeles Olympics) and three more times in the future (*Daily Mail*, 31 January 1982). By July 1982, in the United States the film (released in October 1981) had taken £49.4 million in takings, making it the biggest money-making foreign film in U.S. box-office history (*The Times and Glasgow Herald*, 15 July 1982).

Commercially, critically (at least in terms of the industry's own criteria), popularly, the film was a global whopper of a hit. In the early Summer of 1984 television reviewers had a chance to re-view the film, on the occasion of its first television showing. Julie Davidson, in the *Glasgow Herald*, wrote:

> ... we saw exposed a very ordinary, often tedious film which contained all its inspiration in the opening credits and the theme music. (*Glasgow Herald*, 28 May 1984)

Peter Waymark in *The Times* recollected its first impact:

> The theory put around at the time of its initial success was that Chariots represented a throwback to an older and more wholesome type of film to which the whole family could safely be taken without fear of violence, full-frontals or four-letter words. (*The Times*, 21 April 1984)

Waymark also wondered whether the film represented a throwback to heroes rather than anti-heroes, or an affirmation of the old amateur spirit, in a time when audiences have tired of the tantrums of today's rich sportsmen. "One day", he concluded, "a clever sociologist may come up with the answer".

No sociologist, of course — clever or otherwise — will be able to come up with a definitive answer. And it is somewhat disingenuous of a clever journalist to list the best answers and then pass the buck of proof to the academic. But the answers cannot be definitively proven, for the phenomenon of popular consciousness defies precise delineation. We know that *Chariots of Fire* is in many senses an optimistic story of human endeavour. Maybe audiences were ready for this after a diet, in the late 1970s, of disaster movies and extra-terrestrial adventures. Maybe audiences wanted heroes. Colin Welland, the screenplay writer, in discussion with me, has said that Abrahams and Liddell are his versions of comic-book heroes of the past, such as Alf Tupper (the Tough of the Track) and the Great Wilson. Liddell himself actually became, posthumously, a cartoon-strip hero in the *Victor* (see Magnusson, 1981: facing page 96).

But the most convincing explanation for the popular success of the movie is its evocation of a simpler, more noble past, in which moral dilemmas were soluble and negotiation was possible. *Chariots of Fire* offered audiences a particular image of sport and sporting values, and did so in 1981, the year following the 1980 Moscow Olympics at which no USA athletes had competed, and a year of extraordinary events and tensions in Britain. Without offering background as some crude explanatory focus, it is worth exploring the *context of impact* of the movie

241

itself. What was it, in the USA of late 1981 and the UK of early 1981 onwards which might help us understand more fully the impact of *Chariots of Fire*? To answer this adequately would involve more detailed analysis of audience readings/interpretations, and discussion of the film itself as text[1]. Here, I offer some speculative preliminary responses to the question.

In the United States the New York Times critic David Derby called the film, on its opening at the New York Film Festival, "handsome, well-acted and frequently charming"; in art-house style, a:

> … cautious, distinguished, slightly boring good movie … Apart from a few mild digs at Cambridge anti-Semitism, *Chariots of Fire* is imbued with a kind of low-key pride and patriotism that shone from British movies of the forties and the fifties. It celebrates an England that is gentle, modest and brave — an England essentially good. (*New York Times*, 5 November 1981)

Much of this, for North American viewers, focused around Kent, Cambridge, London and Edinburgh — major stopping-off points in the Grand Tour of Britain. Landscapes in the film are of centuries-old halls of learning and apparently permanent natural landscapes — the Highlands, the coast. Set on the eve of the modern period, the film evokes a visually trans-historical Britain, a sense of environments and institutions almost beyond history. Doing this in terms of the Olympic ideal, too — modernity's attempt to carve out a classical pedigree for itself — the film offered up to North American viewers a simple story of human endeavours, set in the landscapes of a Tourist Guide to the old country. *Chariots of Fire* is a visual dithyramb on pre-modern Britain, an innocent hymn in praise of essentially traditional values. Despite the prominence of the USA/American motif in the film, Americans are noble participants/losers rather than unscrupulous winners. Locked into Cold War politics, absent from the Moscow Olympics, fully-fed on a diet of human-interest alien moves and human disaster tales, a Glossy Tourist Brochure featuring old-time values and ideals was, for the USA viewer, both an escape from the social issues of the day, and an idealization of a recent simpler past.

242

In Britain the film's appeal is perhaps easier to explain. Not so long ago in Britain the two ancient universities were producing crops of Olympians and world-record holders. The film is a reminder of this history, of this legacy of diminishing importance. In the figures of Seb Coe and Steve Ovett in middle-distance running Britain still had world-level middle-distance runners who could be portrayed as within a long-established tradition (even though their forms of funding, support and sponsorship by state-bodies such as a university, or by commercial deals, might have been aeons away from any amateur ideal). Scot Alan Wells had beaten the Russians in Moscow the previous year to win the 100 metres Olympic gold medal, and so British prominence in the 'dash' was re-established. It is possible that in 1981 the public consciousness of the runner was as high as at any time in British history up to that date.

1981 was also a complex point in British — and, primarily, English — culture, the year of the Toxteth and other inner-city riots, the year of the Royal Wedding between Prince Charles and Lady Diana Spencer, the year of Ian Botham's 'boy's own' achievements in the Ashes against the Australian cricketing tourists. It was a year in which many contradictions and tensions attested to both the divisions in British society and the binding forces of nationalist feeling and historicized pride. Many of these were to be dramatically and tragically inflected in the Falklands affair early the following year.

Chariots of Fire, in revealing to the British public a set of social divisions and inner conflicts, and then providing a resolution in the form of nationalist integration, offered a metaphor of adaptation and equilibrium. If *Chariots* operated as a Tourist Brochure to the USA viewer, it operated as a nostalgic evocation of traditional values to the British viewer. Although the scriptwriter Colin Welland has claimed (in personal interview) that the film represents two-fingers to the establishment, it is much more a reminder that though the British boat might rock we can all find our place aboard without the craft sinking. Disapproving of Abrahams' tactics in employing a coach, the Cambridge masters are nevertheless not slow to claim his victory as theirs. The two Britons win for a simpler Britain, threatened but lustily surviving, willing to strike bargains for the sake of stability and continuity.

243

In the age of an increasingly privatised consumer culture one of Britain's most successful television advertisements, for Hovis, worked on a generation's nostalgia for its cultural and geographic roots:

What Hegarty had done for Hovis, using picturesque street-scapes, sentimental music and a north-country voice-over, was to create an overwhelming impression of British 'goodness'. (Bayley, 1986: p. 93)

Hugh Hudson, director of *Chariots*, and his cameraman, David Watkins, were both experienced image-makers from the world of advertising. *Chariots of Fire* is indeed a series of nostalgic images of a glowing national culture, a resilient culture of compromise in an era of negotiated tolerance. The British Art of Losing Well (and casting disapproving looks the way of non-British world-class winners) could find a rousing echo in the nostalgic images of reasonable and heroic success in Puttnam's film.

In this sense, and on both sides of the Atlantic, the success and impact of *Chariots of Fire* shows how sport, and images of sport, can offer temporary resolutions to social and cultural tensions and divisions. And in this particular case, with Frank Keating's Emperor in Cream Clothes just around the corner with his smoothly prepared copy for the world press, the charm of the self-made hero is clear. *Chariots of Fire* is best understood not by any simple search in it for an historical truth, but by the interpretation of it as an interpretation of an age of simpler heroism. In sport the popular memory — reminiscent and nostalgic as it is — so often positions the past not just as a different but as a preferable world. The success of *Chariots of Fire* is explicable primarily in terms of how such an imaginative reconstruction works by contrast in an era when the sporting culture and the sport-media complex is about to produce Carl Lewis, and when heroes and heroines of the track acquire tragic ambiguities of fame, as in the case of Florence 'Flojo' Gaynor Jones, remodeled and anatomically and artificially resculpted for victory at Seoul in 1988, but dead of a heart attack ten years later.

Note

1   As an aid to this, a slide-set and slide notes on *Chariots of Fire* are available from the BFI (British Film Institute), London. See Tomlinson, 1988.

IV

Representations of Masculinity

13 Sports Fiction as Critique: The Novelistic Challenge to the Ideology of Masculinity

It was his remarkable body that occupied virtually all my thoughts. I loved the way he had no visible neck, his head being permanently stove into his shoulders from leading with it in blocking and tackling. I worshipped his chipped front teeth and mangled upper lip from the time he'd dropped the barbell on his face while trying to press 275 pounds. I adored the Kirk Douglas cleft that made his chin look like an upside-down heart, which cleft was actually a crater from an opponent's cleat. I admired the way his left eye had only half an eyebrow from once when he had hit the linesman's stake after being tackled. Joe Bob was evidently indestructible .... (Lisa Alther, 1977: pp. 37-38)

In the morning Creed sent us into an all-out scrimmage with a brief inspirational message that summed up everything we knew or had to know.
    'It's only a game', he said, 'but it's the only game'. (Don DeLillo, 1973: p. 115)

Opening Remarks

This essay combines propositions concerning how we theorize literature, with readings of three novels which I found in second-hand bookshops, some time after they had all been out of print. So the discussions will not be purely random. They are books that I had heard about, sometimes read about, but which I had not actually got hold of until the serendipity of the second hand book store[1]. They are considered here as sources potentially illuminating of the meanings and values of sport.

Sport is the stuff of dreams, of larger than life possibilities, of fantasy. In sport, in identifiable moments structured by agreed-upon ways of acting, things can be achieved on a scale unthought of in everyday life. Few walks of life allow comebacks the like of which are witnessed on the field of play. Yet in sport the margin between success and failure, between glory and grief, is a fine one, and the fickleness of fandom can confirm the fragility of the sporting hero's fame. Prominent sporting figures are both reflexive of the character of their public, yet at the same time larger than life. This makes them both greatly loved and vulnerable. They embody the hopes of their followers and yet, at a moment's notice, can become a focus for despair. The everyday functions of sports are far from simple ones. What then, is sports fiction actually doing in its representation of sports events, sports personnel and sports experience?

To grasp the significance of sports fiction in terms of more than just its own literary characteristics, it is essential to explore it in terms of its societal referents. In this sense sports fiction must be seen as cultural expression within a particular social structural setting.

The use of sports as metaphor has been quite widely exploited in literature. When William Carlos Williams wanted to talk about the 'spirit of uniformity' and the permanent, serious absence of thought characteristic of a great many people, he turned his attentions upon the 'ball game'. To Auden, wanting to capture the difference between the symmetry of external appearances and the unevenness of what actually goes on behind the facade, the runner offered an ideal image. And to A.E. Houseman — that most melancholic of English ruralists — the image of the prematurely dead athlete is a perfect means of evoking a spirit of nostalgic loss[2]. In drama, too, the sports motif is a significant one, one writer arguing that the analysis of this symbolic motif in contemporary dramas is illuminating "because universal humanistic relationships were portrayed" (Ingram, 1979: pp. 128–140). In developing work on sports motifs in fictional/dramatic forms this oversimplification — this universalization of the socially specific — must be opposed. For sports motifs appear in different types of literature in different types of societies. Allen Guttman has argued that sports writing in Western Europe is qualitatively distinct from even American writing[3]. This is the key point. Sports fiction is not some sort of free-floating expression of the human spirit.

When Clifford Odets wrote about claustrophobic human relationships he recognized that such circumstances were rooted in a social setting — one of inequality, exploitation and oppression. In his *Awake and Sing*, he wrote that "all of the characters ... share a fundamental activity: a struggle for life amidst petty conditions"[4]. Popular music fulfils precisely the same function in this play as does sport in *Golden Boy*. The records of Caruso represent an escapist evasion of face-to-face human relationships, whilst at the same time embodying a form of hopeful romanticism. Boxing represents hope for a better future, and is chosen as a route for potential mobility at the expense of the young boxer's real love, the violin. Both these popular cultural phenomena operate in comparable ways within the respective dramatic pieces. They reveal the 'petty conditions' with which Odets was so concerned, yet they offer little more than a fantasy-based escape from these conditions on the one hand, and an exclusive Hobbesian escape for the lucky individual on the other. In both settings, the 'petty conditions' remain unchanged. Odets used popular cultural forms such as sport and music in socially specific ways in his drama. The individual dilemmas are portrayed as social questions, issues and problems. In Depression America a Marxist playwright is doing more than evoke universal values. He is offering specific critique.

The use of the sports motif is not always employed in such an explicitly tendentious way, yet the effect can still be powerful. Mae's equation of irresponsibility with sports in *Cat on a Hot Tin Roof*; and the unsuccessfully, ineffectively channelled sporting aggression of Willy Loman's sons Happy and Biff in *Death of a Salesman* — these are examples of how sports can be used as a metaphor for ineffectiveness and failure[5]. In poetry and in drama, then, the notion of the sportsman, of the sports event, can be drawn upon to amplify the writer's main theme. In the cases I have mentioned the sports motif could certainly be replaced by another motif. There are passive crowds, physical beauties, tragically premature deaths, and failed dreams in other spheres of social life too. But the sports motif in literature is a particularly powerful one because it plays upon a socially significant sports motif in lived experience. It cannot be fully understood without looking at what sport represents in terms of cultural values. The poets and playwrights mentioned in these opening remarks are writing about mass anonymity (Williams), the transitoriness of human beauty (Houseman), the relation between appearance/essence (Auden), stunted class consciousness (Odets) and frustrated personal ambitions and dreams (Williams and Miller). They are not writing, in the first instance, about sport. They are using sport as a way of making their own particular points. In doing this, they assume a degree of givenness concerning what sport actually is in the real world. This makes it impossible to categorize their work as some easily identifiable form of sports fiction. For what the respective writers take for granted about sports might vary greatly. But sport has provided an effective and powerful source because of the breadth of its cultural meanings, and because of the dramatic contradictions that characterize lived sports cultures.

Cultural Values and Sports; Contradictions in Sporting Experience

The novels considered in detail later in this essay illustrate the extent to which sports fiction can be a form of critical social consciousness. The question has to be asked, though, critical of what? It is this 'what' which must be explored or, at the very least, acknowledged if any reading of sports fiction is to have any sociological significance. Literary motifs and images might have their own autonomy within the literary form itself, but we understand them fully only in terms of their derivation from a social context and a material base. And the cultural values embodied in sports, a vital part of that material base, are the raw materials for the writer of sports fiction.

Allen Guttman (1978) has classified sports in terms of different social structural contexts, and in so doing has highlighted in a useful way the distinctive features of modern sports. As Table 1 below shows, modern sports are utterly separate from primitive or mediaeval sports. Only the Greeks or Romans have approximated the modern sports forms. Guttman is working with a conceptual model here, and concedes that things can go a little awry when looking at the contemporary state of affairs (p. 26); he actually makes this point when talking about equality. So he is perfectly aware that the ideal-typical conceptualization can be contradicted in actual affairs as he calls them.

Table 1:   The Characteristics of Sports in Various Ages
[*Source:* Guttman, 1978: p. 54]

	Primitive Sports	Greek Sports	Roman Sports	Mediaeval Sports	Modern Sports
Secularism	Yes & No	Yes & No	Yes & No	Yes & No	Yes
Equality	No	Yes & No	Yes & No	No	Yes
Specialization	No	Yes	Yes	No	Yes
Rationalization	No	Yes	Yes	No	Yes
Bureaucracy	No	Yes & No	Yes	No	Yes
Quantification	No	No	Yes & No	No	Yes
Records	No	No	No	No	Yes

The usefulness of Guttman's conceptualization, though, lies in its appropriateness as a guide to what dominant sports values are. For Guttmann, sports are not reflexive of any explicitly religious function; they are contested in theoretically equal terms; they are increasingly specialized; they are based upon officially drawn-up rules and extraordinarily sophisticated approaches to the doing of them; they are run by organizational personnel; they are measured in unprecedentedly detailed ways; and they stress the unsurpassable, the far horizon, the stretching of limits. That, then, is the ideal type; now to the other side of the coin.

Actual accounts of sporting practice, and demystifying investigations of the nature of sports deal with what the meaning of sports actually is[6], both to those who practise them, and to those who consume sports in the market-place. These sources stress not just the dominant values in an unproblematic way. Rather, they raise the question of how far and in what ways sports can represent subterranean or oppositional values. Thus the 'value' of equality is contradicted by, say the 'revolt of the black athlete' and by accounts of working-class culture[7]. The secularism of sports is questioned by material on the spiritual side of sports practice, such as the 'inner-game'[8]. There is a contradiction between the specialization of the modern sportsman and the general incapacity to participate of those who idolize him. Although sports are rationalised the great appeal of sport can often reside in the irrational, the unknown, the unexpected, the spontaneous[9]. A bureaucratic base to modern sports does not prevent individual sports performers, or groups of them, from coming into conflict with the organization[10]. Quantification does not undermine the important fact that in sports contests the winner is the one who is remembered; it is the event, the spectacle, the performance which engraves itself upon the memory of those who go and see it[11], and the attempt in, say, gymnastics and ice-skating, to quantify the aesthetic does not destroy our appreciation of the artistic beauty of the performance. It is similar with the final characteristic; an obsession with records does not wholly obscure the fact that in sports the performers, at the end of the day, want to beat each other.

It is clear, then, that dominant values are not unproblematically dominant. The cultural values stressed in Guttman's typology are revealing in terms of how general processes characteristic of a modern society implant themselves upon a particular cultural phenomenon. But, looking closely, that phenomenon is a complicated beast. Dominant cultural values are challenged, contested, disputed at the grass roots. Lived experience suggests that appropriation is more than a one-way process. What practitioners may have had taken away from them at a particular historical moment, their successors are often prepared to fight to reappropriate at a later stage. In answer to the earlier question 'critical of what?', the answer 'critical of dominant values' can be offered.

A scrutiny of sports cultures reveals a range of contradictions. In team sports, for instance, it is often the prima donna, the outstanding individual, who wins the contest. In athletics it is often the strongest and the biggest who are really the emasculated ones — in Paul Hoch's memorable words, we see the "production of plastic Superman with no balls" (Hoch, 1972: p. 15). The contradiction here is between fitness and physical well-being and wholeness. The realm of sports is run through with such contradictions. Individualism defies collective responsibility; spontaneity defies routinization; play defies the development of the work effort; participation can defy the urge to win. And, most revealingly of all perhaps in terms of the novels to which I turn in the following section, breakdown, collapse or self-doubt can defy the ideology of masculinity, the notion of what it is to be a man and a winner. Behind the veil of machismo in the sports world there often lurks the always vulnerable, sometimes gibbering and potentially oppositional representative of alternative values.

In Paul Gardner's words, the prominent values over-lapping between US culture and sports are "competitiveness, the frontier virtues of strength and shrewdness, the cult of bigness, attitudes towards laws, and the dislike of inaction" (Gardner, 1974: pp. 62–63). In many ways this corresponds to Guttman's typology. It is simply put less formalistically. What Gardner does emphasize, though, is the cultural context of the single country. The frontier ideology in the United States adds a further dimension to the Guttman typology. It is arguable that sport and space (the moon and so on) constitute the USA's two major frontiers in the contemporary period. Both involve races with other advanced societies; both involve some confrontation with the unknown; both are minutely planned yet to a certain extent unpredictable; both are of little material worth to most of us in our everyday life; and both involve the preparation and production of what are presented to us as genuinely extra-ordinary individuals. In many respects sport and space could well represent atavistic and futuristic variations upon the same ideological theme — a theme which can be pinpointed in its most general form as the ideology of national superiority which is experienced within the society as an ideology of masculinity[12].

The ideology of masculinity combines gut individualism with a brand of corporate loyalty. It stresses achievement, toughness, confidence, single-mindedness and winning. Ideologies are, essentially, sets of clusters of values distorted or moulded into a particular view of the world. The view of the world as a world of big, confident, aggressive winners dominates both USA culture generally and its particular sports forms. If we add the notion of the conqueror of the frontier to Guttman's list, and the notions of masculine and sexuality to Gardner's list, we have a comprehensive account of the ideology of masculinity in the contemporary US. The three novels discussed in the following section highlight the often suppressed contradictions in these values, contradictions which make of sports such a complex ideological form. It is in identifying these dominant values, in exposing the contradictions, that sports fiction is often at its most revealing.

De-stereotyping Masculinity in Three US Sports Novels

The novels offer critiques of dominant sports ideology from three different perspectives. Don DeLillo's *End Zone* (1973) offers the perspective on the position of the individual within the team setting. Leonard Gardner's *Fat City* (1972) deals with the individual sport, as opposed to the team sport. And Frederick Exley's *A Fan's Notes* (1970) comprises the 'fictional memoir' of a fan.

In *End Zone* the narrator, Gary Harkness, is a star player for the football squad of Logos College in West Texas. Gary, a "piece of string that does not wish to be knotted" (p. 16) was a challenge to his father and his teachers. His father, follower of "the simplest most pioneer of rhythms — the eternal work cycle" (p. 17) had played some college football but had great ambitions for Gary. Gary moves from one university to another, through Syracuse, Pennsylvania, Miami and Michigan, playing outstanding football at each one until withdrawing into a complex inner-life bordering on the paranoically insane. He arrives at Logos College as one of a collection of other institution's rejects, led by the coaching reject Emmett Creed. Creed, driven out of big-time coaching after assaulting one of his players, builds his team up by recruiting players who have failed to settle in elsewhere.

This includes Taft Robinson, the first black student to be enrolled at the College. At the end of the novel these two star players are no longer playing football. Taft is constructing a kind of private metaphysical universe in his own room. Gary is well on the way to the infirmary and a life-support system. Coach Creed is crippled in a wheelchair. Tom Cook Clarke, an assistant coach kills himself and the Principal of the College, Mrs. Tom, is dead after a plane crash. The novel is peopled with a memorable supporting cast. These include Zapalac the eco-biologist lecturer; Major Staley, teacher of military studies; and Myna, girlfriend of Gary. The language of football predominates and is embodied in Coach Creed's simplistic view of things, and in the work of his assistants. Their 'ruthlessness of mind' and 'fantastic single-mindedness' (p. 49) are seen as characteristics of modern figures such as the systems planner and the management consultant. The coach is the industrial expert, with a clarity of mission as to what is needed in order to produce the required goods.

Several characters — above all Taft and Gary — reveal a complexity of make up that disputes the validity of any simplistic masculine code. Gary's dreams of wars, destruction and suffering and Taft's obsession with atrocities of all kinds, reveal a metaphysically-derived manic side to the sportsman. The game has represented an "illusion that order is possible" (p. 112), and the whole of the second part of the novel (pp. 111-142) comprises a detailed and ordered account of Logos' climactic defeat at the hands of Centrex. But the human relations both in and around the actual activity of the game are much less prone to such order.

Coach Creed himself had managed to recruit the star black player Taft Robinson not by stressing how much he appreciated his athletic prowess, but by offering "nothing but work and pain" (pp. 236-7). The coach's stress on pain and sacrifice was what drew these players in, an offer to a group of uncontrollables that there might be one further chance of redemption.

There are no stereotypically pure strong young athletes in *End Zone*. Many of the characters cannot live without football, yet know that there is more to life than just football. This is their dilemma. The novel is

257

peopled with thoroughly atypical sports people, with individuals who talk to each other more in the style of grass-roots philosophers than hulking jocks. Toughness, strength, competitiveness are at the heart of the novel — but they are in considerable danger of being disputed, or channelled into non-sporting spheres, by individuals for whom the conventional masculine values do not offer enough. The marginality, and sometimes madness, of *End Zone's* main characters constitutes a warning as to what complex dilemmas may lie behind the stereotypical facade.

Leonard Gardner's *Fat City*, set in the late 1950s, reveals the underbelly of the male world of boxing. Ruben Luna runs the Lido Gym in Stockton, Northern California. He is a no-hoper full of hope, an ex-fighter to whom life begins in the gym. At home he is impatient with the "nonsensical monologues of his children" (p. 17) and he passes his days driving a forklift truck in the port. As a trainer Ruben has a will "like a pure and unwavering light that burned even in his sleep. It was more a fatalistic optimism than determination, and though he was not immune to anxiety over his boxers, he felt he was immune to despair" (p. 46). Ruben knows that he can last, but knows too that his fighters are 'less dependable'.

Fat City chronicles the swaying fortunes of two of the gym's characters — young eighteen year old boxer Ernie Munger, and washed-out old timer Billy Tully. Billy has discovered the young Ernie in the local YMCA, and it is in response to his advice that Ernie has joined Ruben's group of amateurs and small-time pros. At this time Billy is working as a fry cook in a Main Street lunch-room, a long way removed from his peak when he was winning fights, and when he also won the affections of his wife Lynn. But six fights with nationally rated opponents showed Billy his limitations, and these were further emphasized by a knockout, after a six month break, by an unrated opponent. At 29, then, Billy has hit the bottle, has lost his wife and various jobs in factories, and finds consolation in lonely hotel rooms and seedy bars.

Ernie Munger chases success and views his baptism in the ring as the moment when he joins "the company of men" (p. 16). Gym talk and dressing-room talk about sex is far removed from his own experience with his girlfriend Faye, to whom he feels obliged to express a total love in order to get her to engage in full sex. Faye — the fairy, the elusive spirit — thus ties down Ernie and an enforced marriage due to her pregnancy casts its inhibiting spell over Ernie's fighting ambitions.

Ernie's dilemma as an eighteen year old amplifies Billy's twenty-nine year old condition. This circuit of small-time boxers is a grey world of small crowds, dingy gyms, tiring journeys and failed dreams. When they are both desperate for money and temporarily disillusioned with the game, Billy and Ernie meet, both working in a group of casual labourers:

> In the midst of a phantasmagoria of worn-out, mangled faces, scarred cheeks and necks, twisted, pocked, crushed and bloated noses, missing teeth, brown snags, empty gums, stubble beards, pitcher lips, flop ears, sores, scabs, dribbled tobacco juice, stooped shoulders, split brows, weary desperate stupefied eyes under the light of Center Street, Tully saw a familiar man with a broken nose. (p. 81)

Ernie and Billy work together, tree-beating and nut-sacking. They decide to get back in training. Billy has been eking out a living picking anything, onions, nuts, tomatoes — and the ring offers an obvious pull to him, an escape from the inevitability of his life "being swept in among those countless lives lost hour by captive hour scratching at the miserable earth" (p. 55), an outlet from the drudgery of "all the hated work he had ever done" (p. 54).

Ernie's 'career' has followed the usual pattern of the small-time fighter. Stopped with a broken nose in his first fight, he had then gone on to win three fights, but in his next one he is slugged by a strong fighter, reminding Ruben of the death of one of his fighters in gym training. Faye has spirited Ernie away from the world of the pseudo-macho, where the seventeen year old fighter Wes, after four bottles of soda in a Mexican cafe in Salinas, says of the married waitress: "'Shit. I wish I could get her out in the car … I'd fuck her to death'" (p. 36).

Both Ernie and Billy win the last fights featured in the novel. Billy beats the Mexican survivor of close on a hundred bouts, Arcadio

Lucero, a man who lives comfortably well away from his origins as the shoeshine-boy son of a Zapotec Indian, a man who has learnt when to stay down in order to protect his body, his livelihood (p. 95). Ernie crosses the Nevada desert alone, unseconded, for a 50 dollar purse in Salt Lake City. The novel ends with Billy and Ernie as winners in the ring. Ernie even feels that he is "on his way" (p. 126). But if Ernie symbolizes hope, this is always haunted by the presence of Billy, for whom life offers little beyond a sense of loss, pain and minor restoration. After his victory Billy disappears, unable to work out whether he wants the woman Oma or not. Whatever optimism is conveyed through Ernie's hopes is diluted by the feeling that Ernie will follow in Billy's footsteps to nowhere. Billy's life in the bars and hotels of Stockton is the warning that Ernie still ignores. Two figures have lasted — the Filipino asparagus cutter Esteban Escobar, a fighting contemporary of Billy's, (p. 78) as well as Arcadio Lucero — but their survivalism simply highlights the main sense that pervades the novel, the feeling of desperate hope combined with painful loss.

In its evocation of the painful experience of the sportsman dreamer, Gardner's novel successfully employs Hemingway-like 'iceberg' writing. A taut style conveys the grand themes of deprivation, loss and failure. Stockton is no city of fat and plenty for the central characters in the novel, and their experience emphasizes how sporting lives can be just as much a matter of rags to rags as rags to riches, and how inside that tough macho boxer there is often the uncertain individual plagued by self-doubt and trammelled with all the worries of the outcome of that game lying beyond the ring itself — the game of human relationships and social relations. Stockton is overlooked, from the top of one of its twelve-storey sky-scrapers, by a sign publicizing 'California Western States Life Protection' (p. 57), an ironic comment upon the developing Ernie-Faye relationship and, more generally, upon the experience of the novel's main characters — the losers, the unprotected and the weak ones in this sport of the tough.

Spectators as well as participants can become obsessed with and reliant upon sports. In *A Fan's Notes* the eponymous protagonist finds that sport — watching the New York Giants and, especially his old University of California contemporary Frank Gifford — becomes his only reality, his only means of giving some sort of order to the chaos that is life and, more particularly, the madness that is the contemporary US.

A Fan's Notes reconstructs the route away from the realization of the American dream experienced by Ex, who had left University in the early 1950s to tackle New York and to make a successful career out of writing. Fifteen years later Ex suffers what he thinks is a heart attack whilst watching the Giants on television in his regular Sunday afternoon haunt. This is not a heart attack, though, it is simply a black-out as a result of far too regular and intensive drinking. Ex's experience over the fifteen years — easy jobs, successful philandering, breakdown leading to three periods of hospitalization in mental asylums, marriage, drink, bumming, and, at the last, in an intensively self-reflexive confessional form, writing — is contrasted with the experience of his father, Earl Exley, and his college contemporary Frank Gifford.

Earl Exley had been a legendary footballer, a local sporting hero, so much so that his relationship with his son suffered from his achievement. Simulating pain by "parodying how a lesser man might react to iodine" (p. 37) Earl's playing up to the crowd had "[driven] a wedge" into Ex's "narrow circle of love" (p. 37) early on in his life. Earl had died of cancer at the age of forty, passing on to his son "this need to have my name whispered in reverential tones" (p. 39).

There are two truths with which Ex has come to terms: the fact that he is destined to watch not do, to be a fan and not a performer (p. 326); and the recognition that we are all dying (p. 320). His alter ego, Frank Gifford, becomes a star for the Giants and represents all that Ex has not managed to achieve (p. 71), yet at the end represents the same truths. He slows down, loses his reflexes, retires and makes a comeback. In his celebrity's role he still comes to represent the weaknesses of the mass of anonymous men.

Ex starts down the road to individual madness when he fails to raise an erection for Bunny Sue, his dream girl, his Miss America. This is the point at which he stands back from prevalent US values such as respectability, competitiveness, success. After this unconsum-mated relationship, Ex retires to his mother's davenport for six months, the beginning of years of insanity in which truths are searched for and the only source of human communication is football and the Giants.

Ex sees in his every gesture a statement of defiance:

> In a land where movement is virtue, where the echo of heels
> clacking rapidly on pavement is inordinately blessed, it is a
> grand, defiant and edifying gesture to lie down for six months.
> (p. 173)

He talks to the television, and carries out a critique of US social values
in response to the offerings of the medium. The American housewife
is a 'witch without motive', their husbands — afraid to raise their voices
— are no more than soft-spoken ball-less men (p. 186). The davenport
becomes Ex's form of transport away from the "bright-eyed, clean-
jawed men in galactic journeys" towards "a new and different man"
(p. 174). From having, in the words of a prospective employer whom
he spurns, "a hard-on for the world" (p. 52), Ex goes on to fail to have
anything for Bunny Sue, and eventually comes to recognize his own
truths. Near the end, when he is teaching, he condemns the schools
which refuse to teach that "even in America *failure is part of life*" (p. 14).

For Ex football has represented life and success. Its simplicity
allows that someone always succeeds. At the end, it represents also the
truth of failure and mortality. Early on in this confessional text, this
personal outpouring from the analyst's couch, Ex tells us what the
attraction of football is; and then confirms this later in a part of the
narrative:

> Why did football bring me so to life? I can't say precisely. Part
> of it was my feeling that football was an island of directness in
> a world of circumspection. In football a man was asked to do
> a difficult and brutal job and he either did it or got out. There
> was nothing rhetorical or vague about it; I chose to believe that
> it was not unlike the jobs which all men, in some sunnier past,
> had been called upon to do. It smacked of something old,
> something traditional, something unclouded by legerdemain
> and subterfuge. It had that kind of power over me, drawing me
> back with the force of something known, scarcely remembered,
> elusive as integrity — perhaps it was no more than the force of

a forgotten childhood. Whatever it was, I gave myself up to the Giants utterly. The recompense I gained was the feeling of being alive. (p. 15).

… sometimes at these moments, when the play on the field seemed astonishingly perfect, we just fell quiet. That was the most memorable picture of all. We were Wops and Polacks and Irishmen out of Flatbush, along with one mad dreamer out of the cold, cow country up yonder, and though we may not have had the background, or the education, to weep at Prince Hamlet's death, we had all tried enough times to pass and kick a ball, we had on our separate rock-strewn sandlots taken enough lumps and bruises, to know that we were viewing something truly fine, something that only comes with years of toil, something very like art. (p. 126).

Football offers community, collective identity: a form of cultural expression that can be anchored in the relation between the performer and the watching group. To Ex and his fellow fans sport is no peripheral activity; it is that which, more than anything else, invests their lives with meaning. Football and the experience of being a fan offer Ex a vision of community that is nowhere else available. But it is a fickle community, and the realization of such visions is never much more than a fleeting experience. Sport offers Ex a temporary haven away from the madness of the modern world, but this collectively lived refuge is never much more than transitory.

Ex is not unreservedly romantic about the game. The former coach Steve Owen, who dies in relative obscurity, is an important influence, and Ex is sure that it is to Owen that he owes his own recognition of the limitations of success. The second section of the novel is built around the figure of Owen: "It was Owen who over the years kept bringing me back to life's hard fact of famelessness" (p. 71).

Ex is drawn to outsiders and marginal men throughout his adult life. His university friends were outcasts like himself (p. 41). In his spells in the Avalon Valley mental asylum he is with the formally branded outsiders, of whom Paddy the Duke is his teacher, his example of how

263

to struggle towards some sort of truth (pp. 97-111) — thus, Ex recognizes the poet in the illiterate Irishman. Ex's literary influences are Hawthorne, the explorer of the pervasiveness of evil, and Edmund Wilson, leftover critical spirit of the 1920s. And his greatest friend is the Counsellor, a lawyer who eventually finds himself debarred and thus wholly on the outside of respectable America. An absurdist episode involving the weird Mr. Blue, salesman of aluminium siding, his main ambition to discover the joys of cunnilingus (p. 236-265) shows the fine line between being the acceptable insider and the unacceptable outsider. Mr. Blue dies, his "carotid artery … severed by flak from a jumbo-sized can of mentholated shave cream" (p. 273). For Ex, Mr. Blue stands for the absurdity that is modern civilization:

> Mr Blue tried to undo empyrean mysteries with Seedy and his red carpet, with his elevated alligator shoes, with the ardent push-ups he seemed so sure would make him outlast time's ravages, with his touching search for some golden pussy that would yield to his lips the elixir of eternal life. And like Joyce's Leopold Bloom, like Quixote, Mr. Blue had become the perennial mock-epic hero of this country, the salesman, the boomer who believed that at the end of his American sojourn of demeaning doorbell-ringing, of faking and fawning, he would come to the Ultimate Sale, conquer, and soar. (p. 273)

In football, the Ultimate Sale is accessible — the unprecedented play, the inimitable catch. This is its function in *A Fan's Notes* — to illustrate the scale of a man's achievements and, at the end, his limitations. It is in both reflecting and rendering open to criticism the dominant US values of rugged masculinity that football is such a revealing backcloth to Frederick Exley's account of individual madness and social insanity. Ex's rejection of dominant values is focused upon central images within the culture, and often operates through media images in particular. When reading the features on scantily-clad girls in newspaper magazines, Ex feels that he could 'truncheon them to death'; he rejects them as part of America's grotesque disposable plenty (p. 22). He also condemns an America which is 'drunk on physical comeliness', dedicated to the perpetuation of 'the carmine-hued, ever-sober "young-marrieds" in the Schlitz beer sign' (p. 77). Working as a publicist for an aircraft corporation, Ex can take no more when his colleague Harold is praised for producing a script/peptalk for the company's sales force, drawing upon all the conventions of the television show and the Pepsodent advertisement (p. 198). And the 'coveted America' which Ex rejects is best represented in a massive Kodak advertisement full of 'toothy smiles without warmth' (p. 222). It is the figure of the exploited sexual female that also represents, for Ex, the futility of the contemporary culture.

Literature as Portrayal and Critique: Sports Experience and Artistic Expression

A Fan's Notes is a dazzling structure of polarized moments in the life of the one individual, a complex reconstruction of a complicated but, at the last, chillingly simple life. It demonstrates the power of the sports metaphor in the life of the individual. Whether focusing on the insane fan, the burnt out individual sportsman or the maladjusted team player the three novels discussed above expose the contradictions lying behind dominant values. All of them show what failed dreams in the worlds of both sport and the more general macho culture can lead to. All of them plead for more permanent integrity in human relationships. Sports fiction such as this says — 'that is not what sport is really like. Look at what it really means. Look what sports can really be like, what they can really mean to those who are involved in them and close to them'. In life we hear most about successful sportsmen. Who buys the memoirs of a loser, or an ex-champ, apart from students of culture or sociologists of sport? Sports fiction which both draws upon the social referent — the dominant values epitomized by sport — and renders such values open to criticism, constitutes a potentially counter-ideological form. 'Masculine' values are shown to have a vulnerable side to them; a frailty lurks behind the rigid toughness of the male ideal.

Of course, the dominant ideology is able to ward off many challenges to its dominance. This goes on in quite subtle and socially significant ways. People who live out particular ideologies, for instance, will be more receptive to unreflexive versions of that ideology than to a radical and potentially subversive counter-ideology. The ideology of masculinity is, therefore, more frequently perpetuated than challenged by forms of sports fiction; the novels I have discussed in this paper are, a very distinctive kind of sports fiction. Such counter-ideological cultural phenomena are destined to find a less enthusiastic response than are unreflexive, purely reflective and pro-ideological phenomena. Ideologies of masculinity are, in social and cultural life perpetuated more often than they are challenged. Put crudely, the 'story' of the successful, tough sportsman told in a gutsy stereotypical manner will sell more copies than that of the mad fan or the crazy philosophizing player.

Sports fiction is not usually critique, then. It is more often a cultural form which perpetuates the elements within the dominant ideology. What art generally, and literature in particular, sometimes does, though, is to act as portrayal and critique simultaneously. Sports fiction is not a single, simple category or cultural form. Social consciousness, as manifested in literature, can be generated in a variety of ways which are specific in social-structural terms. It is not the cultural analyst's task to rate the form of sports fiction as superior to any other. Rather, we must pinpoint the specific characteristics of the particular cultural object and its social referent. Too many neo-Marxist cultural critics work with models of the art-society relationship which are bound up with their chosen view of what social consciousness can and should be. The genuine task of the cultural analyst must be to identify the mediating factor in any society-art relationship. In the novels discussed here there is a critical world-view aimed at a dominant ideology. In other kinds of sports fiction there will be other mediating world-views or *weltanschauungen*. The identification of the range of these can only take place on the basis of a recognition of the particularity of a piece of fiction's relationship to a given time and moment. Literature operating as both portrayal and critique can be socially illuminating on the level of critical consciousness and counter-ideology. On the very general level of a particular ideology — that of masculinity — and its relation to three selected novels, this essay has illustrated the potential richness of 'sports novels' for the cultural analyst. Other examples of sports fiction beyond those considered in this essay can represent the social consensus, even particular types of ideology such as the 'social mobility' motif. Exploration of this range of sports fictional types will reveal the dominant values of the society and the contradictions within and around those values as they are lived and, in the imagination, represented in various spheres of that society's cultural life.

Notes

1   Perhaps I frequent particularly good second-hand bookshops. Two of the three books which I consider in detail are examined in Neil David Berman (1981), a study which is premised upon a recognition of the significance of sport as a reflection of culture, but which then discusses the novels in terms of a 'play attitude' which is seen as potentially redemptive. The complexity of the imaginative literary form is thus underestimated in what is in the end a plea for the power of play. The cultural unit becomes cut off from the social unit in a normative reading such as this.

2   See Higgs and Isaacs (eds) (1977). Part One includes readings on 'Contending Myths: the athlete in literature'. The poems I referred to are on pp. 28-29, 90-91 and 66 respectively.

3   "The dominant tone of the fiction concerned with baseball is comic. The dominant tones of the European stories is tragic", p. 153 of Guttman (1978).

4   See Clifford Odets (1963: p. 117). All of Odets' plays are variants — materially rooted variants — upon this biblical call-to-arms.

5   See Tennessee Williams (1957, p. 113). And here is Happy Loman talking about his boss to brother Biff: "Sometimes I want to just rip my clothes off in the middle of the store and outbox, outrun, and outlift anybody in that store, and I have to take orders from those common petty sons-of-bitches till I can't stand it any more", in Arthur Miller (1961, p. 8).

6   The first I would want to subsume under the label of ethnography, the second under the label of analysis/interpretation, though these of course at times overlap. Novak (1976) calls experiential texts his 'hagiography', and separates them from those which 'add elements of theory'. His hagiography is a valuable guide to sources which point to the contradictions with which I am concerned.

7   See Edwards (1969); and Clarke, Critcher and Johnson (eds) (1979): the 'studies' in part two include contributions by Paul Wild on recreation in Rochdale, and Chas Critcher on football since the war.

8   See Novak (1976); and, for a social psychological interpretation of the 'inner-game' material, Ken Starkey's 'Attitudes to Running: three sources of leisure motivation', in Tomlinson (ed) (1981).

9   This is the appeal of the careless creativity of a George Best figure. The great Northern Irish footballer, on a diet of alcohol, women and sleeplessness, could torment the most fanatically prepared ordinary defender, and could defy the most carefully prepared and rational tactical plan.

10   Indeed, bureaucratization can easily lead to organizational anarchy when grown adults are treated as if they were incompetent infants. Examples of this abound in sports, and become manifest most often in the form of conflicts between the gerontocracy within a sport and its (usually more youthful) practitioners. Examples of 'play-power' in soccer are interesting in this context. In the summer of 1977, for instance, ten players of Newcastle United's most successful first division team for over a quarter of a century demanded transfers. Most of the first team squad had, earlier in the year, passed a vote of no confidence in the club's board. The club was happy to see a promising team disintegrate as long as bureaucratic control could be reasserted. See this volume, Chapter 7.

11   Thus, Sebastian Coe simply *had* to beat Steve Ovett in their second meeting in the 1980 Moscow Olympics. Not to have done so, would have given him a reputation as a great runner against the clock, but an inadequate contestant in a genuine race.

12   On the 'right stuff' characteristic of the first generation of astronauts/space pilots, see Tom Wolfe's riveting book *The Right Stuff* (1981): "Manliness, manhood, manly courage … there was something ancient, primordial, irresistible about the challenge of this stuff, no matter what a sophisticated and rational age one might think he lived in" (p. 22).

14 Ideologies of Physicality and Masculinity: Comments on *Roy of the Rovers*[1]

> Men do, of course, inherit patriarchal identities, and reproduce these identities in their own lives. The language of patriarchy thus perpetuates the oppression of women. (Tolson, 1977: p. 141)

> The embedding of masculinity in the body is very much a social process, full of tension and contradiction ... even physical masculinity is a historical, rather than a biological, fact ... constantly in process, constantly being constituted in actions and relations, constantly implicated in historical change. (Connell, 1983: p. 30)

Introduction

The theme of the social construction of femininity was prominent in social scientific periodicals of the early 1980s. Pieces noted how teenage girls inherit different social worlds to those of teenage boys, in terms of sexuality and the guarding of reputations (Lees, 1983; Lees, 1984). Analyses of television content revealed what any regular viewer was aware of — that "women are the main stars of about 14% of mid-evening programmes. Most women shown in television are under 30" (Durkin and Akhatar, 1983) and tend to be housewives or, if in paid work, secretaries or nurses. The researchers of this study also showed a clip of a Superman film to young children, and in answer to one question were told by the children that a Superwoman could never equal the hero's display of bravery, even if she could fly and was endowed with super-powers. Why not? The children confidently responded to this: "'Cos', in the words of one boy, 'mans are stronger'". So even if the powers are supernaturally derived, the woman is still seen as inferior to the man. Femininity is something inextricably interwoven with, and often defined by, a masculine view of the innate superiority of the male.

The question of femininity was also covered in terms of the different contexts in which it is experienced and reproduced. Women's experience in different settings was studied, and, depending of course on the particular characteristics of one setting or another, such research reports showed how a sensibility to gender and inequality had yet to penetrate mainstream social institutions. Listen to one young British Army wife on her husband: "He's a typical male chauvinist pig, my husband ... and proud of it. He says women are a lower form of life. If they had any brains they'd be dangerous" (Chappell, 1983). Where it is acknowledged that girls do indeed have brains, there too, it has been widely claimed, one particular version of that brain is given strong emphasis. In schools, engineering is still seen as 'not nice' or 'not normal' for girls; cooking and sewing are the 'normal' activities for them (Steinberg, 1983)[2].

Not just the issue of femininity is raised in pieces such as these. For women's experience is so often defined by men — in the family, the school, the workspace, the place of leisure — that femininity is actively reproduced, within gender relations, by masculinity itself. Young men to whom the inclination to 'fuck well and often' (or at least to claim to do so) is a sign of status, will define as non-feminine any female who is similarly inclined. A lot of work on femininity helps us see not just what women experience, but also how men perceive both women and themselves. This latter perception is rooted in a negative identity learnt by males, in childhood: an identity in which masculinity is seen to comprise 'non-femininity'; and one in which men can be seen as learning to dread women, to actually go in fear of women, and all that is seen as feminine[3]. Studies of women's experience, then, are informative sources for an understanding of masculinity critical to an understanding of the processes whereby boys learn to become men in a male-dominated society. This might reveal an interesting set of contradictions, of discrepancies between the ideology of masculinity and the actual lived experience of being male.

If ideologies of gender are to be at all adequately understood then the processes whereby gender identities are constructed and experienced must be given detailed empirical consideration. To this end, I offer in this essay an analysis of the image of masculinity on offer within a boys' football (soccer) comic in Britain in the mid-1980s. My argument is quite straightforward. I argue that in sports activities and in representations of sports activities (of which as an example I take boys' comics), contradictions inherent in an ideology of masculinity as lived in everyday life are transcended and resolved into idealized fantasies in which masculinity is conceived as an unproblematic, natural — and crucially — non-feminine state of affairs or condition.

"They're always scoring goals and it's always the same"
[Alys, aged 8, on casting aside a copy of *Roy of the Rovers*]

Parodying a classic text in the field of popular cultural analysis, this section might be subtitled 'How to Read *Roy of the Rovers*'. In their analysis of imperialist ideology in the Disney comic, Dorfman and Mattelart noted that the emphases in comic strip storytelling are often made at the expense of other possible emphases. Disney's stories are told in terms of avoidances just as much as in terms of issues which are dealt with. Thus the Disney comic strips avoid the realities of sex and children, producing parentless, sexless narratives — Disney's characters are 'eunuchs' who "live in an eternal foreplay with their impossible virgins" (Dorfman and Mattelart, 1975: p. 39). My critical analysis of masculinist ideology in a comic strip soccer magazine in contemporary Britain adopts a comparable approach, focusing on three major questions: how do particular types of ideological motifs recur within and across narratives?; how do such narrative constructions rest upon particular kinds of avoidances or absences or exclusions?; and how do these narrative constructions, often caricaturing one social category or another, relate to the everyday lives of the young people who read them?

273

I have used some copies of *Roy of the Rovers* in my teaching, and before revealing to a class that the session would involve looking at comics, I have sometimes asked them what the phrase ('Roy of the Rovers') meant to them. In one class made up of 15 or so adults, all the eight men, aged between 30 and 70, could offer a 'definition' of the term. Only one of the seven women (aged between 30 and 50), had the slightest idea what it meant. The men gave as definitions phrases like 'heroic performance', 'last-minute heroism', 'super-human achievement', 'skills which can win matches from out of the blue at the last minute'. The one woman to whom the phrase had any meaning at all was the mother of a young son, from whom she had received a sense of Roy of the Rovers as some kind of 'special football hero'. It is therefore important to recognize the fact that in Britain the phrase 'Roy of the Rovers' can generate this almost exclusively male-rooted sense of heroism in sports.

It has been suggested that the 'Roy of the Rovers' adventure or romance is a version of the giant-killing myth, in which a team of Davids humbles one of "the tournament's Goliaths" (Wren-Lewis and Clarke, 1983: p. 130). Although there is an interesting giant-killer motif in some of the stories in the comic, the 'Roy of the Rovers' romance is also the romance of the immortality of the overdog, not the momentary triumph of the underdog — in the eponymous comic strip, at least. The David/Goliath theme is just one version of the 'Roy of the Rovers' romance. Exceptional goal-scoring by anyone is referred to by players, sports commentators and fans as 'real Roy of the Rovers stuff'. The meaning of the term now resonates far beyond the comic text with which I am primarily concerned. But what it implies, generally, is the reaffirmation of a supra-ordinary male heroism — the continued triumph of the dominant, whatever respective odds or challenges have to be faced.

Roy of the Rovers started life as a weekly comic devoted to soccer adventure tales in September 1976. 'Roy' is Roy Race, a star soccer player with Melchester Rovers. He first appeared, as a comic strip hero, in the first issue of the comic *Tiger*, on September 11, 1954.

In season 1983–84 Roy was still going strong, as a player-manager, still able to score heroic one-man goals and to contribute to overall team moves and scores in an unselfish fashion. By the middle of the 1980s Roy Race had featured in the weekly life of readers for over 30 years. He had, like all popular cultural heroes in fictional forms, performed miracles of chronology as well as of sports performance. In 1983 he was still characterized by an eternal youthfulness. He was a sporting Peter Pan, never needing to grow up. His face had become a little fuller; he may have become burdened by the pressures and obligations of club management and marriage respectively, but he weathered all this well — not just to survive, but to survive as the legendary hero of a big-selling weekly.

Many things happened to Roy in this 30 year spell at the top. First of all, ironically, as he aged he played more active football. In earlier years he was as much an adventure hero off-pitch as on. Later his heroism was mostly on field. He has also been "married, separated, shot, fathered three children, fallen into a coma and starred with Sharron Davies and Suzanne Dando in a Christmas panto. It's tough at the top" (Brown, 1984: p. 5). (Sharron and Suzanne were Britain's contemporary 'sexy' superstars, from the worlds of swimming and gymnastics respectively). For 13 years Roy's team went unbeaten, but in 1967 a more realistic emphasis introduced the notion of defeat, and consequently, the element of restoration, into the Melchester narrative. In a more contemporary world Roy is given his fair share of problems: family, age, defeat. But his main protagonists were still the unsportsmanlike hard-men of the football world: hatchetmen, often from foreign lands.

The comic in its mid-80s form was made up of nine stories, a 'Roy Race Talk-In', a quiz, soccer jokes, and a team chart through which to keep tabs on your favourite real-life team. It was produced by IPC Magazines as one of a number of 'boys' adventure titles'. The comic was not categorized as a sports magazine, but an adventure comic, along with comics on war and science fiction. According to circulation figures for January-June 1983, *Roy of the Rovers* was selling 101,972 copies each week. The sports magazine *Shoot*, a feature and documentary weekly on soccer, was selling 176,753 weekly. Soccer and sports stories also featured in several other of IPC's weekly comics. Although *Roy of the Rovers* was not one of IPC's highest selling weeklies, for a one-sport

275

comic its sales were huge. IPC magazines also produced a *Roy of the Rovers* Annual, for the Christmas-present market. This ran for many years, from well before Roy himself had his own comic. But in the early 1980s the Annual abandoned its focus upon sporting activities beyond just soccer. Earlier editions of the Annual included more prose/photo features, on a variety of sports, than comic strip narratives. The 1984 and 1985 Annuals were almost totally made up of extra-long comic strip stories — a bumper edition, really, of the weekly comic. It is likely that the success of the 'magazine format' (as in *Shoot*) polarized the forms: the comic-strip publication is precisely that, making few concessions to the non-visual, or to the exploration of the 'real world' in features. All the stories are about soccer. What image of maleness and sport was being produced in this re-presentation of Britain's national game?

Three concerns are covered in this interpretation of the comic: first, recurrent motifs in the narrative; second, significant absences; and third, text/reader relations. With some reference to others among IPC's comic listings, I will look at how six recurrent motifs within the stories construct particular types of meanings. First, stories in the comic strip are both rooted in the experience of its young readership, yet simultaneously rendered timeless. The cyclical/ever-recurring nature of the sports season or calendar offers the sense that if you don't triumph this time, then there's always the next match, tournament or season. A second motif, that of mobility, emphasizes that with hard work or real determination, as well as talent, the young sportsman can 'go all the way' to the top.

A David and Goliath fantasy is present, as a third motif implying that the little bag of bones can beat, outwit and humiliate the bigger bully figure. The bully, Bert, and his cronies are humiliated by Tommy Barnes, the determined 'Skinny' and the bespectacled 'Ginger'. Magic is sometimes central to this theme. Simon Benson has an accident and, with an implant, becomes a 'Bionic Boy' (*Roy of the Rovers*, 18 August, 1984). In a comic in which Roy of the Rovers previously featured (Searcher), 'Billy's Boots' were endowed with the skilful qualities of a great player of the past. Billy Dane was to bring his magic to later editions of *Roy of the Rovers*, keeping alive the legendary prowess of the owner of the boots, 'Dead Shot Keen'.

Fourth, the theme of restoration is a fairly prominent one. As mentioned earlier, this is a regular theme embodied in the sporting 'comeback'. If Melchester lose, there's always the next game, competition, or season. More supra-normally, restoration works very much in the fashion of the classical fairy-tale motif. Mysterious individuals with hidden pasts, or para-normal influences emanating from great figures of the past, remind the young reader that his heroes are historically rooted ones. A man wanders into a football club with haunting and as yet imprecise memories 'from his past'. Here, history is magically recycled as the basis of a 'natural' order of things in the here and now — a mysterious yet almost natural inheritance.

Fifth, the motif of eternal but responsible youthfulness reminds us that we can stay young and dominant even when ageing, most particularly if we can groom an appropriate type of successor. In the early 1980s Roy Race, as player-manager of his new Walford club, is clearly the model for Rob Richards, the new young golden-haired clone of Roy himself. Here, should the 'Roy of the Rovers' image lose some credibility through time, a ready-made substitute could be slotted in smoothly to take Roy's place.

Sixth, the embodiment of the male hero is widely cast. Physicality in the male protagonist is not narrowly conceived. The muscle-bound hero, the fat misfit, the skinny waif — these are all presented as capable of male heroism or stardom. In these motifs, around one or more of which just about all the stories revolve, we see some of the ideological work which a particular 'telling of the story' can do.

Beyond the narrative motifs, my second concern in this interpretation of the comic's meaning is with how a story can be told and given a particular ideological direction by the decision to leave out particular elements, or to present them in a highly specific way. To see how this is done, it is illuminating to concentrate upon questions of work, and of women. I will spend most time on the latter.

The work involved in sustaining life as a professional sportsman is given a particular gloss. Roy and his men of Melchester are rarely depicted hard at work, despite the mobility motif. When they are, it is usually to highlight some personal drama. A training session, for instance, might be the place where a recalcitrant member of the squad

— whose refractoriness is usually based in entrenched jealousy of Roy Race's talents and skills — attempts to undermine Roy's authority. Systematic and sustained physical work, though, is not presented as the prerequisite for the glories in the public arena. This gives the top-level action — the main focus of the Roy narratives — a quality of effortlessness. New generations of readers receive the impression that success comes easily. In training sessions it is only clashes of personality that prevent the smooth flow of preparation: pain, resentment, tedium, boredom, physical exploitation — these are rarely featured. Interestingly, in popularity charts of stories in *Roy of the Rovers* (based on readers' own votes) the two least popular stories/items were (late in 1983) 'The Apprentices' and 'The Best of Roy the Rovers'. The latter (old stories of Roy in the past) may be diachronically confusing for a readership in the here and now; and in 'The Apprentices', the very centrality of work (about young professionals whose job is mainly work and whose success is never glamorous, with perhaps the sole exception of Rob Richards) threatens the glamour and romance which is at the heart of the *Roy of the Rovers* stories. The Roy of the Rovers myth works around a romance of physicality in which physical decay does not set in, and injuries are easily overcome. Physicality as labour — sport as work — is significant in its very absence.

But it is in their presentation of the place and the role of women that such comics ply most effectively their ideological trade. Usually, women are simply absent, or unobtrusive, in the background. But they are also given some central spaces, and it is in such spaces that images of female-ness are evoked in such a way as to reaffirm the desirability of being male. The background is one of servicing. Melchester's secretary is a woman, presented in part as a career woman; representing, though, concessions made, in the world of masculine sports, which work towards the retention of male hegemony. Also, players have wives and mothers, working away invisibly in the background, providing the domestic services which are an important basis from which our sports heroes launch themselves on their adventures.

When women are given roles within the centre of the narrative, two major types are featured. First there is the female ogre, the tyrannical and sometimes physically gigantic termagant with threatening powers over a potentially demasculinized client group. A strange, absurd character called Kevin Mouse ('Mighty Mouse') is constantly threatened by the Matron in the hospital in which he is a footballing medical student — a matron of enormous proportions going by the name of Mad Annie.

Second, there is the interfering battle-axe of a wife or mother, the female who for one reason or another lets slip the smooth servicing role. Roy Race himself has been threatened by this type in the shape of what is seen as the fussing interference of his wife. In both these cases the ideological effect is the same. The smooth reproduction of male success in sport is threatened by women abandoning their appropriate and 'natural' position in the social order. Mouse's livelihood and game are constantly threatened by Mad Annie's intention to replace him and her strategy to keep him off the playing field. Roy's game is suffering because of his 'unreasonable' wife. Once away from Mad Annie, Mouse's squeak turns into the lion's roar. Once Mrs. Race is no longer a nagging presence in Roy Race's life, Roy starts finding the net again.

My third and final major concern in looking at *Roy of the Rovers* is with how the construction within the text might relate to the everyday lives of young people. Comic strip heroes are not confined within the pages of the comic itself. They are picked up, like the stars of soap operas, and used in everyday life and other genres. In one of D. C. Thomson and Co.'s adventure comics *Victor and Buddy* there appeared a long established footballing hero called Leslie Thomson, striker with Darbury Rangers. Despite the physical disability of a limp, Leslie ('Limp-Along Leslie', No.1180, Oct.1, 1983) can round up stray rams on the remote farming land, and a scene or two later burst through the country's top soccer defences. Terry Venables, in his soccer novel *They Used to Play on Grass* (co-written with Gordon Williams, Hodder and Stoughton, 1971) calls a slow-moving, physically disabled club hireling 'Limp-Along Leslie'. When I interviewed Colin Welland, screenwriter of the movie *Chariots of Fire*, about sporting heroes, one of his comments referred to another couple of long established athletic heroes, Alf Tupper and The Great Wilson. Tupper, the Tough of the Track, still featuring in *Victor and Buddy* in the wake of the Marathon craze (see 'The Tough on the Marathon Trail', *Victor*, No. 1230, Sept. 15, 1984),

279

usually triumphed upon the basis of a diet of fish and chips, a totally unstructured training schedule, and a very deep-rooted aversion to the 'toffs' in established sport. The Great Wilson was a mysterious reincarnation of a past athletic champion, a pure spirit undiluted by the crises of the contemporary world. Welland's heroes — two comic strip characters embodying the mythical timelessness of the male romance of physicality.

Textual constructions, then, live on in the consciousness of the readers. They fuel and refuel conceptions of masculinity, of male heroism, operating inter-textually and across the boundaries of textual representation and lived experiences. They become in a real sense themselves lived. Welland and I smiled indulgently in a shared male conspiracy of romance at the mention of such names. Welland said simply, after we had spent some time talking about Harold Abrahams (one of the athletic heroes of *Chariots of Fire*): "The Tough of the Track and the Great Wilson — they were our heroes".

Conclusion

Some very simple points must be made here. Boys constituted 88% of the readership of *Roy of the Rovers* in 1982, and many continued to read the comic through their mid-adolescent years. IPC's figures to 1982 showed this unambiguously: 57% of the readership was within the age band 11–14, but 9% were 7–8 and 18% were aged 9–10; 15–16 year olds made up 6%, and 10% of the readership was made up of 17–19 year olds. There was clearly a drop-out rate, but comics circulated among brothers, sisters, school-friends. And one in six of these male readers was of or beyond school-leaving age. It is doubtful that any comic for girls would have followed this pattern. *Bunty* was a long established comic for pre-pubescent girls. *Jackie* targeted mid-adolescent girls (Dunne, 1982; McRobbie, 1977). Work on these two comics has shown how an assertive physicality in pre-pubescence is superseded by an emphasis on girls' main work — the construction of themselves as objects of potential consumption by men. A brand new comic in the British market in early 1985 (*Nikki*) combined elements of both *Bunty* and *Jackie* and demonstrated that the ideology of adolescent femininity could be successfully marketed for even younger markets. The girls' comic market looks as if it is cunningly plotted by a team of developmental psychologists, subtly sensitive to the crises of femininity and sexuality of the adolescent female. *Roy of the Rovers*, read fervently by boys from 7–19, embodied no such dilemma of gender identity. Being male, surviving with an unquestioned maleness, achieving male heroism — the message was that this was normal enough for the boy-soon-to-become-man.

This pattern of readership was exclusive to *Roy of the Rovers*. IPC's rival 'Boys adventure' comic, *Victor*, had a readership which faded at 13/14, and which, astonishingly, rose again at 17/19. It is almost as if boys of 13/16 think that they have grown up or become adult, before recognizing that the essence of masculinity is not growing up at all. The magazine/feature soccer publication *Shoot* lost its readership dramatically at 17/19. Pseudo-realism is displaced again by fantasy, by idealized fictional heroes. Similarly, the specialist science-fiction comic 2000 AD was taken up again by 17–19 year olds, after a mid-adolescent fall in readership. As I have said elsewhere, sport and space offer similar sets of possibilities within the masculinist landscape (see this volume, Chapter 13). Not growing up, the constant sense of masculinity as adventure and glory — these are the key elements in the representation of sport and adventure in boys' comics.

Roy of the Rovers tells boys and youths that life is a game and that male dominance is sometimes problematic but can be taken-for-granted. Young people's own dilemmas of self-identity, sexuality and so on, might carry a different message. But such 'experienced' differences do not necessarily overcome the myth. They might in fact be smoothed over by the constantly reiterated potency of the myth itself.

The Roy Race narrative, over time, has offered the post-war generation of British male soccer fans a remarkable romance. What is clear enough, though, is that the relation between representation in the text and aspects of the everyday life of young males is a symbiotic one. The *Roy of the Rovers* text offered a weekly recipe of dramatic heroic achievement (not infrequently against the odds); thus idealizing as normal what only rarely happens in everyday life itself[4].

Notes

1 A version of this paper was originally presented to an International Interdisciplinary Symposium on 'Gender, Leisure and Cultural Production' at Queen's University, Kingston, Ontario, Canada (30 September—2 October, 1983). I would like to thank Rick Gruneau for encouraging me to produce this piece in written form. An extended analysis of the Roy of the Rovers trope is in A. Tomlinson and C. Young, 1999).

2 There is, of course a wide literature on how schooling reproduces gender identities. For a summary of this literature as it stood in the early 1980s see Madelaine MacDonald (1981).

3 I have summarized, here, the main points in the early work of Ruth Hartley and the feminist work of Nancy Chodorow, as presented in Madelaine MacDonald (1981), pp. 9-16.

4 The romance faded in 1993 when falling sales halted production. But a special monthly was launched a few months later after much protest from *Roy of the Rovers* enthusiasts. Many of the protesters were adult males regretting the loss of one of their post-War myths. Unfortunately, after 19 issues this venture attracted too few subscribers, and in March 1995 *Roy of the Rovers* Monthly (Fleetway Editions) was closed down.

Bibliography

Adair, G. (1986) 'The light ages', *Myths and Memories*. London: Flamingo.

Allied Dunbar (1991) 'Activity matters — the facts', in *Allied Dunbar National Fitness Survey — a summary of major findings and messages from the Allied Dunbar National Fitness Survey*. London: Allied Dunbar / Health Education Authority / Sports Council.

Alt, J. (1983) 'Sport and cultural reification: from ritual to mass consumption', *Theory, Culture and Society — Explorations in Critical Social Science*, Vol. 1, No. 2, 1983: pp. 93–107.

Alther, L. (1977) *Kinflicks*. Harmondsworth: Penguin.

Anderson, B. (1983) *Imagined communities — reflections on the origin and spread of nationalism*. London: Verso.

Armstrong, R. (1977) 'The less appealing side of Nulty', *The Guardian*, 19 October: p. 20.

Atkin, R. (1982) 'Heavenly twins going solo', *The Observer* (Sport and Leisure), 28 November: p. 43.

Bailey, P. (1978) *Leisure and class in Victorian England — rational recreation and the contest for control 1830–1885*. London: Routledge and Kegan Paul.

Bakhtin, M. (1998) 'Carnival and the carnivalesque', in J. Storey (ed) *Culture theory and popular culture: a reader* (2nd edition). London: Prentice Hall.

Ball, P. (1977) 'Gowling: the reluctant rebel with a cause', *The Times*, 24 November: p. 10.

Banks-Smith, N. (1984) 'Where eagles dare', *The Guardian*, 30 July: p. 9.

Barclay, P. (1977a) 'McGarry puts the boot in', *The Guardian*, 28 July: p. 18.

—— (1977b) 'Board see players', *The Guardian*, 29 July: p. 18.

—— (1980) 'Wallace's law of the jungle', *The Guardian*, 13 February: p. 25.

Barker, M. (1991) 'Review of John B. Thompson *Ideology and modern culture*', *Sociology*, Vol. 25, No. 4: pp. 721–723.

Barnes, D. (1982) *World Cup, Spain 1982 — the game of the century*, London: Sidgwick and Jackson.

Barnett, S. (1990) *Games and sets: the changing face of sport on television*. London: British Film Institute Publishing.

Bayley, S. (1986) *Sex, drink and fast cars — the creation and consumption of images*. London: Faber and Faber.

BBC South (1982) *The Ian Wooldridge Interview: Laurie McMenemy*, 25 June.

BBC Television (1978) *Maestro — reminiscences of a master sportsman (Tom Finney talks to Desmond Lyman)*.

Berger, P. (1966) *Invitation to sociology — a humanistic perspective*. Harmondsworth: Penguin.

Berger, P. L. and Luckmann, T. (1971) *The social construction of reality — a treatise in the sociology of knowledge*. Harmondsworth: Penguin.

Berman, N. D. (1981) *Playful fictions and fictional players*. USA: Kenniket Press.

Bishop, J. and Hoggett, P. (1986) *Organizing around enthusiasms — patterns of mutual aid in leisure*. London: Comedia Publishing Group.

Bonnet, R. (1992) 'The missed opportunity': *Special Assignment*, BBC Radio 4, 6 November.

Bourne, R. (1977) *The radical will — selected writings 1911—1918* (preface by Christopher Lasch; selection and introduction by Olaf Hansen). New York: Urizen Books.

Brady, L. (1980) *So far, so good — a decade in football*. London: Stanley Paul.

Brooks, R. (1992) 'BSkyB targets Wimbledon', *The Observer*, 24 May: p. 1.

Brown, M. (1984) 'Wallop! Goal! Roy's still over the moon at 30', *The Sunday Times*, 9 September: p. 5.

Bull, D. and Wilding, P. (eds) (1983) *Thatcherism and the poor*. London: Child Policy Action Group.

Bull, S., and Tomlinson, A. (1987) Analysis of questionnaire returns for CCPR Committee of Enquiry into Amateurism in Sport, July/August (unpublished). London: Central Council for Physical Recreation.

Burawoy, M. (1979) *Manufacturing consent: changes in the labour process under monopoly capitalism.* Chicago: University of Chicago Press.

Burn, G. (1986) *Pocket money — bad boys, business trends and boom-time snooker.* London: Heinemann.

Carrington, B. (1998) 'Sport, masculinity and black cultural resistance', *Journal of Sport and Social Issues,* Vol. 22, No. 3: pp. 275–298.

Central Statistical Office (1985) *Social Trends 15.* London: Her Majesty's Stationery Office.

—— (1986) *Social Trends 16,* London: Her Majesty's Stationery Office.

Chappell, H. (1983) 'Married to the Army', *New Society,* Vol. 66, No. 1098: pp. 354–357.

Clarke, C., Critcher, J. and Johnson, R. (eds) (1979) *Working class culture — studies in history and theory.* London: Hutchinson.

Clarke, J. (1991) *New times and old enemies — essays on cultural studies and America.* London: Harper Collins Academic.

Clarke, J. and Critcher, C. (1984) *The devil makes work — leisure in capitalist Britain.* London: Macmillan.

Cohen, P. and Robins, K. (1978) *Knuckle sandwich: growing up in the working-class city.* Harmondsworth: Penguin.

Conn, D. (1997) *The football business: fair game in the 1990s?.* Edinburgh: Mainstream Publishing Projects.

Connell, R. W. (1983) 'Men's bodies', in R. W. Connell, *Which way is up? Essays on sex, class and culture.* London: Allen and Unwin.

Corrigan, P. (1979) *Schooling the Smash Street kids.* London: Macmillan.

Critcher, C. (1979) 'Football since the war', in J. Clarke, C. Critcher and R. Johnson (eds), *Working-class culture: studies in history and theory.* London: Hutchinson.

—— (1992) 'Is there anything on the box? — leisure studies and media studies', *Leisure Studies,* Vol. 11, No. 2: pp. 97–122.

Davies, H. (1972) *The glory game.* London: Weidenfeld and Nicholson.

Deem, R. (1986) *All work and no play?: a study of women and leisure.* Milton Keynes: Open University Press.

DeLillo, D. (1970) *End zone.* London: Andre Deutsch.

Dickstein, M. (1977) *Gates of Eden — American culture in the sixties.* New York: Basic Books.

Dorfman, A. and A. Mattelart (1975) *How to read Donald Duck: imperialist ideology in the Disney Comics.* New York: International General.

Doyle, R. (1993) 'Republic is a beautiful word — Republic of Ireland 1990', in N. Hornby (ed) *My favourite year. A collection of new football writing.* London: H. F. & G. Witherby.

Dunne, M. (1982) 'An introduction to some of the images of sport in girls' comics and magazines', in M. Green and C. Jenkins (eds) *Sporting fictions.* Birmingham: Centre for Contemporary Cultural Studies/ Department of Physical Education, University of Birmingham, England (September).

Dunphy, E. (1977) *Only a game? The diary of a professional footballer.* Edited, and with a postscript, by Peter Ball; with a preface by Brian Glanville. Harmondsworth: Penguin Books.

—— (1991) *A strange kind of glory — Sir Matt Busby and Manchester United.* London: Heinemann.

Durkin, K. and P. Akhatar (1983) 'Television, sex-roles and children', *New Society*, Vol. 64, No. 1064: pp. 10–11.

Easthope, G. (1974) *A history of social research methods.* London: Longman.

Eastman, S. T. and Land, A. M. (1997) 'The best of both worlds: sports fans find good seats at the bar', *Journal of Sport and Social Issues*, Vol. 21, No. 2: pp. 156–178.

Edwards, H. (1969) *The revolt of the black athlete.* New York: Free Press.

Edwards, R. (1979) *Contested terrain — the transformation of the workplace in the twentieth century.* London: Heinemann.

Elias, N. (1978) *What is sociology?* London: Hutchinson.

Elias, N. and Dunning, E. (1986) *Quest for excitement — sport and leisure in the civilising process.* Oxford: Basil Blackwell.

Evans, J. (1986) *Physical education, sport and schooling — studies in the sociology of physical education.* London: The Falmer Press.

Exley, F. (1970) *A fan's notes — a fictional memoir.* Harmondsworth: Penguin.

Filler, L. (1943) *Randolph Bourne.* Washington: American Council on Public Affairs.

Fishwick, N. (1989) *English football and society 1910–1950.* Manchester: Manchester University Press.

Fleming, S. (1995) *'Home and away': sport and South Asian youth.* Aldershot: Avebury.

Fynn, A. and Guest, L. (1991) *Heroes and villains — the inside story of the 1990–91 season of Arsenal and Tottenham Hotspur.* Harmondsworth: Penguin.

Galbraith, J. K. (1962) *The affluent society.* Harmondsworth: Penguin Books in association with Hamish Hamilton.

Gardner, L. (1972) *Fat City.* London: Panther.

Gardner, P. (1974) *Nice guys finish last — sport and American life.* London: Allen Lane.

Gent, P. (1973) *North Dallas Forty.* New York: Signet.

Giddens, A. (1979) *The constitution of society.* London: Macmillan.

—— (1982) *Sociology: a brief but critical introduction.* New York: Harcourt Brace Jovanovich.

—— (1989) *Sociology.* Cambridge: Polity Press.

Glanville, B. (1980) *The history of the World Cup.* London: Faber and Faber.

Glassford, R. and Redmond, G. (1979) 'Physical education and sport in modern times', in E. F. Zeigler, *History of physical education and sport.* Englewood Cliffs: Prentice Hall.

Glyptis, S. (1983) 'Business as usual? Leisure provision for the unemployed', *Leisure Studies*, Vol. 2, No. 3: pp. 287–300.

Glyptis, S. and Riddington, A. C. (nd) 'Sport for the unemployed: a review of local authority projects', *Sports Council Research Working Paper* 21. London: Sports Council.

Golby, J. M. and Purdue, A. W. (1984) *The civilisation of the crowd — popular culture in England 1750–1900.* London: Batsford.

Goudsblom, J. (1977) *Sociology in the balance: a critical essay.* Oxford: Basil Blackwell.

287

Gowling, A. (1977) *Football inside out*. London: Souvenir Press.

Gramsci, A. (1971) *Selections from the prison notebooks*. London: Lawrence and Wishart.

Granada Television (1981) *City!* Manchester: Granada Television.

Greaves, J. (1979) *This one's on me*. London: Arthur Barker.

Green, G. (1960) 'The Football Association', in A. H. Fabian and G. Green (eds), *Association Football, Volume One*. London: The Caxton Publishing Company Limited.

—— (1974) *Soccer in the 50s*. London: Ian Allan Ltd.

Gruneau, R. (1976) 'Sport as an area of sociological study: an introduction to major themes and perspectives', in R. Gruneau and J. G. Albinson (eds), *Canadian sport: sociological perspectives*. Ontario: Addison Wesley.

—— (1983) *Class, sport and social development*. Amherst: University of Massachusetts Press.

—— (1988) 'Modernisation and hegemony: two views on sport and social development', in J. Harvey and H. Cantelon (eds), *Not just a game — essays in Canadian sport sociology*. Ottawa: University of Ottawa Press.

Guttman, A. (1978) *From ritual to record: the nature of modern sports*. New York: Columbia University Press.

Haines, J. (1988) *Maxwell*. London: Macdonald.

Hall, M. A. (1996) *Feminism and sporting bodies — essays on theory and practice*. Champaign, Illinois: Human Kinetics.

Hall, S. (1980a) 'Cultural studies: two paradigms', *Media, Culture and Society*, Vol. 2, No. 1: pp. 57–72.

—— (1980b) 'Cultural studies and the centre: some problematics and problems', in S. Hall, D. Hobson, A. Lowe and P. Willis (eds), *Culture, media, language — working papers in cultural studies 1972–79*. London: Hutchinson.

Hargreaves, Jennifer (1994) *Sporting females — critical issues in the history and sociology of women's sports*. London: Routledge.

288

Hargreaves, John (1982) 'Sport, culture and ideology', in Jennifer Hargreaves (ed), *Sport, culture and ideology*. London: Routledge and Kegan Paul.

—— (1986) *Sport, power and culture — a social and historical analysis of popular sports in Britain*. Cambridge: Polity Press.

Hargreaves, John and Tomlinson, A. (1992) 'Being there — cultural theory and the sociological study of sport', *Sociology of Sport Journal*, Vol. 9: No. 2: pp. 207–219.

Harris, D. (1992) *From class struggle to the politics of pleasure — the effects of Gramscianism on cultural studies*. London and New York: Routledge.

Hart, S. and McInnes, H. (1992) 'The consultation document *Sport in the 90s — new horizons*', in C. Brackenridge (ed) *Body Matters: leisure images and lifestyles (LSA Publication No. 47)*. *Eastbourne*: Leisure Studies Association.

Haylett, T. (1992) 'Premier Gate blow', *The Independent*, 22 September: p. 34.

Haywood, L. (1977) 'The function of games and sport — a review of some theories', *Momentum — A Journal of Human Movement Studies*, Vol. 2, No. 2: pp. 1–11.

Heath, A. and Edmundsen, R. (1981) 'Oxbridge sociology: the development of centres of excellence', in P. Abrams, R. Deem, J. Finch and P. Rock (eds) *Practice and progress: British sociology 1950–1980*. London: Allen and Unwin.

Hebdige, D. (1979) *Subculture: the meaning of style*. London: Methuen.

Henley Centre for Forecasting (1985) *Leisure Futures* (Autumn). London: Henley Centre.

—— (1986) *Leisure Futures* (Autumn). London: Henley Centre.

—— (1992) *Leisure Futures* (Autumn). London: Henley Centre.

—— (1997) *Leisure Futures* (Spring). London: Henley Centre.

Henry, G., Thorpe, M. and Mullin, J. (1992) 'Soccer chief says no to ITV rematch', *The Guardian*, 22 May: p. 1.

Higgs, R. J. and Isaacs, N. D. (eds) (1977) *The sporting spirit — athletes in Literature and Life*. New York: Harcourt Brace Jovanovich.

Hill, C. R. (1991) *Olympic politics*. Manchester: Manchester University Press.

...ip off the big game: the exploitation of sports by the power elite. ...ndon: Anchor Books.

...art, R. (1958) *The uses of literacy — aspects of working class life with special reference to publications and entertainments*. Harmondsworth: Penguin.

——— (1970) '"The dance of the long-legged fly": on Tom Wolfe's poise' in R. Hoggart, *Speaking to each other: Volume II About literature*. London: Chatto and Windus.

Hollands, R. (1985) *Working towards the best ethnography*. Birmingham: Centre for Contemporary Cultural Studies, University of Birmingham.

Holt, R. (1981) *Sport and society in modern France*. London: Macmillan.

——— (1989) *Sport and the British: a modern history*. Oxford: Oxford University Press.

Houlihan, B. (1997) *Sport, policy and politics: a comparative analysis*. London: Routledge.

Hughes, R. (1977) 'Newcastle: a family at war', *The Sunday Times*, 8 May: pp. 30–31.

Ideology/Power, Canadian Journal of Political and Social Theory Vol. VII, Nos. 1–2, Winter/Spring 1983.

Inglis, S. (1988) *League football — and the men who made it*. London: Willow Books/Collins.

Ingram, A. G. (1979) 'Symbolic use of sport in three dramas by contemporary playwrights', *Review of Sport and Leisure*, Vol. 4. No. 2: pp. 128–140.

James, C. L. R. (1977) 'Fiction and reality' [1953], in *The future in the present*. London: Allison and Busby.

Jhally, S. (1984) 'The spectacle of accumulation: material and cultural factors in the evolution of the sport/media complex', *The Insurgent Sociologist*, Vol. 12, No. 3: pp. 41–57.

Johnson, R. (1979a) 'Histories of culture/theories of ideology: notes on an impasse', in M. Barrett, P. Corrigan, A. Kuhn and J. Wolff (eds) *Ideology and cultural production*. London: Croom Helm.

——— (1979b) 'Three problematics: elements of a theory of working-class culture', in J. Clarke, C. Critcher and R. Johnson (eds), *Working class culture — studies in history and theory*. London: Hutchinson.

——— (1986/7) 'What is cultural studies anyway?', *Social Text* 16: pp. 38–80.

Kellner, D. (1995) *Media cultures — cultural studies, identity and politics between the modern and the postmodern*. London: Routledge.

Kidd, B. (1989) 'Overview of the Olympicmedia relationship'. in R. Jackson and T. McPhail (eds) *The Olympic movement and the mass media: past, present and future issues*. Calgary: Hurford Enterprises.

King, A. (1995) The Premier League and the new consumption of football. PhD Thesis. Institute for Social Research, University of Salford.

—— (1998) *The end of the terraces: the transformation of English football*. London: Leicester University Press.

Kirk, D. (1992) *Defining physical education: the solid construction of a school subject in postwar Britain*. Lewes: Falmer Press.

Lees, S. (1983) 'How boys slag off girls', *New Society*, Vo. 66, No. 1091, 13 October: pp. 51–53.

—— (1984) 'Nice girls don't', *New Socialist*, No. 16: pp. 16–21.

Lord Killanin and Rodda, J. (eds) (1976) *The Olympic Games — 80 years of people, events and records*. London: Barrie and Jenkins.

Lovejoy, J. (1990) 'Maxwell's threat to withdraw his millions', *The Independent*, 23 November: p. 32.

Lowerson, J. and A. Howkins, A. (1981) 'Leisure in the thirties', in A. Tomlinson (ed), *Leisure and Social Control*. (LSA Publication No. 19). Eastbourne: Leisure Studies Association.

MacAloon, J. (1981) *This great symbol: Pierre de Coubertin and the origins of the modern Olympic Games*. Chicago: University of Chicago Press.

—— (1984) 'Olympic Games and the theory of spectacle in modern societies', in J. MacAloon (ed) *Rite, drama, festival, spectacle: rehearsals toward a theory of cultural performance*. Philadelphia: Institute of the Study of Human Issues.

MacDonald, M. (1981) *Class, Gender and Education, Units 10–11*, in Block 4 of Open University Course E353 ('Society, Education and the State') The Open University: pp. 15–30.

Magnusson, S. (1981) *The flying Scotsman*. London: Quartet Books.

Mailer, N. (1977) *The fight*. London: Panther Books.

291

Mandell, R. (1971) *The Nazi Olympics*. London: Souvenir Press.

—— (1976) *The first Modern Olympics*. Berkeley: University of California Press.

Mangan, J. A. (1981) *Athleticism in the Victorian and Edwardian public school — the emergence and consolidation of an educational ideology*. Cambridge: Cambridge University Press.

Manning, M. (1990) 'Tottering Hotspur', *New Statesman and Society*, Vol. 3, No. 128, 23 November: p. 10.

Mappledeck, J. (1978) *Wilf Mannion*. BBC North East.

Mason, T. (1980) *Association Football and English society 1863–1915*. Sussex: The Harvester Press.

McFee, G. and Tomlinson, A. (1999) 'Leni Riefenstahl's *Olympia*: aesthetics, ideology and the body', in J. A. Mangan (ed) *Shaping the superman*. London: Cass.

McIlvaney, H. (1979) 'Motivation', *The Observer*, 18 November: p. 30.

—— (1983) 'Marauder of North End: the magic touch', *The Observer* (*Sport and Leisure*), 17 April: p. 43.

McMenemy, L. (1979) *The diary of a season — Lawrie McMenemy's account of the 1978–1979 season as manager of Southampton Football Club*. (Introduced and edited by Brian Scovell). London: Arthur Barker.

McRobbie, A. (1977) *Jackie: an ideology of adolescent femininity*. Stencilled Occasional Paper, Women Series SP No. 53. Birmingham: Centre for Contemporary Cultural Studies, University of Birmingham, England.

—— (1982) '"*Jackie*": an ideology of adolescent femininity', in B. Waites, T. Bennett and G. Martin (eds), *Popular culture: past and present*. London: Croom Helm.

McRobbie, A. and M. Niva (eds) (1984) *Gender and generation*. London: Macmillan.

Midwinter, E. (1981) *W. G. Grace: his life and times*. London: George Allen and Unwin.

Miller, A. (1961) *Death of a salesman*. Harmondsworth: Penguin Books.

Mills, C. W. (1970) *The sociological imagination*. Harmondsworth: Penguin.

Mullin, J., Henry, G. and Thorpe, M. (1992) 'Late winner leaves ITV sick as parrots', *The Guardian*, 22 May: p. 3.

Novak, M. (1976) *The joy of sports — end zones, bases baskets, balls and the consecration of the American Spirit.* New York: Basic Books.

Odets, C. (1963) *Golden Boy; Awake and Sing!; The Big Knife.* Harmondsworth: Penguin Books.

Orwell, George (1968) 'The sporting spirit', in *Collected essays, journalism and letters of George Orwell, Volume IV, In Front of Your Nose (1945–50).* London: Secker and Warburg.

Page, C. (1973) 'The world of sport and its study', in J. T. Talamini and C. Page (eds), *Sport and society — an anthology.* Boston: Little, Brown and Company.

Parker, S. R. (1971) *The future of work and leisure.* London: Macgibbon.

Parrish, B. (1972) *They call it a game.* New York: New American Library.

Philips, D. and Tomlinson, A. (1992) 'Homeward bound: leisure, popular culture and consumer capitalism', in D. Strinati and S. Wagg (eds), *Come on down: popular media culture in post-war Britain.* London: Routledge.

Plimpton, G. (1964) *Paper lion.* New York: New American Library.

—— (1974) *One for the record — the inside story of Hank Aaron's chase for the home-run record.* New York: Harper and Row.

Prendergast, S. (1978) 'Stoolball: the pursuit of vertigo', *Women's' Studies International Quarterly*, Vol. 1: pp. 15–26.

Priestley, J. B. (1972) 'Introduction' to Thomas Wolfe *The web and the rock.* Harmondsworth: Penguin.

Rapoport, R. and Rapoport, R. (1975) *Leisure and the family life cycle* (with the collaboration of Z. Strelitz). London: Routledge and Kegan Paul.

Rigauer, B. (1992) 'The "true value" of sport is its commodity value: a critical discourse of ideology', *Innovation in Social Studies Research*, Vol. 5, Issue 4: pp. 63–69.

Rollin, J. (1982) *Jack Rollin's complete World Cup guide.* London: Sphere Books.

Roy, D. (1960) 'Banana-time: job satisfaction and informal interaction', in G. Salaman and K. Thompson (eds) *People and organisations.* London: Longman.

Bibliography

Salaman, G. and Thompson, K. (eds) (1973) *People and organisations*. London: Longman.

Saunders, E. (1976) 'Towards a Sociology of Physical Education', *Momentum — a journal of human movement studies*, Vol. 1, No. 2: pp. 46–60.

Schissel, L. (ed) (1965) *The World of Randolph Bourne — an anthology*. New York: E. P. Dutton & Co. Ltd.

Shipley, S. (1983) 'Tom Causer of Bermondsey: a boxer-hero of the 1890s', *History Workshop — a journal of socialist and feminist historians*, Issue 15: pp. 28–59.

Skeat, W. W. (1993) *The concise dictionary of English etymology*. Ware (Hertfordshire): Wordsworth Editions Ltd.

Sontag, S. (1983) 'Fascinating fascism', in *Under the sign of Saturn*. London: Writers and Readers.

Sports Council (1982) *Sport in the community — the next 10 years*. London: Sports Council.

——— (1983) *Digest of sports statistics, 1st Edition*. London: Sports Council Information Series No. 7.

——— (1992) *Sport in the nineties — new horizons: a draft for consultation*. London: The Sports Council.

Stebbins, R. A. (1979) *Amateurs — on the margin between work and leisure*. Beverley Hills: Sage Publications.

Steinberg, J. (1983) 'Nice girls do biology', *New Society*, Vol. 63, No. 1061: pp. 429–30.

Sugden, J. (1994) 'USA and the World Cup: American nativism and the rejection of the people's game', in J. Sugden and A. Tomlinson (eds) *Hosts and champions — soccer cultures, national identities and the USA World Cup*. Aldershot: Avebury / Ashgate Publishing Ltd.

Sugden, J. and Tomlinson, A. (1998) *FIFA and the Contest for World Football — who rules the peoples' game?*. Cambridge: Polity Press.

Sugden, J., Tomlinson, A. and McCartan, E. (1990) 'The making and remaking of White Lightning in Cuba: politics, sport and physical education thirty years after the revolution', *Arena Review*, Vol. 14, No. 1: pp. 101–109.

Talese, G. (1962) 'Joe Louis — The King as a middle aged man', *Esquire* Volume LVIII, No. 6 (Whole No 343), June: pp. 92–98.

——— (1981) *Fame and obscurity*. New York: Dell.

Taylor, I. (1971) 'Soccer consciousness and soccer hooliganism', in S. Cohen (ed) *Images of deviance*. Harmondsworth: Penguin.

Taylor, P. (with Mike Langday) (1980) *With Clough by Taylor*. London: Sidgwick and Jackson.

Thompson, E. P. (1993) 'Time, work-discipline and industrial capitalism', *Customs in common*. Harmondsworth: Penguin Books.

Thompson, H. S. (1972) *Fear and loathing in Las Vegas — a savage journey to the heart of the American Dream*. London: Paladin.

——— (1980) *The great shark hunt — strange tales from a strange time*. London: Picador.

——— (1981) 'The charge of the weird brigade', *Running*, March/April: pp. 23–28 and 83–84.

Thompson, J. (1990) *Ideology and modern culture — critical theory in the era of mass communication*. Cambridge: Polity Press.

Thompson, P. (1963) *The making of the English working class*. London: Gollancz.

Tischler, S. (1981) *Footballers and Businessmen: the origins of professional soccer in England*. New York: Holmes and Meier Publishers, Inc.

Toffler, A. (1981) *The third wave*. London: Pan in association with Collins.

Tolson, A. (1977) *The limits of masculinity*. London: Tavistock.

Tomlinson, A. (1983a) 'Introduction', in A. Tomlinson (ed) *Leisure and popular cultural forms* (LSA Publication No. 20). Eastbourne: Leisure Studies Association.

——— (1983b) 'Introduction', in A. Tomlinson (ed) *Leisure and social control (LSA Publication No. 19)*. Eastbourne: Leisure Studies Association.

——— (1983c) 'The sociological imagination, the new journalism and sports', in P. Donnelly and N. Theberge (eds) *The sociological imagination and sport*. Fort Worth: Texas Christian University Press.

——— (1984) 'De Coubertin and the modern Olympics', in A. Tomlinson and G. Whannel (eds) *Five-ring circus: money, power and politics at the Olympic Games*. London: Pluto Press.

———— (1986) 'Going global: The FIFA Story', in A. Tomlinson and G. Whannel (eds), *Off the ball: the Football World Cup*. London: Pluto Press.

———— (1987) 'Sport and games (in Britain) in the 1980s', BBC Domesday Project, British Broadcasting Corporation.

———— (1988) *Slide-notes to Chariots of Fire*. London: British Film Institute.

———— (1989) 'Representation, ideology and the Olympic Games: a reading of the opening and closing ceremonies of the 1984 Los Angeles Olympic Games', in R. Jackson and T. McPhail (eds) *The Olympic movement and the mass media: past, present and future issues*. Calgary: Hurford Enterprises.

———— (1990) 'Home fixtures: doing it yourself in a privatized world', in A. Tomlinson (ed), *Consumption, identity and style — marketing, meaning and the packaging of pleasure*. London: Routledge.

———— (1996) 'Olympic spectacles: opening ceremonies and some paradoxes of globalization', *Media, Culture & Society*, Vol. 18, No. 4: pp. 583–602.

Tomlinson, A. (ed) (1981) *The sociological study of sport: configurational and interpretive studies*. (LSA Publication No. 18). Eastbourne: Leisure Studies Association.

Tomlinson, A. and Young, C. (1999) 'Golden boys and golden memories: fiction, ideology and reality in *Roy of the Rovers* and the death of the hero', in D. Jones and T. Watkins (eds) *The heroic in children's popular culture*. New York: Garland Press.

Toporowski, J. (1986) 'Beyond banking: financial institutions and the poor', in P. Golding (ed) *Excluding the poor*. London: Child Poverty Action Group.

Turner, B. S. (1992) 'Ideology and Utopia in the formation of an intelligentsia: reflections on the English cultural conduit', *Theory Culture and Society — Explorations in Critical Social Science*, Vol. 9, No. 1: pp. 183–210.

Turner, G. (1990) *British Cultural Studies: an introduction*. London: Unwin Hyman.

Tyrrell, B. (1990) Postmodernism and leisure markets', *Leisure Futures* (August). London: Henley Centre.

Veblen, T. (1953) *The theory of the leisure class — an economic study of institutions* [1899]. New York: Viking Press.

Wagg, S. (1984) *The football world: a contemporary social history.* Brighton: The Harvester Press.

Warde, A. (1990) 'Introduction to the sociology of 'consumption', *Sociology*, Vol. 24, No. 1: pp. 1–4.

Whannel, G. (1982) 'Narrative and television sport: the Coe and Ovett story', in M. Green and C. Jenkins (eds) *Sporting fictions*. Birmingham: Department of Physical Education/University of Birmingham Centre for Contemporary Cultural Studies.

———— (1984) 'The television spectacular', in A. Tomlinson and G. Whannel (eds), *Five ring circus: money, power and politics at the Olympic Games.* London: Pluto.

———— (1986a) 'The unholy alliance: notes on television and the remaking of British Sport, 1968–1985', *Leisure Studies*, Vol. 5, No. 2: pp. 129–145.

———— (1986b) 'Television sport: the archaeology of a professional practice', in J. White (ed) *The media and cultural forms* (LSA Publication No. 26). Eastbourne: Leisure Studies Association.

———— (1992) *Fields in vision — television sport and cultural transformation.* London: Routledge.

Williams, J., Dunning, E. and Murphy, P. (1984) *Hooligans abroad: the behaviour and control of English fans in Continental Europe.* London: Routledge & Kegan Paul.

Williams, R. (1963) *Culture and society 1780–1950.* Harmondsworth: Penguin Books in association with Chatto & Windus.

———— (1977a) *Marxism and literature.* Oxford: Oxford University Press.

————(1977b) 'Literature in society', in H. Schiff (ed) *Contemporary approaches to English studies.* London: Heinemann.

———— (1983) *Towards 2000.* London: Chatto and Windus.

———— (1984) *American society — a sociological interpretation* (Second Edition, Revised) New York: Alfred Knopf (1963).

Williams, T. (1957) *Cat on a Hot Tin Roof.* Harmondsworth: Penguin Books.

Willis, P. (1977) *Learning to labour: how working-class kids get working-class jobs.* Farnborough: Saxon House.

Willis, P., *et al.* (1985) The *social condition of young people in Wolverhampton in 1984.* Wolverhampton: Wolverhampton Borough Council.

Wilson, N. (1988) *The sports business*. London: Mandarin.

Wolfe, T. (1975) *The new journalism*, with an anthology edited by T. Wolfe and E. W. Johnson. London: Picador.

———— (1981) *The right stuff*. London: Bantam Books.

Woods, P. (1976) 'Having a laugh: an antidote to schooling', in M. Hammersley and P. Woods (eds) *The process of schooling: a sociological reader*. London: Routledge and Kegan Paul.

Wren-Lewis, J. and A. Clarke (1983) 'The World Cup — a political football', *Theory, Culture and Society — Explorations in Critical Social Science*, Vol. 1, No. 3: pp. 123–132.

Index

Index

300

F